Frontiers in Pattern Recognition and Artificial Intelligence

Series on Language Processing, Pattern Recognition, and Intelligent Systems

Co-Editors

Ching Y. Suen
Concordia University, Canada
parmidir@enes.concordia.ca

Lu Qin
The Hong Kong Polytechnic University, Hong Kong
csluqin@comp.polyu.edu.hk

Published

Series on Language Processing, Pattern Recognition, and Intelligent Systems — Vol. 5

Frontiers in Pattern Recognition and Artificial Intelligence

Edited by

Marleah Blom
Nicola Nobile
Ching Y. Suen

Concordia University, Canada

World Scientific

NEW JERSEY • LONDON • SINGAPORE • BEIJING • SHANGHAI • HONG KONG • TAIPEI • CHENNAI • TOKYO

Published by

World Scientific Publishing Co. Pte. Ltd.

5 Toh Tuck Link, Singapore 596224

USA office: 27 Warren Street, Suite 401-402, Hackensack, NJ 07601

UK office: 57 Shelton Street, Covent Garden, London WC2H 9HE

British Library Cataloguing-in-Publication Data
A catalogue record for this book is available from the British Library.

Series on Language Processing, Pattern Recognition, and Intelligent Systems — Vol. 5
FRONTIERS IN PATTERN RECOGNITION AND ARTIFICIAL INTELLIGENCE

Copyright © 2019 by World Scientific Publishing Co. Pte. Ltd.

ISBN 978-981-120-335-0

For any available supplementary material, please visit
https://www.worldscienti ic.com/worldscibooks/10.1142/11362#t=suppl

Preface

Frontiers in Pattern Recognition and Artificial Intelligence consists of a collection of topics of general interest within the area of pattern recognition and artificial intelligence. It is of interest to the general public, graduate students and researchers in the field.

This volume brings together a new collection of papers written by a diverse range of international scholars. Papers and presentations were carefully selected from 160 papers from the International Conference on Pattern Recognition and Artificial Intelligence held in Montréal, Québec (May 2018) and an associated free public lecture entitled *Artificial Intelligence and Pattern Recognition: Trendy Technologies in Our Modern Digital World*. The conference and lecture were hosted by Concordia University to mark the 30th Anniversary of the Centre for Pattern Recognition and Machine Intelligence (CENPARMI). The event was well received, with over 300 attendees from 32 countries.

Chapters for this volume were intentionally selected in order to provide readers with an overview of works that highlight the intersection between pattern recognition and artificial intelligence. Chapters are geared to stimulate interest, provide general information and showcase existing applications. Not only do selected works provide information on various topics of interest, readers are invited to become familiar with diverse applications in fields where pattern recognition and artificial intelligence make valuable contributions. These fields include medicine, teaching and learning, forensic science, surveillance, linguistics, computer vision, online rating systems, and object tracking, just to name a few.

The first three introductory chapters provide a foundation of where we have come and where we are at in AI, ways in which artificial intelligence and pattern recognition can be viewed to overlap as well as an overview of the history of natural language processing. Grogono (Chapter 1) provides an overview of artificial intelligence, including a definition, history, key developments and current software technologies and trends. Perspectives held by Barz, Mukherjee, Lall and Vahdati are presented in Chapter 2. These three sets of authors deemed winners of a competition at ICPRAI describe how they each see the relationship between artificial intelligence and pattern recognition. An overview of a sub-field of artificial intelligence, natural language processing (NLP), is then provided in Chapter 3. Amini, Farahnak and Kosseim outline characteristics of natural language before discussing challenges of working with unstructured data, typical applications and the evolution of NLP.

Chapters 4, 5, 6, 7 and 8 centre on online and offline handwriting analysis systems. Khayyat and Nobile (Chapter 4) share an introduction to handwriting recognition, steps involved in the process of handwriting recognition and highlight handwriting recognition applications. Shivakumara, Pal, Lu, Chakraborti and Blumenstein (Chapter 5) propose an automatic system for evaluating descriptive handwritten answers involved in teaching and learning. Xiong, Liu, Wang and Lu (Chapter 6) propose a novel method for Chinese writer identification, which is stated to be an accurate approach to measure the similarity of character pairs. Impedovo and Pirlo (Chapter 7) introduce how handwriting can be successfully used for the assessment of Alzheimer's Disease and Parkinson's Disease. In Chapter 8, Krichen, Anquetil, Girard and Renault describe a pattern recognition and analysis system for Geometry learning in middle school. Not only do the authors express how the proposed digital learning strategy promotes active and collaborative learning in educational contexts, they go on to discuss its relevance in other domains such as architecture plan sketching.

Chapters 9 and 10 centre on the up-to-date use of pattern recognition and artificial intelligence in forensic science, specifically counterfeit coin detection. Sun and Suen (Chapter 9) present the use of a novel visual measurement system that uses image processing, feature extraction and classification to detect fake coins. Hmood and Suen (Chapter 10) describe a counterfeit coin detection method evaluated on a real-life dataset of Danish coins as part of collaborative research with Danish authorities.

Various additional applications, including medical application, detection and tracking systems as well as online rating systems are included in Chapters 11, 12, 13 and 14. Xi, Goubran and Shu (Chapter 11) outline computer aided detection (CAD) of heart murmurs. Chou and Lin's (Chapter 12) work involves details about vehicle detection systems that use surveillance videos. Within the area of computer vision, Li and Hu (Chapter 13) present a robust automatic compressive tracking method. Lastly, Batchu and Battu (Chapter 14) present a prediction system, which applies to rating video games.

The publication of this book would not have been possible without the valuable contributions of the authors.

Contents

List of Contributors

Eric Anquetil
Univ Rennes, CNRS, IRISA
Rennes, France
eric.anquetil@irisa.fr

Hessam Amini
Computational Linguistics at Concordia (CLaC) Laboratory
Concordia University, Montréal, Canada
hessam.amini@concordia.ca

Björn Barz
Friedrich Schiller University Jena
Computer Vision Group, Jena, Germany
bjoern.barz@uni-jena.de

Vishal Batchu
International Institute of Information Technology Hyderabad
Gachibowli, Hyderabad, India
vishal.batchu@students.iiit.ac.iny

Varshit Battu
International Institute of Information Technology Hyderabad
Gachibowli, Hyderabad, India

Marleah Blom
Centre for Pattern Recognition and Machine Intelligence
Concordia University, Montréal, Canada
marleah.blom@concordia.ca

Michael Blumenstein
University Technology of Sydney, Australia
michael.blumenstein@uts.edu.au

Tapabrata Chakraborti

Yan-Lin Chou
Department of Computer Science and Information Engineering
National Taipei University
New Taipei City, Taiwan

Farhood Farahnak
Computational Linguistics at Concordia (CLaC) Laboratory
Concordia University, Montréal, Canada
farhood.farahnak@concordia.ca

Nathalie Girard
Univ Rennes, CNRS, IRISA
Rennes, France
nathalie.girard@irisa.fr

Peter Grogono
Department of Computer Science and Software Engineering
Concordia University
Montréal, Canada

Rafik Goubran
Carleton University
Ottawa, Ontario, Canada

Ali K. Hmood
Centre for Pattern Recognition and Machine Intelligence
Concordia University, Montréal, Canada
a_alfraj@encs.concordia.ca

Wei Hu
Nantong University, School of Electronic and Information, P. R. China
Nantong, P. R. China

Donato Impedovo
Computer Science Department,
University of Bari Aldo Moro, Bari, Italy
donato.impedovo@uniba.it

Muna Khayyat
Centre for Pattern Recognition and Machine Intelligence
Concordia University, Montréal, Canada
muna.khayyat@gmail.com

Leila Kosseim
Computational Linguistics at Concordia (CLaC) Laboratory
Concordia University, Montréal, Canada
leila.kosseim@concordia.ca

Omar Krichen
Univ Rennes, CNRS, IRISA
Rennes, France
omar.krichen@irisa.fr

Brejesh Lall
Indian Institute of Technology Delhi, New Delhi, India
brejeshg@ee.iitd.ac.in

Hongjun Li
Nantong University, School of Electronic and Information
Nantong, P. R. China
lihongjun@ntu.edu.cn

Daw-Tung Lin
Department of Computer Science and Information Engineering
National Taipei University
New Taipei City, Taiwan
dalton@mail.ntpu.edu.tw

Li Liu
School of Information Engineering
Nanchang University, Nanchang P. R. China
liliu033@ncu.edu.cn

Tong Lu
Notational Key Lab for Novel Software Technology
Nanjing University, Nanjing, P. R. China
lutong@nju.edu.cn

Yue Lu
Shanghai Key Laboratory of Multidimensional Information Processing
Department of Computer Science and Technology
East China Normal University, Shanghai, P. R. China
ylu@cs.ecnu.edu.cn

Nicola Nobile
Centre for Pattern Recognition and Machine Intelligence
Concordia University, Montréal, Canada
nicola@encs.concordia.ca

Prerana Mukherjee
Indian Institute of Technology Delhi
New Delhi, India
feez138300@ee.iitd.ac.in

Umapada Pal
Computer Vision and Pattern Recognition Unit
Indian Statistical Institute, Kolkata, India
umapada@isical.ac.in

Giuseppe Pirlo
Computer Science Department
University of Bari Aldo Moro, Bari, Italy
giuseppe.pirlo@uniba.it

Mickaël Renault
Univ Rennes, CNRS, IRISA
Rennes, France
mickael.renault@irisa.fr

Palaiahnakote Shivakumara
Faculty of Computer Science and Information Technology
University of Malaya
Kuala Lumpur, Malaysia
hudempsk@yahoo.com

Chang Shu
National Research Council Canada
Ottawa, Ontario, Canada

Ching Y. Suen
Centre for Pattern Recognition and Machine Intelligence
Concordia University, Montréal, Canada
suen@encs.concordia.ca

Ke Sun
Centre for Pattern Recognition and Machine Intelligence
Concordia University, Montréal, Canada
pincessrr@gmail.com

Elham Vahdati
Centre for Pattern Recognition and Machine Intelligence
Concordia University, Montréal, Canada
g_vahdat@encs.concordia.ca

Patrick S. P. Wang
Northeastern University
Boston, MA, United States
patwang@ieee.org

Pengcheng Xi
Carleton University and National Research Council Canada
Ottawa, Ontario, Canada
pengcheng.xi@nrc-cnrc.gc.ca

Xu-Jie Xiong
School of Electronic and Electrical Engineering
Shanghai University of Engineering Science
Shanghai, P. R. China
xiong@stu.ecnu.edu.cn

Chapter 1

Artificial Intelligence: An Overview

Peter Grogono

Department of Computer Science and Software Engineering
Concordia University
Montréal, Québec

The smart devices that we have become so familiar with—and dependent on—make use of three new technologies: miniaturized computers; the internet; and Artificial Intelligence. In this overview, we provide a definition and a brief history of Artificial Intelligence; mention some of the key developments in formal reasoning, natural language processing, robotics, and games playing; and outline the dominant software technologies in use today. We conclude with a discussion of trends, including the possibility of Artificial General Intelligence.

1. Smart Devices

You don't have to look very far these days to encounter a "smart device". The adjective "smart" has been attached to many things. Here are a few, and you can probably think of more: cameras, coffee makers, diapers, doorbells, fridges, key chains, kitchen scales, light bulbs, locks, loudspeakers, phones, shoes, tablets, thermostats, toasters, toilets, toothbrushes, watches.

What distinguishes devices that are "smart" from other, less well-endowed, devices? A smart device (let's drop the quotes now) has some or all of the following characteristics: it is electronic; it communicates with other devices on a network; it can operate interactively and autonomously; and it incorporates some artificial intelligence.

A traditional watch, for example, is a device that displays the time. It is fairly simple, perhaps consisting of no more than a spring, a few gears, and a dial with hands. A smart watch, on the other hand, may also: change the time according to the time zone; monitor your activities and body movements; handle your email; play audio and video; take photographs; and so on.

Smart devices are just one way in which artificial intelligence (AI) is impinging on our lives. The amount of AI in a smart device is typically quite small, but AI has many other effects in our lives that are less obvious. If someone steals your credit card, for example, its patterns of use will probably change: large amounts will be spent very quickly. This change in usage will be noticed, your card will be cancelled, and you will not be responsible for the charges. It is not a person but a computer that "notices" the changes, and this is an early example of software "learning" to distinguish between regular use and anomalous behaviour.

But AI is not just about smart devices for individuals. AI applications today are affecting entire industries. Activities that are increasingly mediated by computer software include: vehicles that drive themselves; translation between human languages; robots that make their own decisions; analyzing video feeds to anticipate problems; trading on the stock exchange; and making legal judgments.

2. Defining AI

AI is hard to define because it is a moving target. Problems that were hard to solve were said to require "intelligence" but, once they had been reduced to computer programs, the intelligence seemed to evaporate. Reading handwritten words and numbers, understanding speech, driving cars, and playing good chess were all considered at one time to require a high level of intelligence, but are now (or soon will be) routine technologies. Another problem is that people easily perform tasks that are hard for a computer program and *vice versa*. Recognizing a smiling face is easy for a two-year-old but difficult for an AI program: this task has only recently been automated. On the other hand, most people look blank if asked to evaluate an indefinite integral, but computer algebra systems do not find integrals difficult, thanks to an algorithm developed by Robert Risch in 1968.

Hans Moravec put it this way: "it is comparatively easy to make computers exhibit adult level performance on intelligence tests or playing checkers, and difficult or impossible to give them the skills of a one-year-old when it comes to perception and mobility".[1] Moravec's "paradox" is hardly surprising, given that we have had millions of years to evolve seeing and moving but no time at all to evolve skill at checkers.

Nevertheless, we can give a reasonable and not too controversial definition of AI that is sufficient for this introduction:

> Artificial Intelligence is the study of computer systems that
> are able to perform tasks that are traditionally considered to
> require human intelligence, such as reasoning, understanding,
> creating and translating natural languages, recognizing objects
> visually, making decision in complex situations, solving prob-
> lems in mathematics and other technical fields, and skillfully
> playing games.

3. The Early History of AI

If we consider AI to include anything that augments our mental abilities
(as opposed to machines that merely augment our physical abilities), then
calculators are a form of AI. Mechanical aids to calculation include the
abacus (c. 3,000 B.C.), Napier's bones (1617), Pascal's Calculator (1642),
Thomas's arithmometer (1851), Babbage's Difference Engine (started in
1823 but never completed), and many others.

Preceding most of these, the Antikythera mechanism is an artefact found
in a Greek ship that sank around 100 B.C. The mechanism uses at least
thirty-seven metal gears to model the motion of the moon and to predict
eclipses. Unlike other ancient machines that simply performed a task such
as telling the time or pumping water, and calculators that just do arithmetic, the Antikythera mechanism was an aid to knowledge, and in this
sense exhibits AI.

Gottfried Leibniz (1646–1716) was probably the first person to propose
mechanical reasoning. His *calculus ratiocinator* is an early form of symbolic
logic, designed so that it could be executed by a machine. George Boole
(1815–1864) started with Aristotle's system of logic, formalized it as an algebra, and published the results in *An Investigation of the Laws of Thought
on Which are Founded the Mathematical Theories of Logic and Probabilities*, a book now usually referred to more simply as *Laws of Thought* (1854).
Bertrand Russell and Alfred North Whitehead published their monumen-
tal *Principia Mathematica* in three volumes (1910, 1912, and 1913) with
the intention of showing that all of mathematics could be formally derived
from a small set of axioms. In 1930, however, Gödel published his famous
Incompleteness Theorem, establishing that any useful formal theory must
inevitably include true statements that cannot be proved. These results,
showing both what could be done and what could not be done, laid the
foundation for the development of the first symbolic AI programs during

the 1950s.

In the 1930s, mathematicians attempted to formalize (that is, make precise) the notion of *computability* (what can be computed by mechanical application of rules). The three most notable attempts were general recursive functions (Gödel and Herbrand, 1933), lambda calculus (Church, 1936), and Turing Machines (Turing, 1936). Proving that these three formalisms are equivalent (that is, can compute exactly the same things) suggested very strongly that they actually characterize the nature of computation. The *Church-Turing Thesis* asserts that these theories also capture the *informal* notion of computation. The Church-Turing Thesis cannot be proved, because there is obviously no precise definition of "informal computation" but, if true, it strongly suggests that a computer can, in principle, do anything that our brains can do. There is much controversy about this claim, but it also provided foundations and justification for the development of machines that simulate brains.

Turing himself was interested in mechanizing intelligence and, in 1950, wrote a classic paper in which he discussed the question "Can a machine think?"[2] After identifying various problems with this question, he proposed an experiment, now known as the *Turing Test*, which would recognize an intelligent machine. The basic idea is that a person communicating with the machine should not be able to distinguish it from another person. The communication must take place over a channel which doesn't give the game away immediately, and Turing proposed 1950s technology: a teletype machine. So far, no AI program has indisputably passed the Turing Test and, in fact, although the test is still discussed in the literature, it is no longer considered an adequate test of AI.

Even before Turing's paper, McCulloch and Pitts introduced in 1943 "artificial neurons" in an early attempt to model the operation of the brain. An artificial neuron, formally called a *Threshold Logic Unit*, had several inputs and one output. Inputs and outputs were restricted to two values, 0 and 1, and the output was a weighted sum of the inputs. A collection of artificial neurons wired together forms a *neural network* that can be trained to perform tasks by adjusting the weights. The use of artificial neurons constitutes a completely different approach to AI: whereas the symbolic methods described above model the highest levels of brain activity—our ability to reason—neurons model the most basic forms of mental activity.

Grey Walter built the first robots controlled by neural networks in the late 1940s. His robots looked like small tortoises (and were so named) and moved very slowly. Although they had only a small number of "neurons", they exhibited unexpectedly complex behaviour: moving to a power outlet when their batteries ran low; displaying "clumsy narcissistic" behaviour when placed in front of a mirror; and, after the addition of a couple of conditional reflex circuits, able to make associations like Pavlov's dogs.

Neural networks took a further important step with the development of the *perceptron* by Frank Rosenblatt in 1957. Perceptrons were simulated in software at first, but the Mark 1 Perceptron was an actual machine that used 400 photocells for image recognition. Unfortunately, Rosenblatt made exaggerated claims for his machine, leading to hostility from other parts of the emerging AI community. In 1969, Marvin Minsky and Seymour Papert showed that perceptrons could not learn the "exclusive or" function.[3] (Their result holds for single-layer, but not for multi-layer perceptrons.) The Minsky-Papert critique was often cited and contributed to declining interest and funding for neural networks that lasted until the mid-1980s.

Meanwhile, symbolic AI had a grand introduction at the Dartmouth Summer Research Project on Artificial Intelligence, held in 1956 and now widely considered to mark the founding of AI as a legitimate area of research. John McCarthy chose the name "Artificial Intelligence" and proposed a two-month study. Attendees included John McCarthy, Marvin Minsky, Ray Solomonoff, Arthur Samuel, Allen Newell, Herbert Simon, all of whom had major influences on the emerging field.

The period following the Dartmouth workshop has been called the "Golden Era" of AI. Significant advances were made, and generous funding was available. In particular the US Defense Advanced Research Projects Agency (DARPA) invested heavily in AI. As well as neural networks, many researchers developed formal reasoning systems. Much of the work was quite mathematical. For some researchers, however, a more important goal was to communicate with computers in English or, in general a natural language. This area, still important, is now called Natural Language Processing, or NLP.

Even at this early stage, ways of thinking about AI began to diverge. Some researchers studied the ways in which people solved problems and then designed programs that simulated their thought processes. Others believed that it was more fruitful to seek general problem solving methods, based on logic and other formal tools, that might find answers in ways quite different from those used by people. Still others did not believe in general purpose methods, but instead advocated combining numerous *ad hoc* techniques to build expertise.[4]

Unfortunately, AI research suffered a setback and the Golden Era came to an end. The period 1974–80 is now called the "first AI winter". Funding all but ceased, and it became difficult for people who wanted to do research in AI to get good positions at universities. Part of the reason was that AI had been oversold by the researchers themselves: the results they obtained did not match their extravagant claims. But there were other factors: computers of the time were just not powerful enough to do much; solutions were found, but were impractical in the sense that thousands of years of computing time would be needed to find them; Moravec's paradox emerged: it turned out to be relatively easy for machines to do things that people find difficult but extremely difficult to do things that people do easily and without conscious thought. Most people have no difficulty walking upstairs with a cup of coffee, but balk at proving a theorem; for machines, it is the other way round.

Problems within the emerging field of AI were aggravated by criticism and scepticism. Some of the critiques actually came from within the field: we have mentioned the effect of Minsky and Papert's attack on perceptrons. Philosophers such as John Lucas, Hubert Dreyfus, and John Searle attacked the basic assumptions of AI. In the UK, the Lighthill report was highly critical of AI and ended support of research in all but a few universities. Even though many of the philosophical arguments were refuted by AI experts, they cast a pall over AI research.

In the early 1980s, the outlook became brighter. Expert Systems, which mimic the capabilities of a human expert by following a programmed set of rules, achieved successes in several areas. Feigenbaum and his students developed expert systems for analyzing spectrometer readings and diagnosing diseases. By 1985, corporations were spending more than a billion dollars per year on AI, and many new companies were formed to deliver AI products, in both hardware and software forms. Several companies offered computers specifically designed to efficiently execute LISP—the preferred programming language for symbolic AI, invented by John McCarthy. Researchers began to appreciate the importance of *knowledge*, leading to Knowledge Based Systems and Knowledge Engineering. The Japanese government created, and generously funded, the Fifth Generation Project. Neural Networks began to return following the discovery of new techniques by John Hopfield, David Rumelhart, and others.

The bubble burst again in 1987. General purpose computers proved to be more ecoomical than specialized hardware, and the demand for LISP machines and other AI hardware collapsed. Expert Systems turned out to be hard to maintain and upgrade. The Fifth Generation Project failed to meet any of its goals. AI went through its second winter.

In the early 1990s, however, AI once again returned to the mainstream of computer-related research. Between 1995 and the present, AI has made enormous strides. From a niche field familiar to only a few specialists, AI has become omnipresent in our lives. There are a number of reasons for this, but a key contributor to AI's growth and success has been development in computer technology, both hardware and software. No one needs to be told that computers have become smaller, faster, cheaper, and more plentiful, but it is worth while to take a brief look at the remarkable range of these developments.

In 1965, Gordon Moore noticed that the density of transistors in an integrated circuit was doubling roughly every two years; he predicted that this trend would continue. This prediction, now known as "Moore's Law", has held up fairly well. When progress slows, headlines shout "end of Moore's Law", and then a new technology emerges to save it. But, since "atomristors", the newest storage medium, consist of layers one molecule thick, it would seem that Moore's Law will not last much longer. Nevertheless, higher densities enabled the development of computers with exponentially higher complexity, more memory, and lower cost than previously, and thereby had a profound effect on the industry.

The improvements due to Moore's Law and other industrial advances have been so extraordinary that a few comparisons are worth noting. For example, a crude estimate puts the value of real estate in Montreal in 1955 at about half a trillion dollars ($500,000,000,000). If the value of real estate had shrunk at the same rate as computer memory, you could now buy Montreal for about 50 cents. We can also look at this in terms of the amount of data that can be stored in a given space. In 1955, data were stored on 80 byte punched cards. Today, a portable disk drive the size of a bar of soap can store 4 trillion bytes—the equivalent of 75,000 tons of punched cards. Turning to speed, today's computers are up to a million times faster than those of 1976. Software has improved, too, with new algorithms working many times faster than older methods.

Given these performance improvements, it is not surprising that problems that were intractable in the 1950s can be solved easily and quickly today. More importantly, the increases in computational power have encouraged the introduction of new approaches that were inconceivable in the early days. AI today is all about immense quantities of data and enormous computations.

4. AI Landmarks

In this section, we review some of the significant achievements of AI. The discussion is organized around various topics within AI. Historically, communication between these topic areas has often been weak, leading to parallel discoveries and duplicated effort.[5] Recently, however, convergence of techniques has enabled more productive communication between subfields.

4.1. *Formal Reasoning*

People quickly recognized that, although computers were designed primarily to calculate with numbers, they could also manipulate symbols and thereby reason logically. In 1955, the Logic Theorist, a program created by Newell, Simon, and Shaw, managed to prove many of the theorems of *Principia Mathematica*. One of the proofs, shorter and more elegant than the original, even delighted Bertrand Russell. The same group went on to build the *General Problem Solver*, which did not solve many problems but introduced the idea of separating problem knowledge from solving strategy. Gelernter's Geometry Theorem Prover (1958) was true to its name, establishing results in elementary geometry familiar to anyone who suffered through Euclid at school. Slagle's SAINT (1961), which symbolically evaluated integrals, was widely considered to be the first Expert System.

In 1968, Joel Moses introduced Macsyma, an early knowledge-based programming for mathematical reasoning, and the forerunner of modern Mathematica, Maple, and many other "computer algebra" systems. Today, there are many programs that either generate a mathematical proof of a formal claim or check that a purported proof is valid. Computer components are the most complex artifacts ever manufactured, and it is not surprising that most commercial applications of theorem provers center around chip checking.

4.2. *Natural Language Processing*

A "natural language" is a system used by people to communicate: Arabic, Bulgarian, and Croatian are examples. The notations that we use to control computers are called "programming languages" but this is a rather casual usage and programming languages have little to do with natural languages. Following convention, we will abbreviate "Natural Language Processing" as NLP, but it should be noted that this acronym has recently been used for "Neuro-Linguistic Programming".

Using computers to process natural languages is an old idea. A program passes the Turing Test if it communicates in a way indistinguishable from a person; clearly, this requires the program to both understand and generate natural language. Early work often focused on automating translation between natural languages. In the 1950s, when the Cold War dominated politics, funding for translating Russian into English was readily available. As happened in other areas of AI, exaggerated claims made for machine translation were not met, funding collapsed, and research slowed.

However, there are many applications for NLP other than machine translation. These can be divided broadly into two areas, depending on whether the medium is writing or speaking. Since analyzing and synthesizing speech is difficult, it is not surprising that early applications were based on written language.

One way to make progress in a complex domain is to find a simple corner of it and work on that. Joseph Weizenbaum's ELIZA and Terry Winograd's SHRDLU were both developed at MIT during the 1960s. ELIZA simulated a psychotherapist, picking up key words and phrases in sentences and responding, without any understanding. For example, if you said, "My boyfriend made me come here", ELIZA might respond, "Is it important to you that your boyfriend made you come here?" ELIZA was an extremely simple program by modern standards, and Weizenbaum was alarmed to find that many people took it seriously.[6]

SHRDLU enabled the computer to understand simple commands and perform the appropriate actions. SHRDLU worked with a virtual "blocks world" and processed instructions such as "put the blue cone on the red cube". The linguistically interesting feature of SHRDLU was that it maintained context. For example, it would understand that "the cone" in a command referred to the cone used in a previous command. This work was extended in the 1970s to "conceptual ontologies" that converted natural language statements in a limited domain to data structures that could then be used for computer analysis.

Programs that used speech came later, and synthesis preceded analysis. There was a time when your car was likely to say things like "Close the door, please." This brief period has mercifully passed but, instead, we are now expected to tolerate automated telephone answering services.

Early speech recognition systems worked in particular domains with limited vocabularies. At first, such systems recognized isolated words only. The first program that recognized continuous speech (no silences between words) was developed by Raj Reddy in the late 1960s, but it could understand only commands specifying moves in chess. Speech recognition achieved commercial success with Dragon Dictate, a $9,000 program introduced in 1990, that would take dictation for you. Two decades later, such software became obsolete, because you could dictate to your cell phone.

Early work in NLP was mostly based on linguistic principles. Programs analyzed or generated sentences using grammar rules, often influenced by Chomsky's work on natural language and transformational grammars. The Holy Grail of NLP was a universal representation of meaning, such that any human language could be converted to and from this representation, thus solving the translation problem once and for all. This goal was never achieved, and probably never will be, because natural languages have turned out to be much richer and more complex than researchers expected.

We are becoming familiar with "digital assistants" such as Amazon's Alexa, Apples's Siri, Google's Now, and Microsoft's Cortana. All of them use NLP techniques to recognize and synthesize speech in real time, as well as other mechanisms to obtain answers by interrogating a local database or accessing the internet.

Recently, the Chinese company Alibaba demonstrated a program that reads stories and answers questions about them. The stories, questions, and answers were all written in English. The program's performance was not only better than earlier programs, but was also better than the average person. We should not infer from this that the program really "understands", in the deep human sense, better than people, but the performance is impressive nonetheless.

The key to the rapid modern advances in NLP has been the replacement of built-in grammar rules by machine learning. Increasing memory capacity and processor speed, coupled with the rise of the internet, has meant that vast quantities of written and spoken language are available for analysis. This, in turn, has enable programs such as Google Translate to learn translation simply by comparing the same text in different languages, not using any rules at all. Some people feel that Google should pay the human translators who created these texts for their use! Unfortunately, this is unlikely to happen.

4.3. *Robotics*

Self-driving vehicles started to appear in the news only a few years ago, but the first autonomous vehicle was Moravec's Stanford Cart, which wandered around the Stanford AI Lab in the late 1970s. By 1986, Ernst Dickmanns had built robot cars that could navigate along empty roads at realistic speeds. In 1995, one of Dickmanns's vehicles drove from Munich to Copenhagen in traffic at speeds of up to 190 km/h (legal in Europe!). In the same year, Carnegie Mellon's Navlab drove 4,600 km across the USA. NASA needed autonomous robots and, by 2004, Spirit and Opportunity were exploring the surface of Mars. Today, most of the major car manufacturers, and other companies such as Apple and Google, offer vehicles with various degrees of automation.

Machines for tasks other than driving go back 2,500 years or more. For our purposes, however, we are interested only in machines that exhibit some form of intelligence. Amongst the earliest such machines were Grey Walter's tortoises, mentioned above. Industrial robots began to appear in the 1950s with Goertz's remote-controlled arm with force feedback (1951) and Devol's industrial robot UNIMATE (1954).

Many people associate the word "robot" with a machine that looks roughly like a person: a head, a body, two arms and two legs, and so on. The first robots of this kind were pioneered in Japan. Ichiro Kato built WABOT in 1973. It had the same size and structure as an adult human and could move, see, and communicate (in Japanese). His company, the Kato Corporation, introduced WL12RIII, a bipedal robot that could traverse irregular terrain in 1989. Honda has been extensively involved in robotics, building P2 (1996, self-regulating), P3 (1997, completely autonomous), and finally ASIMO (2002), a "personal assistant" that recognizes its owner's face, voice, and name, and can read email.

Modern robotics research has produced machines that would have been thought impossible fifty years ago: flying craft no bigger than an insect; machines that reproduce themselves; artificial fish as fast as a tuna with the navigational skill of an eel; automatic soldiers that can jump over 30-foot obstacles; exo-skeletons that enable paralyzed people to walk and perform other tasks; robots that greet people at tourist attractions; and robots with sensitive and soft "skin" that can cook an egg or defuse a bomb.

4.4. *Game Playing*

The first programs that played games defined by simple formal rules appeared during the 1950s. The Ferranti Mark I computer at the University of Manchester had both a checkers program written by Christopher Strachey and a chess program written by Dietrich Prinz. Arthur Samuel's checkers player was the first program capable of challenging serious human players. By 1968, Richard Greenblatt's MacHack was playing tournament-level chess.

IBM started to develop a chess-playing program in 1985. The project began as ChipTest, in collaboration with Carnegie Mellon University, and evolved first into Deep Thought and eventually to Deep Blue, echoing IBM's nick-name, "Big Blue". Kasparov played against Deep Blue on several occasions, but the crucial match took place in May 1997, when Deep Blue won $3\frac{1}{2}$–$2\frac{1}{2}$ (a drawn match counts as $\frac{1}{2}$). There was some controversy over this match, because Kasparov thought that IBM engineers had modified the program during the match on the basis of a conversation that they overheard. Nonetheless, having an AI program defeat the reigning World Champion was a significant step forward for AI.

All of these programs had built-in strategies but, in 1990, Gerry Tesauro's TD-Gammon demonstrated programs could play Backgammon at championship level just by learning.

A big surprise came in 2016, when AlphaGo, a program developed by Google's DeepMind in London, defeated Lee Sedol in a five-game Go match. As a consequence of this and other competitions, AlphaGo was awarded 9-dan status (the highest ranking) by the Korea Baduk Association and, later, by the Chinese Weiqi Association. This event was significant for several reasons.

Go is played by two players, one with black stones and the other with white stones. Players move alternately by placing a stone on the Go board in one of $19 \times 19 = 361$ positions. Traditionally, a Go teacher instructs a student of the game in one sentence: "You may place your stone on any point on the board, but if I surround that stone, I may remove it." In this sense, Go is much simpler than chess, with its multiple pieces each with different allowable moves. The problem with Go for a computer is that it is very difficult to think ahead when both you and your opponent have the choice of hundreds of possible moves at each step.

AlphaGo used both modern AI methods and sheer computer power to play Go at a high level. First, its neural networks were trained using a collection of expert Go games containing more than 30 million moves. Then it improved its performance by playing thousands of games against itself. Thus AlphaGo *learned* to play Go by, in human terms, studying other players and practicing. This is very different from Deep Blue, which had a vast amount of chess knowledge built into its code, in the form of libraries of opening moves, strategies for the end game, and tactics for mid-game battles. AlphaGo typifies an important modern approach to AI, which is to provide programs with minimal information and allow them to learn.

The learning principle was taken further by AlphaGo's successor, an AI program called AlphaZero. AlphaZero took just 24 hours to achieve super-human performance in chess, shogi, and Go. The "zero" in its name indicates that the program is told nothing about playing strategy, only how to make a legal move and whether it has won. It learns by playing against itself, adjusting its neural networks to favour moves that end in victory.

These two examples, chess and Go, illustrate the development of AI over three decades. IBM used old style AI, sometimes called "GOFAI" (Good Old-Fashioned Artificial Intelligence), in which human expertise is built into the AI program. DeepMind used new style AI, which consists of applying a general purpose learning engine to a particular problem. Learning machines have now reached a level of performance that often makes this approach the quickest and cheapest way of obtaining "intelligence" from a machine.

Chess and Go are games of *total information*: both players can see the board, which tells them everything they need to know about the game. It is not surprising that these and other board games, such as checkers, were chosen as AI challenges. Sceptics pointed to the obvious advantages of total information, and declared that AI program would never compete at games with hidden information. Games such as poker and bridge, in which you cannot see other players' cards, require psychological as well as purely rational reasoning skills.

Libratus (Latin for "balanced") is a poker-playing AI program developed by Tuomas Sandholm and others using supercomputers at the Pittsburgh Supercomputing Centre. In January 2017, Libratus played in a 20-day tournament with four expert poker players. 120,000 hands were played and Libratus won the tournament, ahead by $1,766,250 in chip currency at the end of play. Nevertheless, the human players shared the prize—200,000 real dollars.

Games are a popular target for AI programmers because they do not require physical action. People can enter moves using a keyboard, mouse, or microphone, and the program can display its moves on a screen. Machines have been built to move chess pieces; such machines make it more fun to watch a game but do not affect the reasoning skills required to play. Games involving physical skills present new challenges, but progress is being made. In 2016, a golfing robot hit a hole in one. Forpheus is a robot that plays table tennis, developed by the Omron Corporation in Japan. There are robots that play baseball and pool—though not yet both.

5. AI Technologies

From these summaries of various subfields of AI, we can infer a general pattern: there are two main streams of AI, and their relative importance has varied during the development of AI. The two streams are *symbolic* or *knowledge-based* AI and *machine learning* (ML). Since knowledge-based AI has declined recently, it is often called "good old-fashioned AI" (GOFAI),[7] in spite of the fact that there are still many systems that rely on built-in knowledge.

Both GOFAI and ML emerged early in the history of AI. Arguably, ML came first, with the neural nets proposed by McCulloch and Pitts in 1943. However, from the Dartmouth Conference of 1956 until the return of neural nets around 1990, most of the research focused on GOFAI. As we have seen, the goal was to convert knowledge of mathematics, mechanics, medicine, linguistics, and other areas into a form in which programs could manipulate it. "Knowledge Representation" was the mantra of the period. This approach culminated with Expert Systems, built by translating human knowledge acquired from texts and living experts into a system of rules.

Abstractly, solving any AI problem involves *searching*. There is an imaginary "space" containing all of the solutions to a problem, along with many more non-solutions. The AI program searches this space, rejecting the non-solutions, until it finds a solution. For some problems, any solution will do; for others, the program must find the "best" solution in some sense, or, at least, a "good" solution. The difficulty for AI program is that the search space is usually very large. If getting to a solution requires 10 steps, and there are 10 possible actions at each step, the search space has 10^{10} or ten billion states. These numbers actually correspond to quite a small problem: both the number of steps required and the number of choices at each step may be much larger in practice. This "combinatorial explosion" can defeat even the fastest algorithms. We can see different approaches to AI as different ways of exploring the search space.

Current approaches to AI can be summarized in four main categories: symbolic AI, Bayesian networks, deep learning, and evolutionary algorithms.

5.1. *Symbolic AI*

The idea that human intelligence is based on symbolic reasoning is old, going back to the work of philosophers such as Hobbes, Leibniz, Hume,

Kant, and more recently the Physical Symbol System Hypothesis of Newell and Simon: "A physical symbol system has the necessary and sufficient means for general intelligent action".[8]

Symbolic AI is not an especially effective way of exploring a large search space; combinatorial explosion led to many disappointments for symbolic AI. Many programs showed encouraging performance on simple problems, but could not be scaled up to solve realistic problems. The key to avoiding combinatorial explosion is to use techniques that quickly reject large numbers of non-solutions, and methods based on non-symbolic techniques, such as machine learning and evolutionary programming, eventually turned out to be better at this than symbolic reasoning. Nevertheless, there are some domains in which symbolic AI remains superior. Computer algebra systems and theorem-proving assistants, for example, incorporate mathematical knowledge in the form of thousands of precise rules; it is more efficient to code the rules explicitly than to expect a machine to learn them. Software engineering tools perform extensive symbolic computations on source code; while some of these are straightforward application of standard algorithms, others involve heuristic techniques that may legitimately be considered to be AI.

5.2. *Bayesian Networks*

Thomas Bayes (1701–1761) was a philosopher, statistician, and theologian who never published the work for which he is most famous. Bayes' Theorem quantifies the idea that we modify our beliefs when we receive new evidence. Bayesian *inference* requires starting with a guess about the nature of the solution (more technically, the *prior probability distribution*, or just "prior") and then using training data to refine the guess, obtaining a posterior probability distribution. Critics of Bayesian techniques, both during the eighteenth century and now, see the prior as a subjective human judgment, out of place in a mathematical process. Despite the critics, Bayesian techniques have proven to be very effective.

Turing used Bayesian methods to decode messages enciphered by the German Enigma machines during the Second World War. Judea Pearl introduced Bayesian Networks to the AI community in 1985. A Bayesian Network is a directed acyclic graph in which nodes represent variables and edges represent dependencies. The most direct application of a Bayesian network is to observe the values of some variables and infer the values of others. In a learning situation, training data would be used to establish connection coefficients, and the trained network would then be used to make inferences from other data. Alternatively, we can derive a Bayesian network from given data, thus obtaining dependencies rather than mere correlations. Books published in the late 1980s established Bayesian networks both as a field for research and a basis for practical AI applications.[9,10]

Today, Bayesian networks have applications in many fields, including genetics, medicine, document classification and retrieval, image processing, and biology. If you use a filter that you have trained to remove spam from your email, it probably uses Bayesian techniques. The advertisements you see on web pages may well have been chosen by AdSense, which uses a Bayesian network with more than 300 million connections.[11]

5.3. *Evolutionary Algorithms*

As Darwin showed, biological organisms evolve by natural selection. Each organism reproduces, that is, creates approximate copies of itself. There are always more offspring than can survive, giving a tendency for each generation to be "fitter" than its parents. Evolutionary methods imitate this process, by simulating the reproduction and selection of either data ("genetic algorithms") or actual programs ("evolutionary programming").

Simulated evolution was first used by Fogel in 1960 for AI applications. Since then, evolutionary techniques have achieved widespread use in both AI and other areas. For example, optimization problems, which involve choosing the best (or, at last, a good) solution from a large collection of possible solutions, are often solved most effectively by simulating evolution. Some people, however, do not consider optimization to be AI, because it is "just" a search, not requiring intelligence.

But evolution has been used in other areas, notably design, where it is considered to be a type of AI. For example, Jason Lohn and others used evolutionary programming to design the ST5 antenna for NASA spacecraft. This antenna, little more than an inch high, looks like a paper-clip twisted by a bored child. Engineers accustomed to designing antennas were skeptical that the ST5 would perform at all, but it turned out to be superior to antennas design by experienced engineers. John Koza has used evolutionary techniques to design circuits, lenses, and other artifacts. On several occasions his programs discovered inventions that were already patented and, in a few cases, came up with inventions that were awarded new patents.[12]

5.4. *Deep Learning*

In recent research, machine learning has become dominant. Thanks to faster computers, larger memories, and improving algorithms, deep learning techniques started to dominate AI research around 2012. Early experiments in machine learning were limited by small learning sets and hardware limitations. As mentioned, AlphaGo was taught to play Go by first showing it 30 million moves made by expert players and then allowing it to play against itself, learning from the results. Programs that classify images, for example to find faces, are trained using millions of images, easily obtained on the internet. These tasks would have been infeasible only a few years ago because of the amount of data and computation required.

There is no general agreement about which kinds of ML project are more or less likely to succeed, but we can make one general observation. In a "closed world" situation, where formal and structured knowledge is required, ML will probably be effective; AlphaGo Zero is an example. In an "open" situation, in which criteria are less well defined and examples are numerous, ML may have difficulties. Deciding whether an image contains a smiling face, for example, is still a hard problem for ML.

Most machine learning is performed by Artificial Neural Networks (ANN). Previously called Connectionist Systems, neural networks originated with McCulloch and Pitts' artificial neurons. Modern neural networks maintain the basic plan, in which "neurons" are linked together by "synapses" to form a network, but are much larger and much more complex. The quotes are a reminder that neurons and synapses are biological entities bearing little resemblance to their artificial counterparts.

The dominant form of ML in AI today is *deep learning*. The meaning of "learning" is fairly clear: AI programs acquire expertise by analyzing data. The qualification "deep" is more ambiguous. For some, it means no more than the architecture of the program: a *deep* learning program is a program based on a *deep* neural net, as described below. For others, it is the learning itself that is "deep": a deep learning system can learn at multiple levels of abstraction.

A link between neurons A and B has a *weight*, w. A small (or large) value of w indicates that A has a small (or large) effect on B. The ANN learns by adjusting the weights of its links. The performance of an ANN depends on its topology (how the neurons are connected) and the algorithm that it uses to update the weights. A key advance in the development of ANN was the introduction of *backpropagation* algorithms, discovered independently by various researchers during the 1970s. As the name suggests, backpropagation works by observing the error at the output neurons of the ANN and, by changing weights, distributing errors backwards through the ANN to the input neurons.

A simple ANN has one *layer* of neurons. Input signals are fed to the neurons: for example, there might be one neuron for each pixel of an image. Based on what it receives, each neuron sends a signal to the output neuron, which computes a weighted sum of the inputs. More complex ANNs have more than one layer of neurons, with each layer receiving information from neurons in the previous layer and passing filtered information on to the neurons in the next layer. Until about 2006, most ANNs had between two and five layers, because training deeper networks required more data and computing power than was available at that time. Since then, improved resources have enabled the creation of much deeper ANNs. Modern ANNs may have as many as 150 layers.

Layers after the first are supposed to build increasingly abstract representations of the data, often called "features". Features might be similar to those that a person might use—edges or colored regions of a visual image, for instance—or quite different. An ANN with many layers is called "deep" and, partly for this reason, we describe what many-layered ANNs do as "deep learning". However, "deep learning" also suggests a richer kind of learning, and ANNs can do this, too.

As examples of the availability of data, we may consider ImageNet (14 million images); Wikipedia (5 million articles), and Common Crawl, a nonprofit organization that constantly explores the World Wide Web and provides datasets based on more than two billion web pages. Unlabelled images are of little use, of course, but systems such as Amazon's Mechanical Turk provide a low-cost global workforce.

Another difference between older ANNs and more recent examples is the approach to training. At first, characteristic features of the objects to be classified or recognized were chosen by people expert in the relevant domains, and the ANN would be built to recognize those features. Modern ANNs are able to identify key features themselves and then use the discovered features as a basis for classification. There is a risk here that inappropriate features may be selected. For example, there is a popular story about an ANN that apparently learned to distinguish dogs and wolves, but it turned out that classification reduced to the rule "if there's snow in the picture, it's a wolf". Although the story is apocryphal (the work was performed as part of a scientific experiment, not a real application of classification techniques), it illustrates the potential dangers of automatic feature selection.

Current applications of deep learning include:

- Speech processing, including voice recognition, voice modelling, speaker encoding, and voice cloning.
- Image and video processing, including face recognition, handwriting recognition, semantic analysis of images, and fraud detection.
- Autonomous vehicles, including self-driving cars.
- Genome sequencing.
- Numerous medical applications, including radiology (automatic X-ray analysis), dermatology (diagnosing skin conditions), pathology (cancer detection), and identifying diabetic retinopathy (blindness caused by diabetes).

Although deep learning is the dominant paradigm in AI research today, even some of the leaders in the field doubt that this situation will continue. At an AI conference in October 2017, three of the leading researchers in deep learning (Yoshua Bengio, Geoff Hinton, and Yann LeCun) expressed the opinion that deep learning was no longer producing dramatic new results. Gary Marcus, Judea Pearl, and others have pointed to what they feel are fundamental limitations in what deep learning, as currently practiced, can achieve.[13,14]

One of the first lessons that we learn in statistics is that "correlation does not imply cause". For example, the number of Civil Engineering degrees awarded in the USA closely tracks the consumption of mozzarella cheese.[15] But we should not infer from this that eating mozzarella cheese will get you an engineering degree or that civil engineers like mozzarella: the correlation between the numbers is (probably) a coincidence.

But, on the other hand, there *may be* a cause for correlation. When researchers first started to notice connections between smoking and lung cancer in the 1930s, skeptics (and tobacco companies) were quick to point out that correlation is not cause. Carefully designed studies, starting in 1952, showed that there actually was a cause behind this correlation: smoking does increase your chances of contracting lung cancer.

Most deep learning programs are simply discovering correlations between numbers in very large data sets. For example, AlphaGo seeks moves that correlate with winning the game. AlphaGo succeeds because, in this particular case, correlation *is* cause: good moves lead to wins. But we cannot always rely on this. Working with data alone, even "big data", can establish only correlation. In many cases, we would like to have a deeper understanding. One emerging approach is to use *causality networks* to provide a framework for the analysis of big data.

6. The Future: Artificial General Intelligence?

Successful AI programs are invariably highly specialized: they can play chess, or trade in stocks, or fly an aircraft very well, but they can do nothing else. When we are told that a person is an expert chess player, we assume that he or she can do many other things as well, such as breathing, eating, walking, talking, and generally surviving in a complex world. We say that people have "common sense", "folk psychology", or know "naive physics". Because we have this kind of knowledge, either built-in or learned at an early age, we find it hard to imagine what it would be like to live without it.

Even specialized AI programs must be instructed very carefully. If you tell an AI program to "build a tall building using 10,000 bricks", it will give you a narrow tower 10,000 bricks high. You should have asked it to "build a tall *and stable* building using 10,000 bricks" — but then you have to define "stable".

An *Artificial General Intelligence* (AGI) is an AI program with the human ability to solve many problems adequately rather than a single problem very well. We do not expect a single person to write like Shakespeare, compose like Mozart, and play tennis like Federer, but we do expect each individual to perform a wide variety of tasks competently and perhaps a few tasks well.

Our brains have around 100 billion neurons but, more importantly, perhaps 100 *trillion* synapses linking neurons together. Brains rewire themselves as we learn, a phenomenon known as neuroplasticity. Although learning is most rapid during early development, we continue to learn all throughout our lives. Finally, our brains are exposed to a continuous barrage of information coming through the traditional five senses (sight, hearing, taste, smell, and touch) as well as many others that are not so widely recognized, such as temperature, kinesthetic (body position), pain, balance, hunger, thirst, and so on.

In view of the brain's capabilities, it is not surprising that realizing an AGI is a very hard problem. Opinions about if and when we will achieve AGI vary widely. As we have learned more about AI, dreams of an AGI have receded into the future. Few people now would agree with Herbert

Simon who said, after the Dartmouth conference in 1956, "machines will be capable, within twenty years, of doing any work a man can do".

"Strong AI" is a term related to AGI. Some consider strong AI to be equivalent to AGI but others, especially academics, require that a strong AI must have a "mind" and experience "consciousness". Philosophers use the term "zombie" for a machine that has the general intelligence of a person but is not conscious. However, it is not clear that zombies could ever exist: perhaps having the mental capabilities of a person implies consciousness. We don't yet know and, until we do, it is hard to even define an AGI.

Some people have expressed the concern that, once AI exceeds human intelligence and begins to improve itself, it will advance so rapidly that we will lose control. In 1965, I.J. Good speculated that a machine with greater than human intelligence would be built; this machine would design an even more intelligent machine ... and so on, leading to an "intelligence explosion".[16] Vernon Vinge introduced the idea of a "Technological Singularity" (now called just "Singularity") in an eponymous 1993 essay. Ray Kurzweil postulates that the speed of technological change, in analogy to Moore's Law, will increase exponentially, and also supports the Singularity thesis.[17] The philosopher Nick Bostrom has argued that AGI will become skilled at acquiring the resources that it needs for its own purpose and become resistant to shutting down.[18]

Concerns about the future of AI have also been expressed by people who do not explicitly mention the Singularity, such as the late Stephen Hawking and entrepreneurs such as Bill Gates, Elon Musk, and Peter Thiel. Their concern is that a superintelligent AI will assume the dominant role in planetary affairs that humans enjoy now. Such an AI might decide that we are too stupid to be useful and wipe us out. Another scenario that has been proposed is that an AI will be instructed to make paper clips and will become so successful at this task that it destroys the universe. There is sufficient concern about AI, and its military applications in particular, that 2,400 scientists and 26 countries have signed the Lethal Autonomous Weapons Pledge, which declares that "the decision to take a human life should never be delegated to a machine".[19] The implications of artificial superintelligence present interesting problems for philosophers, but it seems likely that we will retain our dominance over machines for a few years to come.

In summary, there are three schools of thought concerning AGI: it may (1) be even better than apple pie; (2) signal the end of the human race; or (3) never happen. It seems best not to lose any sleep over the future of AI for now but you should not hesitate to use your smart device to wake you up tomorrow morning.

References

1. H. P. Moravec, *Mind Children*, Harvard University Press (1988).
2. A. Turing, Computer machinery and intelligence, *Mind*, **49**, 433–460 (1950).
3. M. Minsky and S. Papert, *Perceptrons: an Introduction to Computational Geometry*, MIT Press (1969).
4. M. Minsky, *The Society of Mind*, Simon & Schuster (1986).
5. P. McCorduck, *Machines Who Think*, second edn. A. K. Peters (2004).
6. J. Weizenbaum, *Computer Power and Human Reason: From Judgment To Calculation*, W.H. Freeman (1976).
7. J. Haugeland, *Artificial Intelligence: The Very Idea*, Bradford Books (1989).
8. A. Newell and H. A. Simon, Computer science as empirical inquiry: Symbols and search, *Communications of the ACM*, **19**(3), 113–126 (1976).
9. J. Pearl, *Probabilistic Reasoning in Intelligent Systems*, Morgan Kaufmann (1988).
10. R. Neapolitan, *Probabilistic Reasoning in Expert Systems*, Wiley-Interscience (1989).
11. P. Domingos, *The Master Algorithm: How the Quest for the Ultimate Learning Machine Will Remake Our World*, Basic Books (2015).
12. J. Koza, *Genetic Programming IV: Routine Human-Competitive Machine Intelligence*, Springer (2007).
13. G. Marcus, Is deep learning a revolution in artificial intelligence?, *The New Yorker* (2012).
14. J. Pearl and D. MacKenzie, *The Book of Why: the New Science of Cause and Effect*, Basic Books (2018).
15. T. Vigen, *Spurious Correlations*, Hachette Books (2015).
16. I. Good, Speculations concerning the first ultraintelligent machine, in *Advances in Computers*, vol. 6, Academic Press (1965).
17. R. Kurzweil, *The Singularity Is Near*, Penguin Books (2006).
18. N. Bostrom, *Superintelligence: Paths, Dangers, Strategies*, Oxford University Press (2014).
19. FLI, Lethal autonomous weapons pledge, The Future of Life Institute, Boston, MA (2018).

Chapter 2

Diverse Perspectives on the Relationship between Artificial Intelligence and Pattern Recognition

Björn Barz

Friedrich Schiller University Jena, Computer Vision Group,
Jena, Germany
bjoern.barz@uni-jena.de irst

Prerana Mukherjee and Brejesh Lall

Indian Institute of Technology Delhi
{eez138300, brejesh}@ee.iitd.ac.in

Elham Vahdati

Centre for Pattern Recognition and Machine Intelligence (CENPARMI)
Concordia University, Montreal, Canada
g_vahdat@encs.concordia.ca

The International Conference on Artificial Intelligence and Pattern Recognition (ICPRAI 2018) brought together scholars to celebrate works on artificial intelligence and pattern recognition. In acknowledgment that two terms are closely related and are sometimes used interchangeably, a Competition was set up as part of the conference whereby attendees were invited to submit a response to the following question: What is the relation between Artificial Intelligence and Pattern Recognition? This chapter includes the top three responses as judged by the ICPRAI 2018 Competition Committee. Barz argues that intelligence goes far beyond pattern recognition, while pattern recognition is an essential prerequisite for any intelligence, artificial or not. Mukherjee and Lall outlines the inter-related concepts in AI and PR and various potential use-cases. Lastly, Elham provides her perspective, which includes seeing pattern recognition as a starting point or a principle of discovery of artificial intelligence developments.

1. The Perspective of Björn Barz

The idea of artificial intelligence (AI) has been fascinating mankind for hundreds of years. The ancient myth of Talos (Greek: Τάλως), a giant automaton made of bronze to protect the Greek island Crete from enemy ships, is one of the first known mentions of intelligent artificial beings. In the late 18th century, the world was impressed by an automaton that was apparently able to play chess. This machine is nowadays known as the Mechanical Turk and its intelligence was actually fake, since it was controlled by a hidden human operator. About 200 years later, in 1997, a chess-playing computer named Deep Blue[1] defeated the reigning world champion Garry Kasparov without human intervention. Since then, the benchmarks for AI have continuously been changing: For winning a chess game, sufficient compute power for simulating the consequences of all possible decisions is all that is needed. Thus, one might argue that this is not intelligence, but just number crunching. The game Go has then been considered the last bastion of human intelligence regarding board games for a long time, until one of the world's best players was beaten by a machine learning approach called Alpha Go.[2] Shortly after that, the psychologist Gary Marcus argued that Alpha Go did not learn the game completely on its own, but benefits from a considerable amount of prior knowledge about the game hard-wired into the system by humans.[3] Moreover, though it is capable of playing usual Go games with impressive performance, it could not generalize what it has learned to boards of different size, in contrast to humans.

These examples illustrate the usual shift of requirements imposed on AI: There are problems which are generally considered requiring intelligence for being solved appropriately, but once done by machines, the mechanisms solving the problem are considered as being engineered and not that intelligent after all. AI is hence a moving target without exact definition. This problem is also inherent in the widespread definition of AI, which can, for example, be found in the Encyclopædia Britannica: "the ability of a digital computer [...] to perform tasks commonly associated with intelligent beings".[4] However, once a specialized "intelligent" machine attains such an ability but still lacks the ability to perform other intelligent tasks, the solved task will not be commonly associated with intelligent beings anymore and the machine itself will not be considered an intelligent being either.

But what is intelligence then? One of the best-known benchmarks for intelligence is the Imitation Game proposed by Alan Turing,[5] whose most popular interpretation is nowadays usually referred to as the Turing test. According to the setup of this test, human judges conduct a conversation with another human on the one hand and a machine on the other hand using a text-based chat interface. After five minutes, the testers must judge which of the two dialog partners is the human. If the machine can convince more than 30% of the testers to be human, it passes the Turing test.

Since then the Turing test has been the subject of ongoing debates. In 2014, it was claimed that a chatbot named "Eugene Goostman" would have passed the test, but this was met with a lot of skepticism: The chatbot pretended to be a 13-year-old Ukrainian boy to justify grammatical mistakes and limited conversational skills. Moreover, the software evaded questions requiring world-knowledge or reasoning by asking deflecting questions.

In fact, passing the Turing test does not require real intelligence, but rather a sophisticated imitation of intelligent behavior. According to a thought experiment by the philosopher John Searle,[6] known as the Chinese Room, a computer could simulate intelligence, generating plausible outputs for given inputs, without actually understanding any of them. Imagine a lookup table of all possible sequences of sentences in a certain language— Chinese in Searle's example—and corresponding responses for each sentence. A machine could have a conversation in that language with a human just by looking up the responses, but actually understanding nothing. In Searle's examples, these rules for interacting with the world were assumed to be given. Learning them from examples, on the other hand, would fall in the domain of pattern recognition, which refers to the automatic recognition of structures in data—such as groups, relations, and distinctive features—and learning of complex rules from the data. Although this field has achieved impressive breakthroughs in the recent past, such as mastering the game of Go, contemporary AI systems are, in principle, still similar to Searle's Chinese Room: They learn and recognize patterns in the data, but they do not actually understand them. Digital "smart" assistants recognize spoken language and map it onto a set of request types, but the adequate responses are still produced by manually engineered algorithms. Driver-assistance systems recognize patterns in sensor data, such as traffic signs and weather conditions in images. The reaction on these events is, again, hard-wired and not actually learned.

Of course, these typical responses are also patterns and could, in theory, be learned from data. However, learning and recognizing patterns is only one component of intelligence. The associations machine learning algorithms currently try to learn have their origin in human intelligence itself: language, complex categorizations of the entities of the world, the rules of traffic etc. Real intelligence is less about solving a certain task or learning to recognize a set of patterns, but more about learning how to learn (the part of pattern recognition that is currently done by humans) and abstracting. Intelligence is not only about recognizing concepts, but also inventing them in the first place. It is about curiosity, innovation, and creativity. A contemporary AI system may be able to recognize the writing style of different authors and even to generate new books, but the results will always be an imitation of the existing. Such a machine cannot create its own style. Similarly, machine learning techniques can learn how to play chess and Go, but could they have invented these games and their rules in the first place?

The drivers behind such innovations are often specific needs of humans: The hunger of ancient people led to the invention of weapons for hunting. Language, being the most effective and efficient way for humans to communicate, was a necessary invention for overcoming loneliness and solving tasks that cannot be accomplished alone.[7] And what else could have been the motivation for the creation of art and music if not the human search for joy? Thus, intelligence also involves emotions. Machines, on the contrary, have no motivation to learn beyond what they are told to learn. Moreover, they might be able to recognize the patterns in human behavior, but they will not be able to understand how humans feel and why they act the way they do. However, a machine will only be perceived as intelligent by humans if it can understand them the same way other humans do. Empathy hence is another important component of intelligence, which should not be underestimated. Humans develop this ability through years of social interaction and perhaps even on the basis of innate biological prerequisites.

Empathy is furthermore crucial for understanding how humans make decisions, which is not always rational but driven by emotions, personal opinions and ambitions. This allows us to make decisions even in situations where no optimal solution but multiple equally good or equally bad alternatives are available, from a rational point of view. In such a situation, a strategy suitable for machines would be to flip a coin, but the irrational, emotional aspect in human decision-making gives us confidence to still do the right instead of a random thing. A machine, on the other hand, follows deterministic rules and cannot develop own opinions and personal goals.

Pattern recognition is a fundamental skill of all intelligent beings and a prerequisite for any intelligent behavior: for vision, language understanding and conversation, and for learning complex interrelationships. Therefore, it is currently often used to pretend intelligent machines, but true intelligence goes far beyond this. Besides the recognition and abstraction of patterns, it also involves creativity, innovation, imagination, emotions, empathy, and personality. Whether machines can achieve this at all, is questionable.

2. The Perspective of Prerana Mukherjee and Brejesh Lall

Artificial Intelligence (AI) term as coined by John McCarthy refers to the intelligent agents that can mimic cognitive functions such as "learning" or "problem solving" with explicit programming. The notion is to maximize the success rate for reaching the set goal. The goal could be varied like reasoning, automated learning and scheduling, natural language processing, computer vision, robotics or simply general intelligence. Pattern Recognition (PR) on the other hand refers to the observations or pattern finding ability using the knowledge bases and inference engines. With the huge digital data explosion, the concepts of PR (regression, classification, clustering on structured or unstructured data) is handled by the machine learning (ML) algorithms. If PR capabilities are augmented with feedback it results in learning things thus interchangeably used with the term machine learning. Both AI and PR complement each other in the working principles. AI has leaped a long way ahead from the Turing test and is being applied in domains such as self-driving cars such as Autopilot in Tesla, multi-agent collaborative systems, strategic game systems such as AlphaGo Zero by Google's DeepMind, natural language processing, intelligent personal assistants such as Siri, Alexa, Cortana use AI principles. There are three school of thoughts associated in the domain of PR: i) Neural Net works (1950s–1970s): key to make the machine understand as we do with a tradeoff in speed and accuracy, ii) Machine Learning (1980s–2010s): It is an era predominated by ML zeitgeists, and iii) Deep Learning (Recent trend): Deep learning architectures drive the AI boom. Deep learning has shown unprecedented success in computer vision tasks like 2D object recognition, scene classification, tracking etc. and steers ahead the work in 3D world. AI automates repetitive learning and discovery through data while adding intelligence to the inference engines. Figure 1 depicts the AI vs PR relationship (tools and its applications).

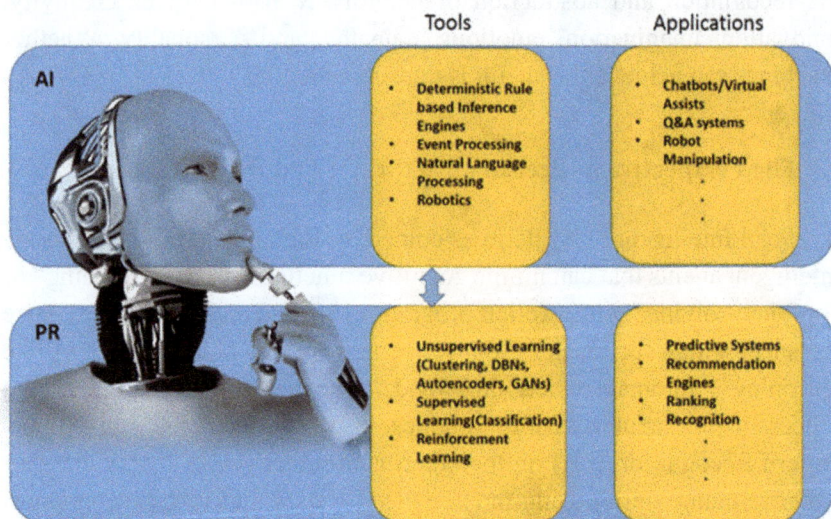

Fig. 1. AI vs PR relationship (tools and its applications).

2.1. *Towards understanding AI and PR concepts*

To apply a style, begin by selecting the text to which the style needs to be the typical AI problems involve reasoning, decision-making, learning, natural language processing, visual perception, object manipulation, routeplanning, affective computing, game theory etc. After a decade of AI shutdown also referred to as the "AI Winter" era when most agencies had retracted from providing requisite funds for AI exploration, it again saw the light of commercial success with the popularity of expert systems. The standard approaches to evaluate AI problems include cybernetics or computational intelligence, symbolic AI, logic programming, embodied or behaviour based, and statistical learning-based methods. Tools comprehensively involve optimization techniques, neural-networks, probabilistic inference engines. The terminologies such as pattern recognition, machine learning, data mining and knowledge discovery in databases (KDD) are highly overlapping in their scope and usage. Machine learning typically refers to the supervised learning techniques whereas KDD and data mining have emphasized on unsupervised strategies and have broad spectrum in business use. Pattern recognition formalizes the pattern visualization discovered in the data whereas machine learning aims at maximizing recognition rates. The three broad learning methods involve: i) Supervised/classification methods handling labeled data, ii) Unsupervised/clustering methods handling unlabeled data, and iii) Semi-supervised methods which uses a combination of labeled and unlabeled data. There is a fourth category known as Reinforcement learning which deals with maximizing the reward while minimizing the penalties. It is both common to AI and PR fields. The classification methods could be further categorized into parametric (e.g. linear discriminant analysis, logistic regression) and non-parametric (e.g. decision trees, support vector machines, naive Bayes) methods. Cluster analysis involves k-means, hierarchical clustering algorithms.

2.2. *Case scenarios and applications*

Artificial intelligence is pervasive and the application domain areas are ubiquitous in nature. Ranging from medical diagnosis or healthcare, autonomous navigation assist, strategic game playing[9] to optimizing search results, personal assistants AI techniques are omnipresent. Pattern recognition goes hand-in-hand with the AI applications[10] such as speech recognition, spam classification, cancer patient classification, target recognition etc. Causal InfoGAN[11] creates plannable representations of dynamical systems such as maze simulations. Count determination with high precision is highly helpful for navigation purposes and can be achieved with deep learning based techniques[12].

2.3. *Conclusion*

The relationship between artificial intelligence and pattern recognition is presented. AI and PR concepts have been outlined to allow the readers to appreciate the advancements in these fields. AI techniques with PR capabilities envisages the futuristic world and expands the knowledge boundaries. Thus, it is extremely important to continuously dwell on the AI and PR advancements and maximize unprecedented benefits to humanity.

3. The Perspective of Elham Vahdati

The main objective of artificial intelligence is to develop a system that learns and solves problems on its own. AI currently leverages state-of-the-art techniques to identify and analyze patterns so that it will be able to predict real-life outcomes. The demand for intelligent machines in areas such as medical diagnostics and biometric security systems, gives researchers an incentive to develop novel methods, and explore new practical applications in this field. In fact, AI involves machines which succeeded in accomplishing tasks that are inspired by the capacities of human intelligence.

One of the salient abilities in intelligent machines is pattern recognition which is considered as a part of the broader area of Artificial Intelligence (AI). The ability of intelligence of machines for environmental perception is peculiar to pattern recognition, whereas cognition, including reasoning, knowledge engineering, and language understanding, can be acquired using other branches of AI. Researchers strive to design intelligent machines that are able to recognize patterns, and then assess their efficacy. Consequently, accurate pattern recognition by intelligent machines would definitely be extremely useful. It should be noted that although human beings are able to distinguish between the aroma of a flower and the odor of an onion or differentiate between handwritten numerals "3" and "8" effortlessly, it is still difficult for computers to solve these perceptual problems[13]. The main reason is that each pattern usually contains a considerable amount of information, which would definitely lead to inconspicuous and high-dimensional structures for recognition problems. Pattern recognition can be considered as a field which deals with a number of typical problems and techniques stemmed from a process of overspecialization. Moreover, Pattern recognition is viewed as a way to provide categorization ("see the one in many")[14]. The primary goal of pattern recognition algorithms is to find an obvious answer for all possible data and to categorize input data based on certain attributes.

It is noteworthy that pattern recognition can be deemed to be a sub-area of artificial intelligence. From a historical perspective, pattern recognition and artificial intelligence have been inextricably intertwined since their emergence. Interestingly, researchers working in the field of pattern recognition are drawn to topics which are of paramount importance, including knowledge representation, inference, search and learning, comprising the core of AI. Furthermore, it is worth mentioning that the recognition and understanding of sensory data such as speech and images, which are of great value in pattern recognition, are also considered as significant subfields of AI. From a scientific point of view, what relates pattern recognition to artificial intelligence is profound dependencies which strongly link categorization to all intellectual activities[14]. Pattern recognition would certainly span a wide range of information processing problems which are of great practical importance. Cross-disciplinary applications of artificial intelligence and pattern recognition range from speech recognition and the classification of handwritten characters to fault detection in machinery and medical diagnosis where fundamental learning techniques, namely classification, regression and clustering, have been extensively employed.

The fact that pattern recognition is significantly correlated to the process of learning was identified since the advent of artificial intelligence.

Pattern recognition which solves the problems of identification and recognition of patterns as well as regularities in data, is also considered as a branch of machine learning[15]. Learning is a process of obtaining information and acquiring skills to discover how to solve new problems or how to deal with new situations. Said differently, Training can be accomplished with feeding data to an algorithm and allowing it to adjust itself and continually improve. In other words, the process of learning would enable an algorithm to evolve based on empirical data. These self-learning algorithms would possess the ability to detect patterns in existing data, identify similar patterns in future data and make data driven predictions. In fact, systems can enhance their ability continuously to recognize patterns without having to be programmed to handle each pattern. As a result, when AI is devoid of learning, a multitude lines of codes along with sophisticated rules will be required to perform a particular task. It is important to note that recent scientific advances in disciplines of pattern recognition and artificial intelligence, have developed emerging techniques, including deep learning, big data and social computing. Therefore, artificial intelligence combined with pattern recognition techniques are growing in importance owing to novel methods and new applications. For instance, automation using artificial intelligence for drug discovery is a promising area of research.

To sum up, pattern recognition would certainly be a starting point or a principle of discovery of artificial intelligence developments. Sophisticated algorithms are employed by AI to learn features from data. Moreover, AI is usually equipped with learning and self-correcting abilities to enhance its accuracy based on feedback. The future role for AI is to be as a brilliant assistant who collaborates with the scientists, and it will definitely enable scientists to achieve bright scientific discoveries. Additionally, pattern recognition and machine learning will be the core constituents of solving the upcoming generation of AI problems.

The following figure illustrates the relation among AI, pattern recognition and machine learning.

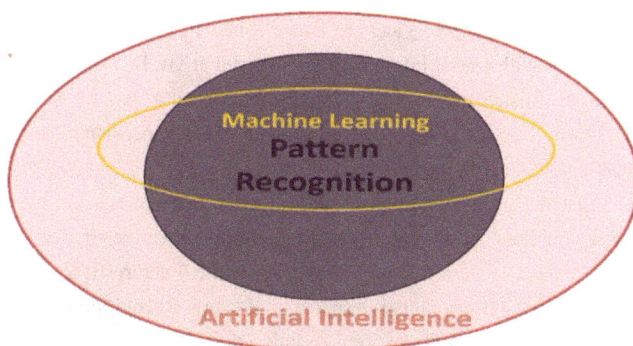

Fig. 2. Relation among AI, pattern recognition and machine learning.

References

1. F.-H. Hsu, *Behind Deep Blue: Building the computer that defeated the world chess champion,* Princeton University Press (2004).
2. D. Silver, A. Huang, C. J. Maddison, A. Guez, L. Sifre, G. Van Den Driessche, J. Schrittwieser, I. Antonoglou, et al., Mastering the game of Go with deep neural networks and tree search, Nature, 529(7587) 484 (2016).
3. G. Marcus, Innateness, alphazero, and artificial intelligence, arXiv preprint arXiv:1801.05667 (2018).
4. B. J. Copeland, Artificial intelligence, *Encyclopædia Britannica* (June 2018). Accessed 16 July 2018. URL: https://www.britannica.com/technology/artificial-intelligence.
5. A.M. Turing, Computing machinery and intelligence, Mind, 59(236) (1950).
6. J. R. Searle, Minds, brains, and programs, Behavioral and brain sciences, 3 (3), 417–424 (1980).
7. S. Pinker, The Language Instinct: How the Mind Creates Language, Penguin Books (2003).
8. H. Kim, P. Garrido, A. Tewari, W. Xu, J. Thies, M. Nießner, P. Pérez, C. Richardt, M. Zollhöfer, and C. Theobalt, Deep video portraits, arXiv preprint, arXiv:1805.11714 (2018).
9. G. N. Yannakakis and J. Togelius, *Artificial Intelligence and Games,* Springer (2018).
10. N. Bonnet. Artificial intelligence and pattern recognition techniques in microscope image processing and analysis, in *Advances in Imaging and Electron Physics*, pp. 1–77 (2000).

11. T. Kurutach, A. Tamar, G. Yang, S. Russell, and P. Abbeel, Learning plannable representations with causal infogan, arXiv preprint arXiv:1807.09341 (2018).

12. H. Laradji, N. Rostamzadeh, P. O. Pinheiro, D. Vazquez, and M. Schmidt, Where are the blobs: Counting by localization with point supervision, arXiv preprint arXiv:1807.09856 (2018).

13. Tohka. What is pattern recognition?, Introduction to Pattern Recognition Course: Lecture 1, Institute of Signal Processing, Tampere University of Technology, Finland. http://www.cs.tut.fi/sgn/m2obsi/courses/IPR/Lectures/IPR_Lecture_1.pdf

14. T. Scantamburlo, Philosophical Aspects in Pattern Recognition Research, PhD thesis, Ca' Foscari University of Venice, Italy (Nov. 2013).

15. H. Liu, J. Yin, X. Luo, S. Zhang, Foreword to the special issue on recent advances on pattern recognition and artificial intelligence, *Neural Comput. Appl.*, 29(1), 1–2 (2018).

Chapter 3

Natural Language Processing: An Overview

Hessam Amini*, Farhood Farahnak* and Leila Kosseim

Computational Linguistics at Concordia (CLaC) Laboratory
Department of Computer Science and Software Engineering
Concordia University, Montreal, Canada H3G 2W1
first.last@concordia.ca

This chapter provides an overview of the field of Natural Language Processing (NLP), a sub-field of Artificial Intelligence (AI) that aims to build automatic systems that can understand or produce texts in natural language. The intended audience is a non-technical reader with no particular background in linguistics or computer science.

The chapter first characterizes natural language and explains why dealing with such unstructured data automatically is a challenge. Examples of typical applications of NLP are then provided ranging from low-level tasks to end-user everyday systems. As much of the work in AI, NLP has gone through three main eras: symbolic approaches, machine learning driven approaches, and more recently, deep learning driven approaches. These three paradigms will be described, with a particular emphasis on the current one, deep learning, which, in only a few years, has led to exciting results and allowed applications, such as conversational agents and machine translation, to become accessible and usable to the public.

1. Introduction

Today, an overwhelming quantity of textual information is available in electronic form. These texts are written in *natural language*, for example, English, French, Spanish, ... but are aimed for human consumption. Developing automatic tools so that machines can understand the content of such documents or produce them automatically is the goal of Natural Language Processing (or NLP). This includes 1) understanding the content of

---

* Authors, listed in alphabetical order, contributed equally.

documents written in natural language, also known as Natural Language Understanding (or NLU) and 2) generating texts in natural language, also known as Natural Language Generation (or NLG). Practical applications of NLP include systems such as web search engines, text summarizers, word completion, question answering systems, conversational agents, sentiment analyzers, ... to name only a few.

1.1. *Natural versus Artificial Languages*

Natural language refers to the language used for human communication such as English, French, ... As opposed to natural language, *artificial language* refers to a language that was designed. These languages may include human-like languages created for entertainment purposes (such as J.R.R. Tolkien's *Elvish* language[1] or David J. Peterson's *Valyrian* and *Dothraki* languages[2]), for specific practical purposes (such as Esperanto), or for technological and scientific reasons (such as programming languages).

Natural languages have several key differences with artificial languages that make them challenging to process automatically:

Natural languages evolve due to human unconscious and conscious factors, including social, historical, and psychological factors. As natural languages evolve, new words and expressions are created and included in the language. A sentence such as *I forgot my iPhone in your SUV* would have been incomprehensible only a few years ago. NLP systems will therefore need to deal with issues such as an open lexicon, unknown words, ...

Natural languages are robust as they are meant for human communication. Syntactic rules, although typically rather complex, are often flexible. If a semi-colon is required by the grammar, one can easily substitute it for a colon, and the reader will still very likely understand the text. If a word is misspelled, or a word in unknown by the reader, the text will still likely be understandable. NLP systems therefore need to address issues such as informally written texts, misspelled words, ungrammatical sentences, ...

Natural languages are ambiguous at many levels. For example, a single word may have different meanings (e.g. a *chair* may be a person or a piece of furniture), a sentence may have different syntactic parses (e.g. in the sentence *The man saw Jane with the telescope*, the phrase *with the telescope* can qualify either the verb *saw* or the noun *Jane*), or a sentence may have different interpretations depending on its context. These ambiguities create challenges for NLP systems. For example, a human will easily understand that in the sentence *the chair cancelled the meeting*, the word *chair* refers to a person, but automatically ruling out the sense of furniture will need to be addressed.

1.2. *Natural Language Understanding versus Generation*

The field of NLP is composed of two sub-fields:

(1) **Natural Language Understanding (NLU)** takes texts as input. NLU tries to develop techniques to understand and interpret texts in natural language in order to perform a variety of decisions: act according to some instructions, extract relevant information from a text, provide an answer to a question, classify or summarize a document, or create an intermediary representation of the text that can be used for further processing in other applications.

(2) **Natural Language Generation (NLG)** produces texts as output. As opposed to NLU, NLG takes as input some representation of the content to communicate (which can be of various forms[3]) and tries to generate as output a human-like textual data such as an answer, an article, an email...

The ultimate goal of NLU is to understand a text as well as a human would; while the ultimate goal of NLG is to produce a text as well as a human would. These two tasks can be seen in action in conversational agents, where the system must understand the user's sentences (NLU) in order to respond accordingly (NLG).

1.3. *Components of Natural Language Processing Systems*

In order to process natural language automatically, systems are traditionally divided into different components, each of which deals with a different aspect of language. Following the field of linguistics, it is standard to consider the following components:

Lexical Analysis studies individual words. Automatically, converting a sequence of characters into a sequence of words and sentences is the task

of lexical analysis. This includes tasks such as tokenization (e.g. *I don't* →
I / don't), lemmatization (e.g. *I / do / not*), sentence boundary detection,
...

Syntax refers to the set of rules that govern how words can be arranged
together in order to form grammatical sentences. For example, in English,
the sentence *I like to read* is grammatical, but the same set of words in
a different order, for example, *like I read to*, is not. Understanding the
underlying structure of a sentence gives very strong cues about its meaning.

Semantics refers to the meaning of words, phrases and sentences and
how these meanings are related. *Lexical semantics* studies the meanings
of individual words and the semantic relations that they have with other
words. For example, lexical semantics is involved when determining that
the word *chair* in the sentence *The department voted for Jane to be the
new chair* refers to a person rather than a piece of furniture. On the other
hand, *compositional semantics* studies how the meaning of larger phrases
and sentences can be composed from the meaning of their individual words
and their relationships with each other.

Discourse goes beyond individual sentences and tries to capture the relations between sentences in order to understand the text as a whole. This
includes the study of referring expressions (e.g. the use of pronouns to refer to entities already mentioned in the text) and discourse relations that
indicate the logical relation between textual elements. For example in *Jack
is hungry, because he did not eat*, it is important to identify that there is a
causality relation between the two clauses.

Pragmatics tries to go beyond the literal meaning and studies how the
context influences the meaning of a text. The context can be linguistic (e.g.
the other words around), cultural, or situtational (e.g. in which situation
the text is written/said). For example, if on the street, someone asks a
passer-by *Do you have some change?*, the questioner does not really want
to be informed if the other has or does not have change; but rather is
requesting to be given some change.

World Knowledge takes into account the assumptions or background
information about the world (such as history, facts, ...) to truly understand

the text. For example, in the sentence *The trophy would not fit in the brown suitcase because it was too big,*[4] a human would easily understand that the pronoun *it* refers to the *trophy*; whereas in *The trophy would not fit in the brown suitcase because it was too small*, the pronoun *it* refers to the *suitcase*.

This knowledge, referred to as *world knowledge* or *common sense knowledge*, is naturally acquired by humans through their living experience. Building systems that understand or produce natural language as well as a human requires to take into account world knowledge.

2. Applications

Let us now explore examples of successful applications of NLP. We categorized these applications into two classes: low-level and high-level applications.

2.1. *Low-Level Applications*

Low-level applications of NLP are typically not used by end-users, but rather compute core linguistic representations that are used in order to develop or improve high-level applications that are used by end-users. Standard low-level applications include:

Part-of-Speech (PoS) Tagging Part-of-Speech tags are grammatical labels that are assigned to words in a particular sentence. Such tags can be general, such as *Noun*, *Verb*, *Adjective*, or more fine-grained, such as *Noun-Singular*, *Verb-be-3rd-Person-Singular-Present*, …

Over the years, a multitude of automatic PoS taggers have been developed following a variety of approaches (see Section 3). Today PoS taggers achieve around 97% accuracy for English.[5] However, PoS tagging is not a solved problem, as these tools are often domain-dependent: a PoS tagger trained on a specific domain (e.g. biology) does not perform as well on another domain (e.g. computer science).

Named Entity Recognition (NER) is concerned with finding and labelling a predefined set of semantic expressions, such as PERSONS, PLACES, ORGANIZATIONS, EXPRESSIONS OF TIME, etc. For example, given the sentence *The meeting with Jane Young, the CEO of ABC inc., was July 3 2017*, an NER system will determine that *Jane Young* is a PERSON, *ABC inc.* is an ORGANIZATION, and *July 3 2017* is a DATE.

Extracting named entities is seen as a segmentation problem and is further complicated by embedded entities. For example, *University of Montreal* is a named entity, but *Montreal* on its own is also an entity. Labelling named entities is also challenging, since the same entity may be labeled differently depending on the context. For example, *Louis Vuitton* can be a PERSON, an ORGANIZATION or a COMMERCIAL PRODUCT. State-of-the-art NER systems achieve a performance of around 90% for English, while for other languages, the performance is significantly lower.[6]

Co-reference Resolution and Generation   In a text, several words or phrases can refer to the same entity. For example, in the sentence *I saw Alex when he was going home*, both *Alex* and *he* refer to the same entity. Finding the referent of expressions is essential to understand a text.

Co-reference resolution aims to identify these co-references automatically. State-of-the-art systems have achieved performances of around 65% to 74% for English,[7] which shows that much work still needs to be done in this field. As opposed to co-reference resolution, co-reference generation (often referred to as *referring expressions generation*) aims to find the most natural words or phrases that an NLG system should use to refer to an entity.[8]

Word Sense Disambiguation   As indicated in Section 1.1, natural language is ambiguous. In particular, one word or expression may have more than one meaning; for example, the word *bass* may refer to a fish or a man with a low-pitched singing voice. Word Sense Disambiguation (WSD) is the task of identifying the sense of a word in its context. For example in *the bass was excellent on the grill* a WSD system will find that most likely *bass* refers to a fish.

Similarly to PoS tagging, WSD can be considered as a classification problem; however, different linguistic features are used. In WSD, the words immediately surrounding the ambiguous word give very strong clues about its meaning. State-of-the-art systems in WSD achieve performances around 95%.[9]

Syntactic Parsing   determines how words in a sentence are grouped into constituents following a specific grammar. The result is one, or more often, multiple, *parse trees*. Finding the proper parse tree of a sentence helps determine what the sentence means, and hence is very useful for applications such as question answering. For example, given the sentence *The man saw Jane with the telescope*, two parse trees are shown in Figure 1.

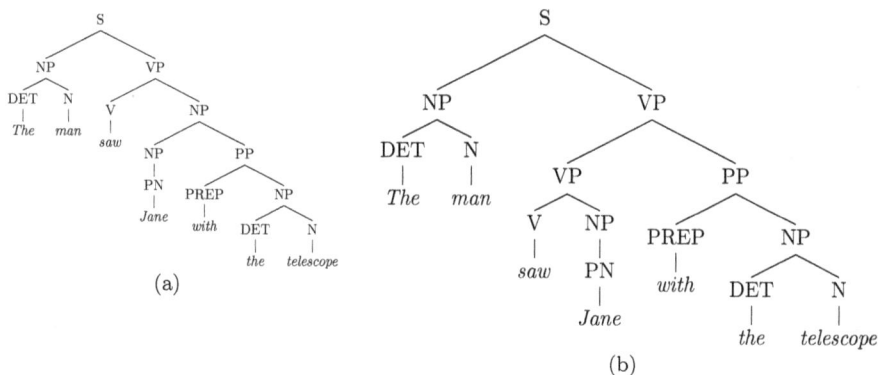

Fig. 1.   Two possible parse trees for the sentence *The man saw Jane with the telescope*.

In Figure 1(a), the constituent *with the telescope* is part of the noun phrase (NP) – in this case, the sentence means that Jane was carrying the telescope; whereas in Figure 1(b), *with the telescope* is part of the verb phrase (VP) – in this case, the sentence means that the telescope was the instrument used to see Jane.

Today, syntactic parsers can reach performances that are comparable to human experts on English texts (with performances near 92%);[10,11] however much work still needs to be done to improve their performance on informal texts, such as tweets, or languages other than English.[12]

Paraphrase Detection and Generation   A paraphrase is a text that states the same meaning as another, but using different words or grammatical structures. For example, the two sentences *Scientists studied this case* and *This case was studied by scientists* are paraphrases.

The automatic detection of paraphrases is crucial for several applications, such as text summarization, plagiarism detection, and question answering. Today, state-of-the-art paraphrase detection systems perform very well on well-written English texts;[13] however, much work still needs to be done to improve their performance on informal texts, such as tweets.[14]

On the other hand, paraphrase generation tries to generate paraphrases automatically. This task is particularly useful for conversational agents in order to vary the output of the system. Recent advancements in deep learning for NLP, in particular sequence-to-sequence models (see Section 3.3) have led to the development of systems that generate paraphrases of very high quality.[14]

2.2. High-Level Applications

As opposed to low-level applications, high-level applications aim to solve problems for the end-user. Typical examples include:

Information Extraction (IE) tries to extract specific structured or semi-structured information from texts.[15] For example, from the sentence *Jane's son, Jim, works at Microsoft*, an IE system would exact the relations CHILD-OF(*Jane, Jim*) and EMPLOYEE-OF(*Microsoft, Jim*).

IE systems typically first use NER and co-reference resolution (see Section 2.1) to identify named entities (*Jane, Jim* and *Microsoft*). Then the semantic relations between these entities are found. These relations can be very general, such as CHILD-OF, EMPLOYEE-OF, ... or specific to a particular domain such as MUTATION-EXTRACTION, MUTATION-TO-GENE-ASSOCIATION, ... in biomedical applications.[16] Finally, many IE systems organize the extracted information by automatically filling slots in pre-defined templates.

Sentiment Analysis automatically detects affective states in a text. The most basic task in sentiment analysis is to identify the polarity of a text – such as positive, negative, or neutral. In a more complex setting, sentiment analysis can extract the emotional state (e.g. happy, sad, angry, ...) regarding a specific aspect or feature of an entity.

Sentiment analysis has a wide range of applications in marketing and customer service, as it allows to mine customer reviews. Other useful applications include recommender systems, where sentiment analysis is used to understand the preferences of online customers or social media users in order to provide them with appropriate advertisements or recommendations.

Summarization is the task of automatically creating a summary from a natural language text that includes the most important points of the text. Two main approaches are typically followed: *extraction-based summarization* and *abstraction-based approach*. Extractive summarisation creates a summary by identifying and extracting key parts of the original text. On the other hand, abstractive summarization first tries to represent the content of the original text, and then produces a summary using NLG techniques.

Question Answering (QA) tries to automatically provide a specific answer to questions that are asked in natural language. For example, given the question *Where is the Eiffel Tower*, a QA system will search through a document collection and extract the answer *Paris*. QA can either be closed-domain or open-domain. Closed-domain QA systems focus on answering questions in specific domains (e.g. law, medicine, ...), while open-domain QA systems are capable of answering more general questions on any domain.

Conversational Agents (also known as *dialogue systems*) are applications that are able to hold coherent conversations with humans. Conversational agents should be capable of understanding the user's intentions and responding appropriately and fluently.

Two types of conversational agents have been developed: *task-oriented bots* and *chatbots*. Task-oriented bots are aimed at performing a specific task, such as placing an order, booking a hotel/flight, or scheduling an event, via a conversation. On the other hand, chatbots are mostly designed for entertainment purposes. Today, thanks to advances in deep learning for NLP (see Section 3.3), the performance of conversational agents has reached a level that allows them to be used in our daily life for simple tasks.

3. NLP Techniques

NLP is a sub-field of Artificial Intelligence (AI). As such, it followed the same technical trends of the field of AI. In this section, we will describe the three main approaches used in NLP over the years: *symbolic NLP*, *statistical NLP*, and *deep learning for NLP*.

3.1. *Symbolic NLP*

The field of NLP dates back to the early years of Artificial Intelligence (AI) in the 1950's, when Alan Turing published the seminal paper *Computing Machinery and Intelligence*[17] in which he directly relates machine intelligence to the ability to communicate with humans through natural language.

From the 1950's to the 1990's, NLP was performed by experts versed in both linguistics and computer science. Following the trend in AI in those days, NLP used a rule-based, prescriptive approach, where experts developed rules by hand to describe how language ought to be. These techniques were also known as *knowledge intensive* approaches, because experts would manually encode their knowledge into symbolic logical rules in order to perform NLP tasks. Developing hand-crafted rule-based systems was time consuming and expensive. Prototype systems were developed, but very little high-level applications made their way to the end-users. On the other hand, many theoretical and fundamental issues were addressed.[18] For example, the work of Noam Chomsky on the structure of language[19] set the groundwork for much advancement in NLP in these days.

3.2. *Statistical NLP*

In the mid-1990s, the field went through its first major paradigm shift. Large annotated corpora became available, and statistical methods and machine learning became more and more attractive to describe how language was actually used in practice. The era of statistical NLP was born.[20] Machine learning techniques were applied to large document collections to automatically identify discriminating linguistic features that were useful for the specific NLP applications to develop. The need for linguistic expertise shifted from writing rules by hand to describing useful linguistic features, and the machine learning algorithms would develop the rules automatically. The use of machine learning was much less time-consuming and expensive, and the heavy use of large corpora allowed the development of more robust low-level as well as high-level NLP applications such as part-of-speech taggers,[21,22] syntactic parsers,[23,24] and named entity taggers.[25,26]

3.3. *Deep Learning for NLP*

Around 2010, the field of NLP, and AI in general, went through another major parading shift: the era of deep learning. The resurgence of neural networks led researchers to push the boundaries even further and eliminate the need to develop hand-crafted features for the machine learning algorithms. The emergence of deep models and end-to-end learning algorithms led to NLP techniques that automatically learn a representation of useful linguistic features. The field went from writing rules by hand, to learning rules automatically (but still hand-crafting linguistic features), to automating the entire process: automating the rules and finding the linguistic features (also known as representations) automatically. In only a few years, deep learning methods have led to impressive improvements to most NLP tasks and have led to the development of many end-user applications such as conversational systems, question answering, more accurate machine translation systems, ... [27–29]

Due to the success of this new paradigm, we will describe these techniques in more detail in the next sections.

3.3.1. *Language Models*

The first successful and wide use of deep learning for NLP was is the area of *Language Modelling*. A Language Model (LM) is used to compute the probability of a sentence being used in a specific language. For example, an LM could determine that the probability of the sequence of words (or sentence) *I will find out* in English is 0.003, but the probability of *I will fine out* is much lower (e.g. 0.0001).

LMs are used in many NLP applications such as machine translation,[30] speech recognition,[31] ... Hence, being able to better estimate the probability of a sentence through a more accurate LM, often directly leads to improved results in many end-user applications.

From the 1990s to 2010, most LM methods were based on a method called *ngram modelling*[20,32] where a large collection of texts was used to count how many times a word follows a specific sequence of previous words.

Early efforts to use neural networks to create LMs date back to the early 1990's (for example[33–35]); but it was only in 2010 that significant improvements over the standard n-gram method was achieved through the use of Recurrent Neural Networks (RNNs).[36] An RNN is a special type of neural network particularly appropriate to deal with sequences, such as sequences of words or sentences. With the concurrent success of deep learning in other domains (such as speech recognition[31] and image classification[37]) researchers started to investigate the use of these models for a variety of NLP tasks such as machine translation,[38,39] text analysis,[6] conversational agents[40,41] and image captioning.[42]

3.3.2. *Language Representation*

Before major breakthroughs could be achieved by deep learning in NLP, another important issue had to be addressed: neural networks require as input a vector of numbers that does not lend itself well to sequences of words. In order to make better use of neural networks for NLP, an effective way to represent natural language through numbers was needed.

Word Embeddings

Traditionally, to be fed to a neural network, a word was represented as a *one-hot vector*. In such representation, a word is represented as a binary vector of the size of the vocabulary. Only one position in this vector has the value of 1, all others are 0. For example, the one-hot representation of the word *python* may be $[0, 0, 0, 0, 0, 1, 0, 0, 0, 0, 0, \ldots]$ where the length of the vector is in the order of a few thousand elements. The problem with this representation is that similar words such as *python* and *boa* do not have similar vector representations. The distance between all one-hot vectors is identical. Hence a neural network will learn independent regularities of the language if the words *python* and *boa* are used as input without generalizing what it has learned to *snakes* or *reptiles*.

What was needed is a vector representation where similar words such as *python* and *boa* have similar representations and dissimilar words such as *python* and *orange* have dissimilar representations. In addition, by reducing the size of the vectors and allowing decimal values instead of binary values, we create a dense vector and reduce sparsity. Embeddings are an alternative to one-hot vectors where each word is represented by such a dense vector. For example using a word embedding, *python* could be represented by $[0.34, 0.67, 0.04, 0.06, \ldots]$ and the size of the vector is reduced from a few thousand to a few hundred elements. Several methods have been developed to find the values of these embeddings.[43,44] Typically, these methods follow the *distributional hypothesis*, which states that words with similar meanings tend to occur in similar contexts. For example, Word2vec[43] learns the embedding of a word by learning to predict the current word in a text given its surrounding words or vice-versa. Using such embeddings, words with similar characteristics tend to have similar vector representations. In addition, a variety of relations between words seemed to be learned as well. The now famous example of subtracting the vector for *man* from the vector for *king* and adding the vector for *woman* results in a vector that is very close to the vector for the word *queen*: VEC("KING") - VEC("MAN") + VEC("WOMAN") $\approx$ VEC("QUEEN").[43] This captures the gender relation. Another example is VEC("PARIS") - VEC("FRANCE") + VEC("POLAND") $\approx$ VEC("WARSAW") which describes the concept of capital city.

Character Embeddings

Instead of using embeddings for words, another level of granularity often used is the character level. In that case, the size of the dictionary is drastically reduced to the size of the alphabet plus a few special characters, such as punctuation marks. This significantly reduces the computation and memory requirements of word-based models that have to deal with large dictionaries.

Although working at the character level may not seen intuitive on a linguistic point of view, it does alleviate the problem of out-of-vocabulary words.[45,46] In addition a suitable character-level language model can to capture the meaning of some unseen words. For example the fact that the character *s* is often used to indicate the plural form.

Sentence Embeddings

Another possibility is to represent an entire sentence as a vector through sentence embeddings. The difficulty in creating such embeddings is that large amounts of data are required to generalize over all possible sentences.[47,48]

Through embeddings (word, character or sentence based) natural language sentences could be more efficiently processed by neural networks, which made these more and more used for NLP applications and several novel neural architectures then followed.

3.3.3. *Model Architectures*

Once the problem of language representation was solved, and the use of neural networks was wide-spread in NLP, another important problem had to be addressed: natural language exhibits was is called *long distance dependencies* that standard neural network models (including RNNs) do not handle well. For example, in the sentence: *My brother, the math teacher who loves fast cars and travelling, biked to work this morning*, a model should be able to "remember" the information *teacher* to understand where *work* refers to, even if the two words are far away from each other in the text. To alleviate this problem, several new types of neural networks had to be developed.

LSTMs and GRUs

Deep networks, including RNNs suffer from the so-called *vanishing* and *exploding* gradient problems which stops the network from learning when

processing long sentences.[49] One effective way to handle this, is to use
LSTMs (Long Short-Term Memory[50]) or their variant, GRUs (Gated Recurrent Unit[39]). These cells try to control the flow of information using
gates so that important information from the text can be remembered and
others can be forgotten. Today, LSTMs and GRUs are the most common
choices in most works in NLP.[27]

Sequence-to-Sequence Models

With the growing computational power and availability of larger datasets,
more complex neural network models can be used and even combined as
an ensemble. Sequence-to-sequence models follow such an approach. A
sequence-to-sequence model consists of two RNNs: the first one, called the
encoder, reads an input sentence word by word and maps it to a single
vector representation. The second RNN, called the *decoder*, consists of a
language model which generates an output word by word, conditioned on
the encoded vector. Hence the encoder plays the role of an NLU system
and the decoder performs NLG.

Attention Mechanisms

Although LSTMs and GRUs can deal better with long sentences than standard RNNs, they cannot deal with sentences of arbitrary length. For example, in neural machine translation, the performance of a simple encoder-
decoder architecture starts to drop for sentences longer than 20 words.[51,52]
To address this problem, *attention mechanisms* were developed, where the
decoder generates an output word, not only based on the last encoder output and the previously generated words, but also based on all incremental
encoder outputs. This way, the decoder has access to all embedded information for each incremental result of the encoder.

Memory Networks

Although applying attention improves the performance of many NLP
tasks[53–55] and allows to deal with long sentences, the model needs more
computation and memory as the length of the sentence grows. In a task
where a long document should be used as input to the network, the use of
an attention mechanism requires to keep track and perform computations
for a large number of intermediary vectors, which is highly inefficient. One
way to deal efficiently with long documents is to augment the model with
an external memory[56] and instead of keeping track of all the words in the

document, the model only keeps track of the information that might be useful later. Choosing what kind of information needs to be written in the memory can itself be learned using another neural network. Memory-augmented models have achieved impressive results in different tasks such as question answering,[57] sentiment analysis[58] and machine translation.[59]

3.3.4. *Successful Applications*

Deep learning techniques have had a great impact on the field of NLP. Not only have they significantly improved the state of the art in many standard NLP tasks, such as machine translation,[60] question answering[57] and conversational agents[41] (see Section 2), but also they have been applied to new NLP applications such as visual question answering[61] and image captioning.[42] Three notable applications are described below.

Machine Translation is one of the most successful applications of deep learning for NLP. Work in this area has led to a new generation of systems called Neural Machine Translation (NMT).[38,39] NMT is based on a sequence-to-sequence model (see Section 3.3.3) where the encoder reads a sentence in the source language and maps it to a context vector (a representation of the source sentence), and the decoder maps the context vector to its translation in the target language. Attention mechanisms (see Section 3.3.3) are typically used to deal with long sentences.[51,62] The amazing successes of NMT allowed the development of end-user applications such as Google's online machine translation.[60]

Image Captioning is a novel application based on the idea of translation via an encoder-decoder; however, instead of translating from a natural language to another, image captioning translates an image to an English sentence that describes it. An encoder receives an image as input and creates a vector representation for it, and then a decoder takes the vector as input and generates a sentence. This idea has led to impressive novel systems.[42]

Conversational Agents described in Section 2.2, constitute one of the earliest applications of AI.[17] Whereas early chatbots were based on handwritten rules (e.g. Eliza[63]), modern conversational agents such as Google Now or Alexa are based on deep learning techniques. Typically, one or two encoders encode the input sentences and their context into a vector representation, and then a decoder uses this representation to generate a response word by word.[40,41] Although the performance of these new conversational agents is significantly better than their ancestors, they still suffer from several important issues. In particular, these systems tend to generate short and generic responses such as *yes* or *I don't know*.[64] In addition, as these systems do not ground their "understanding" to the real world, they may produce answers that make no sense or are inconsistent. Hence we need to find a appropriate way to take into account pragmatics, discourse information and world-knowledge (see Section 1.3) to generate more natural answers.

4. Conclusion

This chapter has provided a non-technical overview of the field of Natural Language Processing (NLP): one of the earliest sub-fields of Artificial Intelligence (AI) that brings together experts in both computer science and linguistics. We have characterized the complexity of natural language that make its automatic processing much more complex than when dealing with artificial languages. Ambiguity at the lexical, syntactic and semantic levels, as well as the inherent necessity to deal with pragmatic and world-knowledge makes this field of study both challenging and fascinating at the same time.

As much of the work in AI, NLP has gone through three main eras. In the early days (from the 1950's to the 1990's), symbolic computation was the driving paradigm. Hand-written rules developed by linguists and computer scientists drove NLP algorithms. Most systems were developed only at the prototype level as they did not scale well to real-life applications. In the 1990's, as more and more electronic documents became available, more robust statistical and machine learning methods became the norm to mine these large quantities of text collections automatically. Human expertise shifted from writing rules, to hand-crafting linguistic features that were then used by the machine learning methods to discover the rules automatically. Many low-level applications were developed during these days, but only a few made their way to every-day applications. Around 2010, with the advancements of deep learning models, a new era in NLP development was born. A variety of neural-network based approaches were developed to deal specifically with natural language and significantly improved the state of the art in many NLP tasks. Expertise in NLP shifted again from hand-crafting linguistic features, to providing no hand-crafted information at all. The networks discover automatically both the linguistic features and the rules. With the ever increasing availability of data, and new neural-based architectures, such as RNN's, sequence-to-sequence models, ... new applications such as efficient machine translation and conversational agents finally made their way to end-users.

It is an exciting time to work on natural language processing, and future applications are limitless. The holy grail of building automatic systems that can produce or analyze texts as a human would seem more and more reachable today.

References

1. J. R. R. Tolkien, *The Lord of the Rings*, Allen & Unwin (1954).
2. D. J. Peterson, The languages of ice and fire, *Mastering the Game of Thrones: Essays on George RR Martin's A Song of Ice and Fire*, pp. 15–34 (2015).
3. E. Reiter and R. Dale, *Building Natural Language Generation Systems*, Cambridge University Press (2000).
4. H. J. Levesque, E. Davis, and L. Morgenstern, The Winograd schema challenge. In *Proceedings of the Thirteenth International Conference on Principles of Knowledge Representation and Reasoning*, pp. 552–561, Rome, Italy (June 2011).
5. C. D. Manning, Part-of-speech tagging from 97% to 100%: Is it time for some linguistics? In *12th International Conference on Intelligent Text Processing and Computational Linguistics*.
6. G. Lample, M. Ballesteros, S. Subramanian, K. Kawakami, and C. Dyer, Neural architectures for named entity recognition. In *Proceedings of the 2016 Conference of the North American Chapter of the Association for Computational Linguistics: Human Language Technologies, NAALC-HTL 2016*, San Diego, California (June 2016).
7. K. Clark and C. D. Manning, Improving coreference resolution by learning entity-level distributed representations. In *Proceedings of the 54th Annual Meeting of the Association for Computational Linguistics, ACL 2016*, Berlin, Germany (August 2016).
8. E. Krahmer and K. van Deemter, Graphs and booleans: on the generation of referring expressions. In *Computing Meaning: Volume 3 (Studies in Linguistics and Philosophy)*, Springer (2006).
9. A. Moro, A. Raganato, and R. Navigli, Entity linking meets word sense disambiguation: A unified approach, **2**, 231–244 (05, 2014).
10. D. Chen and C. Manning, A fast and accurate dependency parser using neural networks. In *Proceedings of the 2014 Conference on Empirical Methods in Natural Language Processing, EMNLP 2014*, pp. 740–750, Doha, Qatar (October 2014).
11. O. Vinyals, L. Kaiser, T. Koo, S. Petrov, I. Sutskever, and G. Hinton, Grammar as a foreign language. In *Proceedings of the 28th International Confer-*

ence on Neural Information Processing Systems – Volume 2, NIPS 2015, pp. 2773–2781, Montreal, Canada (December 2015).

12. C. Gómez-Rodríguez, I. Alonso-Alonso, and D. Vilares, How important is syntactic parsing accuracy? An empirical evaluation on rule-based sentiment analysis, *Artificial Intelligence Review* (October 2017).

13. B. Dolan, C. Quirk, and C. Brockett, Unsupervised construction of large paraphrase corpora: Exploiting massively parallel news sources. In *Proceedings of the 20th International Conference on Computational Linguistics, COLING 2004*, Geneva, Switzerland (2004).

14. B. Agarwal, H. Ramampiaro, H. Langseth, and M. Ruocco, A deep network model for paraphrase detection in short text messages, *Information Processing & Management*, **54**(6), 922–937 (2018).

15. J. Piskorski and R. Yangarber, *Information Extraction: Past, Present and Future*, In eds. T. Poibeau, H. Saggion, J. Piskorski, and R. Yangarber, *Multisource, Multilingual Information Extraction and Summarization*, pp. 23–49. Springer (2013).

16. A. S. M. A. Mahmood, T.-J. Wu, R. Mazumder, and K. Vijay-Shanker, Dimex: A text mining system for mutation-disease association extraction, *PLOS ONE*, **11**, 1–26 (04, 2016).

17. A. M. Turing, Computing machinery and intelligence, *Mind*, **59**(236), 433–460 (1950).

18. J. Allen, *Natural Language Understanding (2nd Ed.)*, Benjamin-Cummings (1995).

19. N. Chomsky, *Syntactic Structures*, Mouton (1957).

20. C. D. Manning, C. D. Manning, and H. Schütze, *Foundations of Statistical Natural Language Processing*, MIT Press (1999).

21. T. Brants, Tnt: A statistical part-of-speech tagger. In *Proceedings of the Sixth Conference on Applied Natural Language Processing, ANLC 2000*, pp. 224–231, Seattle, USA (May 2000).

22. K. Toutanova and C. D. Manning, Enriching the knowledge sources used in a maximum entropy part-of-speech tagger. In *Proceedings of the 2000 Joint SIGDAT Conference on Empirical Methods in Natural Language Processing and Very Large Corpora: Held in Conjunction with the 38th Annual Meeting of the Association for Computational Linguistics — Volume 13, EMNLP 2000*, pp. 63–70, Hong Kong (2000).

23. A. Ratnaparkhi, A linear observed time statistical parser based on maximum entropy models. In *Second Conference on Empirical Methods in Natural Language Processing, EMNLP 1997*, pp. 1–10, Providence, USA (August 1997).

24. S. Miller, H. Fox, L. Ramshaw, and R. Weischedel, A novel use of statistical parsing to extract information from text. In *Proceedings of the 1st North American Chapter of the Association for Computational Linguistics Conference, NAACL 2000*, pp. 226–233, Seattle, USA (May 2000).

25. A. Borthwick, J. Sterling, E. Agichtein, and R. Grishman, Exploiting diverse knowledge sources via maximum entropy in named entity recognition. In *Proceedings of the Sixth Workshop on Very Large Corpora*, pp. 152–160, Montreal, Canada (August 1998).

26. R. Florian, A. Ittycheriah, H. Jing, and T. Zhang, Named entity recognition through classifier combination. In *Proceedings of the Seventh Conference on Natural Language Learning at HLT-NAACL 2003 — Volume 4, CONLL 2003*, pp. 168–171, Edmonton, Canada (June 2003).

27. T. Young, D. Hazarika, S. Poria, and E. Cambria, Recent trends in deep learning based natural language processing, arXiv preprint arXiv:1708.02709 (2017).

28. Y. Goldberg and G. Hirst, *Neural Network Methods in Natural Language Processing*, Morgan & Claypool Publishers (2017).

29. L. Deng and Y. Liu, *Deep Learning in Natural Language Processing*, Springer, Singapore (2018).

30. A. Vaswani, Y. Zhao, V. Fossum, and D. Chiang, Decoding with large-scale neural language models improves translation. In *Proceedings of the 2013 Conference on Empirical Methods in Natural Language Processing, EMNLP 2013*, pp. 1387–1392 (2013).

31. G. Hinton, L. Deng, D. Yu, G. E. Dahl, A.-r. Mohamed, N. Jaitly, A. Senior, V. Vanhoucke, P. Nguyen, T. N. Sainath, et al., Deep neural networks for acoustic modeling in speech recognition: The shared views of four research groups, *IEEE Signal Processing Magazine*, **29**(6), 82–97 (2012).

32. D. Jurafsky and J. H. Martin, *Speech and Language Processing (2nd Edition)*, Prentice-Hall (2009).

33. J. L. Elman, Finding structure in time, *Cognitive Science*, **14**(2), 179–211 (1990).

34. R. Miikkulainen and M. G. Dyer, Natural language processing with modular PDP networks and distributed lexicon, *Cognitive Science*, **15**(3), 343–399 (1991).

35. Y. Bengio, R. Ducharme, P. Vincent, and C. Janvin, A neural probabilistic language model, *Journal of Machine Learning Research*, **3**, 1137–1155 (March 2003).

36. T. Mikolov, M. Karafiát, L. Burget, J. Černocký, and S. Khudanpur, Recurrent neural network based language model. In *Proceedings of the Eleventh Annual Conference of the International Speech Communication Association*, pp. 1045–1048 (2010).

37. A. Krizhevsky, I. Sutskever, and G. E. Hinton, Imagenet classification with deep convolutional neural networks. In *Proceedings of the 25th International Conference on Neural Information Processing Systems — Volume 1, NIPS 2012*, pp. 1097–1105 (2012).

38. I. Sutskever, O. Vinyals, and Q. V. Le, Sequence to sequence learning with neural networks. In *Proceedings of the 27th International Conference on Neural Information Processing Systems — Volume 2, NIPS 2014*, pp. 3104–3112 (2014).

39. K. Cho, B. van Merrienboer, C. Gulcehre, D. Bahdanau, F. Bougares, H. Schwenk, and Y. Bengio, Learning phrase representations using rnn encoder–decoder for statistical machine translation. In *Proceedings of the 2014 Conference on Empirical Methods in Natural Language Processing, EMNLP 2014*, pp. 1724–1734, Doha, Qatar (October 2014).

40. O. Vinyals and Q. V. Le, A neural conversational model, *CoRR* (2015), URL http://arxiv.org/abs/1506.05869.
41. I. V. Serban, A. Sordoni, Y. Bengio, A. C. Courville, and J. Pineau, Hierarchical neural network generative models for movie dialogues, *CoRR, abs/1507.04808* (2015).
42. O. Vinyals, A. Toshev, S. Bengio, and D. Erhan, Show and tell: A neural image caption generator. In *2015 IEEE Conference on Computer Vision and Pattern Recognition*, pp. 3156–3164 (2015).
43. T. Mikolov, K. Chen, G. S. Corrado, and J. Dean, Efficient estimation of word representations in vector space, *CoRR* (2013).
44. J. Pennington, R. Socher, and C. Manning, Glove: Global vectors for word representation. In *Proceedings of the 2014 Conference on Empirical Methods in Natural Language Processing, EMNLP 2014*, pp. 1532–1543, Doha, Qatar (October 2014).
45. J. Chung, K. Cho, and Y. Bengio, A character-level decoder without explicit segmentation for neural machine translation. In *Proceedings of the 54th Annual Meeting of the Association for Computational Linguistics*, ACL 2016, pp. 1693–1703, Berlin, Germany (Aug. 2016).
46. Y. Kim, Y. Jernite, D. Sontag, and A. M. Rush, Character-aware neural language models. In *Proceedings of the Thirtieth AAAI Conference on Artificial Intelligence, AAAI 2016*, pp. 2741–2749 (2016).
47. D. Cer, Y. Yang, S.-y. Kong, N. Hua, N. Limtiaco, R. S. John, N. Constant, M. Guajardo-Cespedes, S. Yuan, C. Tar, et al., Universal sentence encoder, arXiv preprint arXiv:1803.11175 (March 2018).
48. S. Subramanian, A. Trischler, Y. Bengio, and C. J. Pal. Learning general purpose distributed sentence representations via large scale multi-task learning. In *International Conference on Learning Representations* (2018).
49. Y. Bengio, P. Simard, and P. Frasconi, Learning long-term dependencies with gradient descent is difficult, *IEEE Transactions on Neural Networks*, **5**(2), 157–166 (1994).
50. S. Hochreiter and J. Schmidhuber, Long short-term memory, *Neural computation*, **9**(8), 1735–1780 (1997).
51. D. Bahdanau, K. Cho, and Y. Bengio, Neural machine translation by jointly learning to align and translate, *CoRR* (2014), URL http://arxiv.org/abs/1409.0473.
52. M.-T. Luong and C. D. Manning, Achieving open vocabulary neural machine translation with hybrid word-character models. In *Proceedings of the 54th Annual Meeting of the Association for Computational Linguistics (Volume 1: Long Papers)*, ACL 2016, pp. 1054–1063, Berlin, Germany (August 2016).
53. O. Vinyals, L. Kaiser, T. Koo, S. Petrov, I. Sutskever, and G. Hinton, Grammar as a foreign language. In *Advances in Neural Information Processing Systems 28, NIPS 2015*, pp. 2773–2781 (2015).
54. R. Paulus, C. Xiong, and R. Socher, A deep reinforced model for abstractive summarization. In *Proceedings of the International Conference on Learning Representations* (2018).

55. K. M. Hermann, T. Kočiský, E. Grefenstette, L. Espeholt, W. Kay, M. Suleyman, and P. Blunsom, Teaching machines to read and comprehend. In *Proceedings of the 28th International Conference on Neural Information Processing Systems — Volume 1, NIPS'15*, pp. 1693–1701, MIT Press, Cambridge, MA (2015).

56. A. Graves, G. Wayne, and I. Danihelka, Neural turing machines, *CoRR* (2014). URL http://arxiv.org/abs/1410.5401.

57. S. Sukhbaatar, A. Szlam, J. Weston, and R. Fergus, End-to-end memory networks. In eds. C. Cortes, N. D. Lawrence, D. D. Lee, M. Sugiyama, and R. Garnett, *Advances in Neural Information Processing Systems 28, NIPS 2015*, pp. 2440–2448 (2015).

58. P. Chen, Z. Sun, L. Bing, and W. Yang, Recurrent attention network on memory for aspect sentiment analysis. In *Proceedings of the 2017 Conference on Empirical Methods in Natural Language Processing, EMNLP 2017*, pp. 452–461 (2017).

59. Y. Feng, S. Zhang, A. Zhang, D. Wang, and A. Abel, Memory-augmented neural machine translation. In *Proceedings of the 2017 Conference on Empirical Methods in Natural Language Processing, EMNLP 2017*, pp. 1390–1399 (2017).

60. Y. Wu, M. Schuster, Z. Chen, Q. V. Le, M. Norouzi, W. Macherey, M. Krikun, Y. Cao, Q. Gao, K. Macherey, J. Klingner, A. Shah, M. Johnson, X. Liu, L. Kaiser, S. Gouws, Y. Kato, T. Kudo, H. Kazawa, K. Stevens, G. Kurian, N. Patil, W. Wang, C. Young, J. Smith, J. Riesa, A. Rudnick, O. Vinyals, G. S. Corrado, M. Hughes, and J. Dean, Google's neural machine translation system: Bridging the gap between human and machine translation, *CoRR* (2016).

61. S. Antol, A. Agrawal, J. Lu, M. Mitchell, D. Batra, C. L. Zitnick, and D. Parikh, VQA: Visual Question Answering. In *International Conference on Computer Vision, ICCV 2015* (2015).

62. T. Luong, H. Pham, and C. D. Manning, Effective approaches to attention-based neural machine translation. In *Proceedings of the 2015 Conference on Empirical Methods in Natural Language Processing, EMNLP 2015*, pp. 1412–1421, Lisbon, Portugal (September 2015).

63. J. Weizenbaum, ELIZA—a computer program for the study of natural language communication between man and machine, *Communications of the ACM*, **9**(1), 36–45 (Jan. 1966).

64. J. Li, M. Galley, C. Brockett, J. Gao, and B. Dolan, A diversity-promoting objective function for neural conversation models. In *Proceedings of the 2016 Conference of the North American Chapter of the Association for Computational Linguistics: Human Language Technologies, NAACL-HLT 2016*, pp. 110–119 (2016).

Chapter 4

Handwriting Recognition Systems and Applications

Muna Khayyat* and Nicola Nobile[†]

*Centre for Pattern Recognition and Machine Intelligence
Concordia University,
Montreal, Quebec H3G 1M8, Canada*
* muna.khayyat@gmail.com, [†] nicola@encs.concordia.ca

A great number of handwritten documents have been digitized, to preserve, analyze, and disseminate them. These documents are of different categories, being drawn from fields as diverse as history, commerce, finance, and medicine. Developing efficient means of analyzing and recognizing these documents is of significant interest. Meanwhile, many devices such as smart phones generate handwritten samples, which need to be recognized and translated to machine code. Therefore, handwriting recognition is an active research area with an increasing number of applications on handwriting. This chapter introduces handwriting recognition, describes the steps of a handwriting recognition process, and finally, summarizes different handwriting recognition applications.

1. Introduction

Handwriting has evolved over thousands of years, where the earliest known pictograph writing was invented in Sumer - present day -Iraq, around 3200 B.C. Later the Sumerian writing system became cuneiform around 2800 - 2600 B.C. Meanwhile, Egyptians used hieroglyphic writing around 3000 B.C. Sequential pictographic inscriptions appeared in 2000 B.C on clay tablets in Crete. Chinese developed ideographs writing around 1500 B.C. Between 1100-900 B.C., Phoenicians spread the precursor of modern Latin alphabet across the sea to Greece. Finally around 800 B.C., Greeks developed the concept of the modern alphabet, with vowels.[1]

Handwriting recognition systems started in the early twentieth century

---

*Corresponding author.

when Emanuel Goldberg[2] developed a system to read handwritten characters and digits and converted then into a telegraph code in 1914. Goldberg continued his work and studies to develop a handwriting recognition system. In 1933, Paul W. Handel was one of the pioneers proposing template matching for handwriting recognition. In 1944, the first primitive computer type optical character recognition system had been proposed to help blind people. In 1985, structural approaches were proposed with statistical methods.[3] Sheer progress in handwriting recognition had been shown following 1990, in which new techniques and methodologies in image processing and pattern recognition had been proposed. Since then, handwriting recognition has always been an active and challenging research area of pattern recognition.

Several international conferences exist with handwriting analysis as one of the themes. Topics commonly discussed in The International Conference on Frontiers in Handwriting Recognition (ICFHR) are: Online/Offline Handwriting Recognition, Signature Verification, Word Spotting, Historical Document Image Analysis, Writer Classification, Postal-Address Recognition, Bank-Check Processing, and Writer Recognition. Other conferences that are involved with some or all of these topics are: The International Conference on Document Analysis and Recognition (ICDAR) and International Conference on Pattern Recognition and Artificial Intelligence (ICPRAI).

There are several research centers and labs around the world that focus on handwriting recognition. The Centre for Pattern Recognition and Machine Intelligence (CENPARMI) has been one of the pioneer groups to recognize handwritten cheques in English, French, and Arabic. The Centre was also early in word recognition and word spotting of Arabic, Dari, Farsi, Pashto, and Urdu handwritten documents. The Center for Unified Biometrics and Sensors (CUBS) was influential in the development of the first handwritten address interpretation system used by the US Postal Service. Researchers of the Computer Vision and Pattern Recognition Unit (CVPRU) group have been actively researching online handwriting recognition and word spotting of Indian scripts.

This chapter is organized as follows: online and offline handwriting recognition tools and technologies are described in Section 2. Section 3 summarizes the challenges in handwriting recognition. The process of recognizing handwriting is described in Section 4, while different applications are described in Section 5. Finally, Section 6 concludes the chapter.

2. Online and Offline Handwriting Recognition

Despite new technologies available to capture and transmit information, handwriting is still regarded as an important means of communication and recording information.[4] The means by which handwritten documents are obtained come in two types: online and offline.

Online handwritings are obtained through devices such as smart phones, tablets, and touch pads. Real-time information on stroke sequences is known as the text is written using a finger or stylus. Offline recognition is used when the temporal information is not available. This is usually the case for scanned documents such as historical documents, cheques, and paper forms.

An advantage of online recognition is of course, the availability of the stroke sequences. Compared to offline, online recognition systems have fewer broken strokes, require little pre-processing, need no noise removal, are better at "learning" an individual writer's style, require low memory storage, and generally have a higher accuracy. Furthermore, the future is leaning towards online as more businesses and governments are making online forms more acceptable and legal.

Offline systems are better suited for scanned images that contain no stroke sequence information. However, storage of the digital scanned images requires a lot more memory space than online data. For example, a typical 8.5 x 11 inch grayscale page, scanned at a resolution of 300 dots per inch, will generate a file size of 8.4 megabytes.[4] This will take longer to load and will have a higher bandwidth for transmission.

Some researchers have combined both online with offline classifiers which have outperformed either individual system.[5] Handwritten digits were written online and this was then converted to an offline image. By combining the results of both the online and offline classifiers, the authors were able to decrease the error rate by 43% when compared to the online results.

Many commercial tools have been developed for online handwriting recognition. Smartphones come with their own built-in systems to recognize a user's "writing", written by using a finger or stylus. The company MyScript[6] have several applications and provide libraries for developers wishing to create their own applications.

There are several offline handwriting classifier tools on the market. ABBYY's FlexiCapture[7] is software that will automatically extract segmented handwriting from forms. Tesseract,[8] used by Google, is a free OCR engine but must be trained to recognize handwriting. Developer libraries, by Hanwang Technology Co., Ltd.,[9] can recognize Chinese and English handwritten lines of text.

3. Handwriting Recognition Challenges

Aside from the billions of variations, handwriting recognition has many challenges that must be overcome for it to be successful. The quality of a handwritten document is dependent not only on the writer, but on the external influences such as the writing instrument, the medium, and the writing surface.

Other outside influences which can hinder handwriting recognition is if the document was photographed or scanned at low resolution, or if the digital image is the result of an nth generation photocopy.[10] Historical handwritten documents usually have some degradation. The age of the document and/or the scanning method may introduce a lot of noise in the digital image. Documents with complex layouts, such as those containing mathematical expressions, are generally more complex to segment since they do not follow general and typical flow of text blocks.

The writers are the source of many writing style variations and odd peculiarities. In fact, many poorly handwritten documents are difficult to understand, even by a human reader. Handwritten documents often have touching and broken strokes. If not using lined paper, the text lines may overlap, be skewed, slanted, or be curvilinear. All of these factors require that a page be pre-processed to correct these anomalies since the recognition stage is sensitive to outlying artifacts.

One last important requirement for handwriting recognition, is the creation of ground-truth information of a database. In order to measure the accuracy of a classifier, a ground-truthing of a database is required. This is usually done manually, or at least, semi-automatically. In any case, a human is needed for final verification of the ground-truth information. For training and test sets consisting of thousands or millions of samples, this can be quite a challenging task to complete.

3.1. *Chinese Handwriting Recognition*

The Chinese script consists of approximately 50,000 characters, where 99.65% of the usage is covered by 3775 common characters. Sentences can be written either horizontally left to right from the top to the bottom of the page, or vertically from top to bottom. Chinese characters are based on strokes where there is an average of about 10.3 strokes per character. Figure 1 shows Chinese handwritten text.

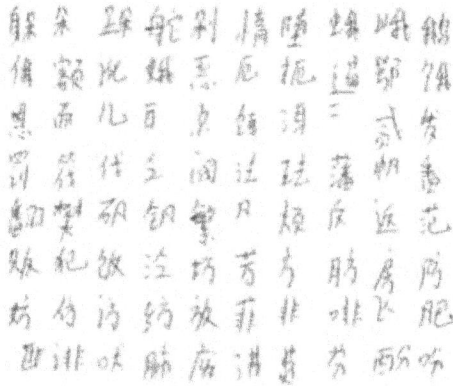

Fig. 1. A Chinese handwritten document.

Chinese characters are made of about 500 component sub-characters called radicals which are written in predefined positions and in a predefined order. This order of writing strokes in Chinese characters is lost in offline handwriting recognition. This increases the challenge to automatically recognize Chinese handwriting. The average word length of a Chinese word is short consisting of 2-4 characters. Furthermore, the characters are always written in print fashion, not connected. Segmentation is often easier in Chinese than in other languages because characters rarely need to be split apart. However, it is sometimes challenging to determine whether two radicals are in fact two separate characters or two component parts of the same character. The greatest challenge is recognizing the large number of Chinese characters. The majority of research has been devoted to overcoming this difficulty. Furthermore, the significant confusion between similar characters, and the distinct handwriting styles across individuals introduces an additional challenge to Chinese handwriting recognition.[11,12]

3.2. *Arabic Handwriting Recognition*

Arabic script is always cursive even when printed, and it is written horizontally from right to left. In Arabic writing, letter shapes change depending on their location in the word. This fact distinguishes Arabic writing from many other languages. In addition, dots, diacratics, and ligatures are special characteristics of Arabic writing. Figure 2 shows two Arabic handwritten documents.

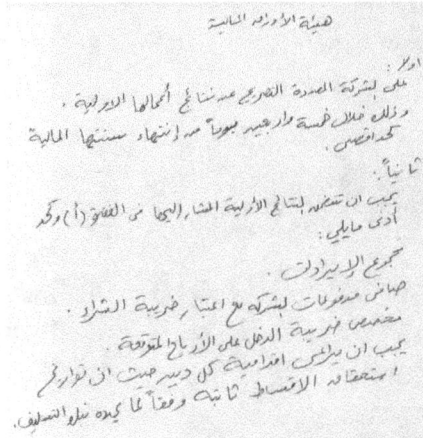

Fig. 2. An Arabic handwritten document.

The Arabic handwriting has 28 letters, where many letters share a primary common shape and only differ in the number and/or location of dots. This means dots play an important role in Arabic writing and other languages that share the same letters such as Farsi (Persian) and Urdu. It is also worth mentioning that more than half of the Arabic letters are dotted. In printed documents, double and triple dots are printed as separate dots, while there are different ways to write them in handwritten documents.

In addition, the shapes of letters change depending on their position in the word. Therefore, each Arabic letter has between two and four shapes. Letters shapes can be isolated, beginning, middle, and ending. However, there are six letters in Arabic that are only connected from the right side. Therefore, when they appear in a word, they cause a disconnect resulting in sub-words or Pieces of Arabic Words (PAW). This fact makes Arabic handwriting recognition and document segmentation into words more challenging.

Ligatures are used to connect Arabic letters. They make it difficult to determine the boundaries of the letters since ligatures are not added according to any writing rule. Ligatures in Arabic can only be found on the baseline because letters are only connected on the baseline.

In Arabic words, there are small markings called "diacritical markers".

These markers represent short vowels, double consonants, and other marks[7] that are added to the letters. There are no Arabic letters with upper and lower diacritics. Adding these diacritics to the Arabic script is not obligatory, so they are not always added, which would introduce a new challenge to the Arabic language handwriting recognition.

4. Handwriting Recognition Process

Figure 3 shows the process of a handwriting recognition system. The system is divided into two parts: training and testing. Training is done before testing in order to build a model to compare an unknown sample. Training begins with collecting many handwriting samples of the target classification type. This could be words, digits, signatures, etc. A database is created by grouping, or labeling, the samples into classes. The raw samples are usually not suitable for a classifier so they need to be preprocessed to conform to a minimal, common framework. For example, some people may write larger than others which would result in a skewed training influence from those samples. The solution is to normalize the samples into a fixed size by width, height, or both. Other preprocessing steps that are commonly employed are noise reduction and slant correction.

Once preprocessing is completed on all the database images, features are extracted from those samples. Different features can be used as discussed in Section 4.1. Each sample image will have a feature vector associated with it. All feature vectors of a class will be combined to form a class model. How they are combined depends on the classifier used - Support Vector Machines (SVM), Hidden Markov Model (HMM), and neural networks are some common classifiers for handwriting recognition as shown in Section 4.2.

Testing an unknown sample follows the same acquisition, preprocessing, and feature extraction steps as the training stage. The extracted feature vector of the unknown sample is applied to the classifier. The classifier will find the closest matching class by using the class models generated in the training stage.

4.1. *Feature Extraction*

Feature extraction is a crucial process in handwriting recognition that aims to minimize a "within class" pattern variability, while enhancing the "between-class" pattern variability. The extracted features represent salient

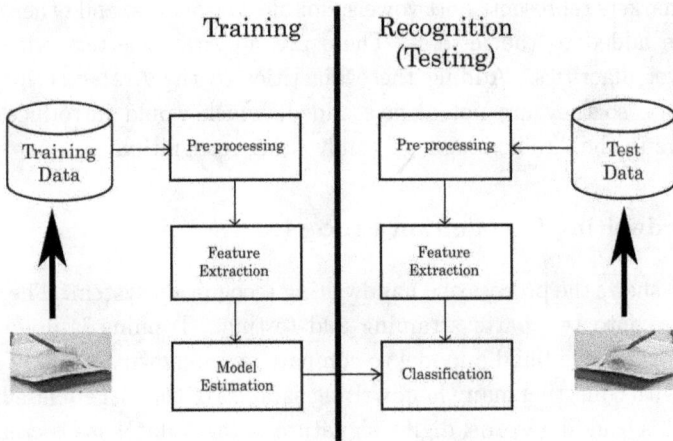

Fig. 3. The process of handwriting recognition.

features of a handwritten character to be recognized, while reducing the significant variation. In the handwriting recognition literature, several features have been extracted from handwritten text. These features are mainly within the following four categories: structural and geometric, statistical, gradient, and transformation and wavelet.

The extracted features can be extracted locally by dividing the handwritten image into zones and extracting features from each zone, or globally in which the features are extracted from the whole image. For example, counting the number of intersection points globally in a handwritten image, or locally, in which the image is divided into zones and the number of intersection points in each zone is counted.

Handwritten characters are rich with their structural and geometric information, which give details about the topology, geometry, and quantitative information of a handwritten image. Structural features facilitate extracting components that are useful in the representation and description of a character shape. Detecting boundaries, skeletonization, contouring, and the convex hull can be powerful tools to set up the image for extracting structural features. There are two types of structural features: Geometric and Quantitative. Geometric features are not sensitive to the varying sizes and slants of the images as they describe the shape of the image. This is done by extracting loops, end points, cross points, intersection points, curves, maxima and minima, lines, ascenders and descenders, strokes and their directions, inflections between two points, etc. However, quantitative features represent structural information by means of quantities.[13,14]

Statistical features can be extracted from handwriting since they are based on statistical distribution of a handwritten character, which tends to adapt to handwriting style variations. The major statistical methods used in handwritten characters representation are: histograms, zoning, projection and profiles, center of gravity, density, crossings, and distances.[15,16]

Gradient features have been widely applied to many handwriting recognition systems. This is because gradient features are language independent and can lead to high recognition rates. These features are extracted by applying a filter to an image. The gradient is then calculated by using the strength and the direction of the grayscale images.[17–20]

Special attention has been paid towards global transformation and wavelets in handwriting recognition systems. Transformations remove redundant information from images. Many mathematical transformations that convert images from the special domain to frequency domains by relying on different functions have been employed in the field of handwriting recognition. Some include: Discrete Fourier Transformation DFT and Fast Fourier Transformation FFT, Discrete Cosine and Sine Transformation DCT and DST, Haar Transformation, and different types of wavelets.[21–24]

Finally, Convolutional Neural Networks (CNN), feature extraction is integrated with the classification by using convolutional layers for dynamic feature extraction. This has shown promising results on handwriting recognition, after which, many researches favoured this approach for feature extraction.[25,26]

4.2. *Classification*

Several classification algorithms have been proposed in the literature of handwriting recognition. Each algorithm was utilized based on the implemented applications. For character, digit, and word recognition, in addition to signature verification, k-Nearest Neighbor, SVM, Neural Networks including CNNs, and Batesian classification algorithms have been successfully used. However, for data sets with a large lexicon, such as Chinese handwriting recognition, Regularized Discriminant Analysis (RDA), Quadratic Discriminant Function (QDF), etc. have been used and shown promising results.

Successful applications that need to trace a handwritten script, in which text line segmentation is needed, are: HMM, Recusant Neural Networks (RNN), Long-Short Term Memory (LSTM) RNN, etc.

5. Handwriting Recognition Applications

Handwriting recognition is considered one of the most challenging research areas in the field of pattern recognition. This includes numerous applications such as, reading aid for the blind, bank cheques, conversion of any handwritten document into a structural text form, and writer identification. As the tools of digitizing handwritten documents are advancing, as well as the devices to capture online handwriting, new applications are being introduced in the field of handwriting recognition. Document analysis and recognition applications are divided into two categories: expertise and handwriting recognition. Expertise includes signature verification and authentication, writer authentication, etc. Handwriting recognition includes Optical Character Recognition (OCR), word spotting, and word and character segmentation. Figure 4 is a diagram summarizing handwriting recognition applications.

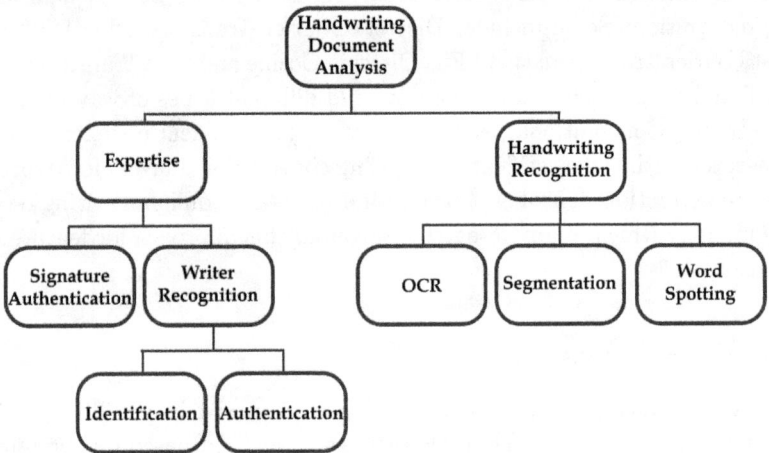

Fig. 4. Handwriting recognition applications.

The following sections include brief summary of the following applications: handwritten character recognition, word and text recognition, signature verification, and finally, handwritten word spotting or indexing.

5.1. *Handwritten Character Recognition*

Many algorithms and classification approaches have been presented to recognize handwritten characters including statistical discriminate approaches such as: Neural Networks, Support Vector Machines, and Convolutional Neural Networks. In addition, nonparametric models, such as K-nearest neighbor classifiers, are widely used. In the literature of handwriting recognition, many data sets has been proposed to evaluate the proposed system. Among these data sets, the MNIST was the most widely used dataset in the handwriting recognition research.[27] This dataset contains real samples as they were collected from the US returned mail, and the writers never knew that these digits will be used to create an experimental dataset. Thus, the dataset was preprocessed and prepared synthetically where each image was resized to (28 × 28) pixels. The dataset includes 60,000 and 10,000 training and testing samples respectively. The dataset includes some difficult samples that are ambiguous to human beings, so even the human readability is not 100%, Figure 5

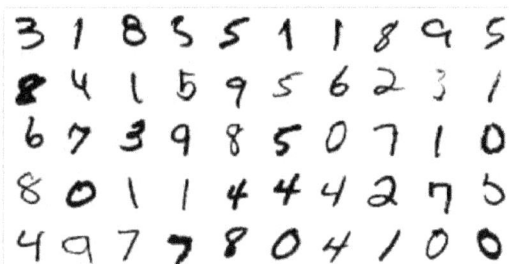

Fig. 5. Some samples of the MNIST dataset.

LeCun et al.[27] have performed the first experiment on the MNIST dataset using a neural network, in which they achieved an 12.00% error rate. Later Ciresan et al.[28] performed an experiment on the MNIST dataset using a convolutional neural network achieving error rate of 0.23%, shown in Table 1. At the time, this showed that the handwritten character recognition problem had been solved.

Table 1. Recognition rates in the MNIST dataset.

Author	Classifier	Accuracy(%)
LeCun et al. 1998	1-layer Neural Backpropagation Neural Network	88.00
Ciresan et al. 2012	Convolutional Neural Network (CNN)	99.77

However, Halkias et al.[29] had implemented an experiment using the three different datasets (MNIST,[27] RIMES[30] and UPS[31]) in order to provide a comparative baseline. Each of which was trained using deep learning algorithms. Then each system was tested using each of the three datasets (MNIST, RIMES, and UPS). The results show that the training and testing the system using the same dataset the systems will perform well with a small error rate. However, when cross training and testing using different datasets, the error rate might be significant, with each around 70%. The results of the experiment and the error rates can be shown in Table 2. This shows that character recognition is still a challenging problem which is unsolved.

Table 2. Error rate for MNIST, RIMES and UPS cross-training/testing.

Train/Test	MNIST	RIMES	UPS
MNIST	1.17	17.25	46.20
RIMES	30.73	0.62	41.45
UPS	69.17	54.81	5.10

Different combinations of features and classification algorithms have been proposed in the literature of handwritten character recognition. This includes the use of Bayesian classifiers,[32] k-nearest neighbor,[33] Support Vector Machines (SVM),[34] and Neural Networks. Kaensar conducted a comparative study to evaluate handwriting digit recognition classifiers and SVM has outperformed both k-nearest neighbor and Neural Networks.[35] Later, deep learning algorithms had been used to recognize handwritten characters and generated very low error rates, thereby outperforming the other classification algorithms including Deep Neural Network (DNN), Deep Belief Network (DBN), and Convolutional Neural Network (CNN).[36] Nevertheless, having a 100% accurate system cannot be achieved, since there are many ambiguous handwritings where even human beings cannot achieve that level of accuracy.

5.2. *Handwritten Text Recognition*

Handwritten books, documents, notes, etc. are difficult to store, access, or search through efficiently. Also, it is not easy to share them with others. A lot of important knowledge gets lost since these documents never get transferred to digital format. Consequently, many of these documents have been digitized in order to keep the knowledge they contain. Many methods have been proposed to transfer the digitized documents into machine code. Figure 6 shows the process of recognizing handwritten text. It starts by preprocessing the document and then segmenting the document into either characters or words. The former segmentation is referred to as the analytical approach, while the latter is the holistic approach. In addition, another approach, which has been inspired from speech recognition, aims to integrate the segmentation with the recognition.

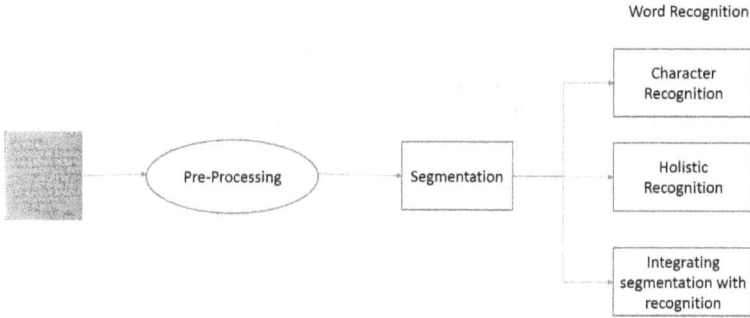

Fig. 6. Text recognition approaches.

The analytical segmentation treats a word or a text line as a collection of sub-units or graphemes such as letters. It aims to segment the text line into letters,[37] and then recognize each character individually. This approach can be applied to scripts consisting of alphabetic characters such as Latin and Arabic languages. Words are segmented into the letters of the language and then each of them are recognized. Classifiers such as the Bayesian classifier, SVM, and k-nearest neighbor, can be used to recognize the segmented characters. The main disadvantage of this method in the difficulty to segment words into characters. This is evident when the handwritten script in cursive causing segmentation errors to be carried over to the recognition step. This method can be applied when the handwritten letters are nicely segmented which minimizes the segmentation error.[38,39] Nevertheless, this method can be used for open lexicon text recognition since the system is trained on the alphabet of the language.

On the other hand, the holistic segmentation, segments the text line into words, and then recognizes the word as a whole or uses shape features to describe a word. The segmentation in these approaches is easy, especially for languages where the words are nicely separated by space such as Latin based languages. However, this approaches can only be used for closed lexicon application such as recognizing the legal amount on a cheque. In addition, it can be used for character based languages (Idiographic) like Chinese and

Japanese. For small lexicons, Neural Networks, SVM, etc. can be used for training and recognition,[40–42] while Modified Quadratic Discriminant Function (MQDF) has shown promising results for large lexicons.[43]

Some approaches attempt to systematically divide an image into many overlapping pieces, or sliding windows, without regard to the contents. Then, the final classification decision is made based on the integration between segmentation and recognition. In the literature of handwriting recognition, these approaches have been often called *"segmentation-free"* as described by Casey and Lecolinet.[44] Time Delay Neural Network (TDNN), Hidden Markov Model (HMM), and Long Short Term Memory Recurrent Neural Networks (LSTM RNN) have been successfully applied to recognize handwritten text.[45–48] Finally, language models have been often used when segmentation was integrated with recognition to improve the performance of the handwritten text recognition systems.[49,50]

5.3. *Signature Verification*

The task of signature verification systems is to evaluate whether unknown signatures are genuine or forgeries. This task is considered one of the oldest biometrics used for forensic purposes. There are generally three ways to gain access to sensitive material: 1. Physical items such as a key or badge, 2. Information, such as a PIN number or password, and 3. Personal identifying characteristics like a fingerprint, retina, or signature.[51]

The first two methods are the least secure since physical items and information can be lost or stolen. There are two types of personal identifying features: physical and behaviour characteristics. It is much more difficult to steal a personal feature of an individual such as a retina or fingerprint. Furthermore, these personal features are unique to each individual and are almost unchangeable and stable during a person's lifetime. Behaviour features may change during a person's lifetime due to age, illness, or injury. Gait, speech, and signatures are some examples of features dependent on a person's behaviour.

No two signatures are alike - even from the same person. There are always slight variations in strokes, speed, pressure, etc. It is more evident when different writing instruments and mediums are used. Figure 7 shows some signature variations from the same person.

Until recently, signature verification had been an offline problem. Important documents requiring signature verification were from cheques, bills, and wills. The goal is to verify if an unknown signature belongs to a specific

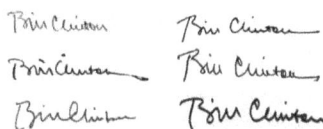

Fig. 7. Signature variations from the same person.

person. One challenge is that only a few known, true samples would exist for any one person. True signatures are usually obtained when a person joins an organization, opens an bank account, or applies for a loan for big purchases such as a car or home.

Online signatures have the benefit of an almost noise-free signature during acquisition. Offline signatures are usually noisy and must go through a more intense pre-processing stage. After a relatively clean signature is obtained, feature extraction begins. For online verification, a mathematical time-function is the feature set. Some function parameters could be the total time taken, the number of pen lifts, the number of endpoints, velocity, acceleration, or the slant of the signature. Choosing the best set of parameters is difficult since there are few true and fake signature samples.

After extracting function parameters of an unknown signature, it needs to be matched with the true signature parameters. Several approaches were considered. One way is to compare the parameters of the unknown signature with each of the parameters belonging to the true signature.

Another method is to divide the sets into segments and then to compare each of those segments. A signature will be considered genuine if there exists a true signature where all the segments match the unknown sample. A third matching method would require that all the segments of the unknown signature match all of the corresponding segments of all the true signature segments. The unknown signature is genuine if all the segments are matched.

Matching two signature parameters, or segments, usually require some distance measure. That is, how far apart two values, or vectors, are. Some common similarity measurements include Euclidean, City Block or Manhattan, and Chessboard. More on similarity measurements can be found in Refs. 52 and 53. A signature parameter, or segment, is considered genuine the distance measure is below a threshold. Thresholds can be fixed, set beforehand, or dynamically set. Dynamic thresholding can take into account specific features of the handwriting such as stroke thickness, amount of broken strokes, etc. and adjust the threshold accordingly.

Offline signature verification is a much more difficult task than online. Aside from missing temporal information, offline images are usually noisier, have to be able to handle degrading paper and faded ink, and must rely on the scanning quality and resolution. Features are more related to the physical aspect of the signature such as stroke thickness, angle, pressure, endpoints, and cross-strokes. Subtle landmarks can give away forgeries such as pauses in strokes and slow movement of writing.

Many methodologies have been proposed. These include using Dynamic Time Warping (DTW) for the features and using Euclidean similarity measurement to compare an unknown signature with a true one.

Ferrer et al.[54] extracted geometric features, such as the interior stroke distribution, in polar and Cartesian coordinates, and sent them through different classifiers. Classifiers used were Hidden Markov Models (HMM), Support Vector Machines (SVM), and an Euclidean distance classifier.

Fang et al.[55] proposed two template matching methods to detect forgeries by understanding that there are always variations in signatures written by the same person. One method would measure the variations in the one-dimensional projection profiles of the signature patterns. The second method determined relative stroke positions in the two-dimension signature patterns.

Das and Dulger[56] trained a neural network using a particle swarm optimization (PSO) algorithm. Geometric features such as width to height ratio, center of gravity, and the normal angle were extracted. Finally, Bhattacharya et al.[57] used a pixel matching technique which was close in accuracy compared to a Neural Network.

5.4. *Handwritten Word Spotting*

As the sheer number of handwritten documents being digitized continues to increase, the need for indexing becomes vital. Word spotting is an approach that allows a user to search for keywords in spoken or written text. While initially developed for use in Automatic Speech Recognition (ASR), word spotting has since been applied to the growing number of handwritten documents for the purpose of indexing. Even though speech is analog in nature, while handwritten documents are spatial, word spotting of handwritten documents has been able to adopt the methods of speech recognition for its use. Eventually, techniques and algorithms specific to handwritten documents have been developed.

Early indexing work started by applying conventional Optical Character Recognition (OCR) techniques, and the results are passed to special search engines to search for words. However, Manmatha et al.[58] designed the first handwritten word spotting system in 1996 because they found that applying traditional OCR techniques to search for words was inadequate. Using OCR in indexing words fails for the following reasons:[59,60] 1) handwriting analysis suffers from low recognition accuracies, 2) the associated indexing systems are hampered by having to process and recognize all the words of a document, and then apply search techniques to the entire result, and 3) the training of OCR systems requires that a huge database be constructed for each alphabet.

Several successful handwritten word spotting systems have been proposed in the literature. These approaches and methods are based on two main approaches: template matching and learning-based.

5.4.1. *Definition*

Handwritten word spotting, also called indexing or searching within documents, is the task of detecting keywords from documents by segmenting the document into word images (clusters) based on their visual appearance. Word spotting systems aim to recognize all occurrences of the specific keyword within a document. The input to the word spotting system is a keyword query, which can be either query by string or query by example. Query by string is a string of letters entered on the keyboard, while query by example uses an image of a word. Initially, most of the word spotting systems start by clustering documents into words. This can be done using different clustering techniques. Afterwards, the word can be described as a whole or it can be segmented into a set of components such as letters, strokes or graphemes. Finally, different algorithms and methods are used to spot words. These methods include learning-based, template matching, and shape code mapping. Figure 8 illustrates different word spotting approaches.

5.4.2. *Input Queries*

In word spotting systems, both query by string and query by example are used to input keywords. Each of these approaches have its pros and cons. Query by string requires learning the alphabet of the language, and then concatenating the letters to form the word model for later matching it with the words in the document.[21,61–63] These systems alleviate some of the

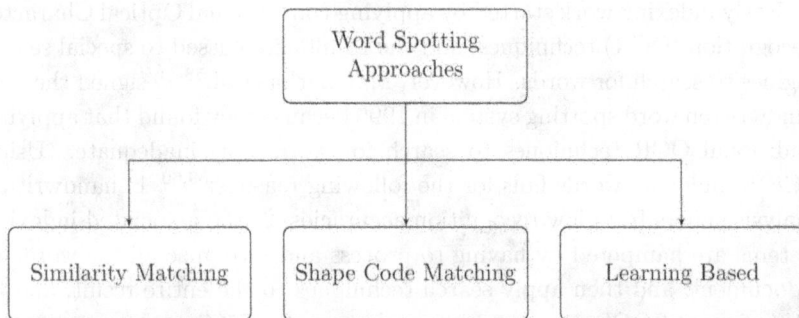

Fig. 8. Word spotting approaches.

drawbacks of traditional handwriting recognition systems, which require huge databases for training. These word spotting systems perform well for lexicon-free approaches,[64] where there are no restrictions on the size of the lexicon.

On the other hand, for query by example, the pixel by pixel or the extracted features of the template image are passed to the system, which is then detected in the document using word spotting techniques. These systems suffer from the drawback that they can be applied only on closed lexicons.[65–68]

5.4.3. *Word Spotting Approaches*

Segmenting or clustering the document into words is considered the first step in many word spotting systems. This can be done using state-of-the-art word segmentation techniques. Various techniques were proposed to establish a threshold for the gap distance between the words in the document, to decide if the gap is within or between words.[65,66,69] Other techniques apply vertical projections and profiles to the lines of the document to find optimal segmentation points, and the document can also be clustered into words using classifiers such as artificial neural networks.[70] However, Leydier et al.[68] found that it is impossible to achieve accurate line or word segmentation. Thus, many successful segmentation-free approaches have been proposed, in which classifiers integrate segmentation with recognition, such as Hidden Markov Models (HMM)[71] and recurrent neural networks.[72]

Handwritten word spotting is a technique which detects words selected by the user in a document without any syntactic constraints.[68] Many methods are used in the literature to detect words. These methods are based on three approaches: template matching, shape code mapping, and learning-based.

Similarity Matching methods are applied in many different studies to spot words. These methods have successful applications with systems of few writers and are also lexicon-free. These methods measure the similarity or dissimilarity between either the pixels of the images or the features that are extracted from the images. Manmatha et al.[58] proposed the first indexing or word spotting system for single writer historical documents. The proposed method was based on matching word pixels. Subsequently, different template matching approaches based on features extracted from word images have been proposed,[67,70,73,74] as well as graph matching approaches.[75] Dynamic Time Warping (DTW) [59,65,76,77] had been successfully applied as an efficient template matching algorithm based on dynamic programming.

Shape code mapping techniques use the character shape code in which each character is mapped into a shape code. Ascenders, descenders, loops and other structural descriptors are used to form the shape code. Each word forms a sequence of shape codes, and query words are mapped into word shape codes. Then, string matching algorithms can be applied to perform the mapping and detect words.[78]

Learning based word spotting systems were introduced to adapt to muli-writers with promising results. However, sufficiently large databases are needed to train the system. HMM is the most common classifier applied to word spotting systems.[21,69,79,80] Other approaches have also been developed; for example, Frinken et al.[72] proposed a word spotting system that uses a bidirectional Long Short-Term Memory (LSTM) Neural Network together with the Connectionist Temporal Classification (CTC) Token Passing algorithm to spot words, which has shown high performance. Khayyat et al.[81,82] have proposed a hierarchical classifier to spot Arabic handwritten words, the classifier integrates classification and language models. A handwritten Urdu word spotting based on Connected Components Analysis[83] has been also implemented. Finally, deep learning has been proposed for word spotting and has achieved state of the art performance on handwritten word spotting.[84]

6. Conclusion

Handwriting recognition is an active research area, which is considered a very challenging problem that is not yet solved. The difficulties in creating ground-truth for thousands/millions of handwritten documents makes handwriting recognition challenging. Nevertheless, being able to create such a large annotated handwritten databases can improve the performance of many handwriting recognition applications, such as text recognition. Finally, the use of contextual information and language models, in addition to the recent incremental use of deep learning algorithms, have had a significant improvement on the performance of the handwriting recognition applications and systems.

References

1. R. Claiborne, *Reading the Past*, University of California Press/British Museum (1990).
2. H. F. Schantz, *The History of OCR, Optical Character Recognition*, Recognition Technologies Users Association (1982).
3. M. Shridhar and A. Badreldin, A high-accuracy syntactic recognition algorithm for handwritten numerals, *IEEE Transactions on Systems, Man, and Cybernetics*, **SMC-15**(1), 152–158 (1985). doi: 10.1109/TSMC.1985. 6313404.
4. R. Plamondon and S. Srihari, On-line and off-line handwriting recognition: A comprehensive survey, *IEEE Trans. Pattern Anal. Mach. Intell.* **22**, 63–84 (2000).
5. A. Vinciarelli and M. Perone, Combining online and offline handwriting recognition. In *Seventh International Conference on Document Analysis and Recognition*, pp. 844–848 (2003).
6. MyScript, `https://www.myscript.com/` Accessed: 2018-07-25.
7. ABBYY, Abbyy® FlexiCapture. `https://my.ufcinc.com/Flexicapture/handwriting/` Accessed: 2018-07-25.
8. Tesseract, Tesseract. `"https://github.com/tesseract-ocr/tesseract/wiki/Downloads"` Accessed: 2018-07-25.
9. L. Hanwang Technology Co. Hanwang technology co., ltd. `https://hanwangt.en.china.cn/` Accessed: 2018-07-25.
10. N. Nobile and C. Suen, *Handbook of Document Image Processing and Recognition*, pp. 257–290 (2014).
11. S. N. Srihari, X. Yang, and G. R. Ball. Offline chinese handwriting recognition: A survey. In *Frontiers of Computer Science*, p. 2007 (2007).
12. X.-Y. Zhang, Y. Bengio, and C.-L. Liu, Online and offline handwritten chinese character recognition: A comprehensive study and new benchmark, *Pattern Recognition*. **61**, 348 – 360 (2017). doi: https://doi.org/10.1016/j.patcog. 2016.08.005. URL `http://www.sciencedirect.com/science/article/pii/S0031320316302187`.
13. K. Huang and H. Yan, Off-line signature verification based on geometric feature extraction and neural network classification, *Pattern Recognition* **30** (1), 9–17 (1997).

14. C. Jou and H.-C. Lee, Handwritten numeral recognition based on simplified structural classification and fuzzy memberships, *Expert Syst. Appl.* **36**(9), 11858–11863 (2009). doi: 10.1016/j.eswa.2009.04.025. URL http://dx.doi.org/10.1016/j.eswa.2009.04.025.

15. A. Boukharouba and A. Bennia, Novel feature extraction technique for the recognition of handwritten digits, *Applied Computing and Informatics*. **13**(1), 19–26 (2017). doi: https://doi.org/10.1016/j.aci.2015.05.001. URL http://www.sciencedirect.com/science/article/pii/S221083271500006X.

16. P. V. Hatkar, B.T. Salokhe, and A. A. Malgave handwritten signature verification using neural network, *International Journal of Innovations in Engineering Research and Technology [IJIERT]* **2**(1) (2015).

17. Y. F. M. Shi, T. Wakabayashi, and F. Kimura, Handwritten numeral recognition using gradient and curvature of gray scale image, *Pattern Recognition* **35**(10), 2051–2059 (2002).

18. N. Bouadjenek, H. Nemmour, and Y. Chibani. Age, gender and handedness prediction from handwriting using gradient features. In *13th International Conference on Document Analysis and Recognition*, pp. 1116–1120 (2015). doi: 10.1109/ICDAR.2015.7333934.

19. Y. Serdouk, H. Nemmour, and Y. Chibani. New gradient features for off-line handwritten signature verification. In *2015 International Symposium on Innovations in Intelligent SysTems and Applications*, pp. 1–4 (2015). doi: 10.1109/INISTA.2015.7276751.

20. B. Wicht, A. Fischer, and J. Hennebert. Deep learning features for handwritten keyword spotting. In *23rd International Conference on Pattern Recognition*, pp. 3434–3439 (2016). doi: 10.1109/ICPR.2016.7900165.

21. V. Lavrenko, T. M. Rath, and R. Manmatha, Holistic word recognition for handwritten historical documents. In *Proceedings of the First International Workshop on Document Image Analysis for Libraries*, pp. 278–287 (2004).

22. J. Chen, H. Cao, R. Prasad, A. Bhardwaj, and P. Natarajan. Gabor features for offline Arabic handwriting recognition. In *Proceedings of the 9th International Workshop on Document Analysis Systems*, pp. 53 – 58 (2010).

23. S. Pasha and M. C. Padma. Handwritten kannada character recognition using wavelet transform and structural features. In *2015 International Conference on Emerging Research in Electronics, Computer Science and Technology*, pp. 346–351 (2015). doi: 10.1109/ERECT.2015.7499039.

24. Y. Xiong, Y. Wen, P. S. P. Wang, and Y. Lu. Text-independent writer identification using sift descriptor and contour-directional feature. In *2015 13th International Conference on Document Analysis and Recognition*, pp. 91–95 (2015). doi: 10.1109/ICDAR.2015.7333732.

25. F. Lauer, C. Y. Suen, and G. Bloch, A trainable feature extractor for handwritten digit recognition, *Pattern Recogn.* **40**(6), 1816–1824 (2007). doi: 10.1016/j.patcog.2006.10.011. URL http://dx.doi.org/10.1016/j.patcog.2006.10.011.

26. D. Cireşan and U. Meier. Multi-column deep neural networks for offline handwritten chinese character classification. In *International Joint Conference on Neural Networks*, pp. 1–6 (2015). doi: 10.1109/IJCNN.2015.7280516.

27. Y. LeCun, L. Bottou, Y. Bengio, and P. Haffner, Gradient-based learning applied to document recognition, *Proceedings of the IEEE* **86**(11), 2278–2324 (1998).

28. D. C. Ciresan, U. Meier, and J. Schmidhuber, Multi-column deep neural networks for image classification, *CoRR*. abs/1202.2745 (2012). URL http://arxiv.org/abs/1202.2745.

29. X. C. Halkias, S. Paris, and H. Glotin, General sparse penalty in deep belief networks: Towards domain adaptation, *LSIS Research Report* (2012).

30. a2iaLab, The rimes database, http://www.a2ialab.com/doku.php?id=rimes_database:start Accessed: 2018-08-13.

31. J. J. Hull, A database for handwritten text recognition research, *IEEE Transactions on Pattern Analysis and Machine Intelligence* **16**(5), 550–554 (1994).

32. K.-W. Cheung, D.-Y. Yeung, and R. T. Chin, A bayesian framework for deformable pattern recognition with application to handwritten character recognition, *IEEE Transactions on Pattern Analysis and Machine Intelligence* **20**(12), 1382–1388 (1998). doi: 10.1109/34.735813.

33. U. R. Babu, Y. Venkateswarlu, and A. K. Chintha. Handwritten digit recognition using k-nearest neighbour classifier. In *2014 World Congress on Computing and Communication Technologies*, pp. 60–65 (2014). doi: 10.1109/WCCCT.2014.7.

34. D. Nasien, H. Haron, and S. S. Yuhaniz. Support vector machine (svm) for english handwritten character recognition. In *2010 Second International Conference on Computer Engineering and Applications*, vol. 1, pp. 249–252 (2010). doi: 10.1109/ICCEA.2010.56.

35. C. Kaensar. A comparative study on handwriting digit recognition classifier using neural network, support vector machine and k-nearest neighbor. In *9th International Conference on Computing and Information Technology*, pp. 155–163 (2013).

36. M. M. A. Ghosh and A. Y. Maghari. A comparative study on handwriting digit recognition using neural networks. In *2017 International Conference on Promising Electronic Technologies*, pp. 77–81 (2017). doi: 10.1109/ICPET.2017.20.

37. S. Madhvanath and V. Govindaraju, The role of holistic paradigms in handwritten word recognition, *IEEE Trans. Pattern Anal. Mach. Intell.* **23**(2), 149–164 (2001).

38. M. Rajnoha, R. Burget, and M. K. Dutta. Offline handwritten text recognition using support vector machines. In *International Conference on Signal Processing and Integrated Networks*, pp. 132–136 (2017). doi: 10.1109/SPIN.2017.8049930.

39. L. Neumann and J. Matas. A method for text localization and recognition in real-world images. In *Proceedings of the 10th Asian Conference on Computer Vision*, pp. 770–783 (2011). URL http://dl.acm.org/citation.cfm?id=1966049.1966110.

40. C. Bartz, H. Yang, and C. Meinel, STN-OCR: A single neural network for text detection and text recognition, *CoRR*. abs/1707.08831 (2017). URL http://arxiv.org/abs/1707.08831.

41. F. Coelho, L. Batista, L. F. Teixeira, and J. S. Cardoso. Automatic system for the recognition of amounts in handwritten cheques, In *Proceedings of the International Conference on Signal Processing and Multimedia Applications*, pp. 320–324 (2008). URL http://www.inescporto.pt/~jsc/publications/conferences/2008FCoelhoSIGMAP.pdf.
42. D. Guillevic and C. Y. Suen, Recognition of legal amounts on bank cheques, *Pattern Anal. Appl.* **1**(1), 28–41 (1998). doi: 10.1007/BF01238024. URL http://dx.doi.org/10.1007/BF01238024.
43. C.-L. Liu. High accuracy handwritten Chinese character recognition using quadratic classifiers with discriminative feature extraction. In *18th International Conference on Pattern Recognition*, vol. 2, pp. 942–945 (2006). doi: 10.1109/ICPR.2006.624.
44. R. G. Casey and E. Lecolinet, A survey of methods and strategies in character segmentation, *IEEE Trans. Pattern Anal. Mach. Intell.* **18**(7), 690–706 (1996).
45. H. Bunke, M. Roth, and E. Schukat-Talamazzini, Off-line cursive handwriting recognition using hidden markov models, *Pattern Recognition.* **28**(9), 1399 – 1413 (1995). doi: https://doi.org/10.1016/0031-3203(95)00013-P. URL http://www.sciencedirect.com/science/article/pii/003132039500013P.
46. R. Mouhcine, A. Mustapha, and M. Zouhir, Recognition of cursive arabic handwritten text using embedded training based on hmms, *Journal of Electrical Systems and Information Technology.* **5**(2), 245–251 (2018). doi: https://doi.org/10.1016/j.jesit.2017.02.001. URL http://www.sciencedirect.com/science/article/pii/S2314717217300156.
47. T. Bluche, J. Louradour, and R. O. Messina, Scan, attend and read: End-to-end handwritten paragraph recognition with MDLSTM attention, *CoRR.* **abs/1604.03286** (2016). URL http://arxiv.org/abs/1604.03286.
48. B. Stuner, C. Chatelain, and T. Paquet, Cohort of LSTM and lexicon verification for handwriting recognition with gigantic lexicon, *CoRR.* **abs/1612.07528** (2016). URL http://arxiv.org/abs/1612.07528.
49. V. Frinken, A. Fornés, J. Lladós, and J.-M. Ogier. Bidirectional language model for handwriting recognition. In *SSPR/SPR* (2012).
50. V. Frinken, F. Zamora-Martãnez, S. Espana-Boquera, M. J. Castro-Bleda, A. Fischer, and H. Bunke. Long-short term memory neural networks language modeling for handwriting recognition. In *Proceedings of the 21st International Conference on Pattern Recognition*, pp. 701–704 (2012).
51. G. Pirlo. Algorithms for signature verification. In *Fundamentals in Handwriting Recognition*, pp. 435–454 (1994).
52. D. Ramu and T. Devi, A comparison study on methods for measuring distance in images, *International Journal of Research in Computers*, pp. 34–38 (2012).
53. S.-H. Cha, Comprehensive survey on distance/similarity measures between probability density functions, *International Journal of Mathematical Models and Methods in Applied Sciences* **1**(4), 300–307 (2007).

54. M. A. Ferrer, J. B. Alonso, and C. M. Travieso, Offline geometric parameters for automatic signature verification using fixed-point arithmetic, *IEEE Trans. Pattern Anal. Mach. Intell.* **27**(6), 993–997 (2005).
55. B. Fang, C. Leung, Y. Tang, K. Tse, P. Kwok, and Y. Wong. Off-line signature verification by the tracking of feature and stroke positions (2003).
56. M. T. Das and L. C. Dulger, Off-line signature verification with pso-nn algorithm, *2007 22nd International Symposium on Computer and Information Sciences*, pp. 1–6 (2007).
57. I. Bhattacharya, P. Ghoshb, and S. Biswasb. Offline signature verification using pixel matching technique. In *International Conference on Computational Intelligence: Modeling Techniques and Applications*, pp. 970–977 (2013).
58. R. Manmatha, C. Han, and E. M. Riseman. Word spotting: A new approach to indexing handwriting. In *CVPR Conference*, pp. 631–637 (1996).
59. J. A. Rodríguez-Serrano and F. Perronnin. Local gradient histogram features for word-spotting in unconstrained handwritten documents. In *Proc. of 11th Int. Conf. on Frontiers in Handwriting Recognition*, pp. 7–12 (2008).
60. J. A. Rodríguez-Serrano and F. Perronnin. Score normalization for HMM-based word spotting using universal background model. In *Proc. of 11th Int. Conf. on Frontiers in Handwriting Recognition*, pp. 82–87 (2008).
61. R. Saabni and J. El-Sana. Keyword searching for Arabic handwritten documents. In *Proc. of 11th International Conference on Frontiers in Handwriting Recognition*, pp. 271–277 (2008).
62. A. Bhardwaj, D. Jose, and V. Govindaraju. Script independent word spotting in multilingual documents. In *Proceedings of the 2nd International Workshop on Cross Lingual Information Access*, pp. 48–54 (2008). URL http://citeseerx.ist.psu.edu/viewdoc/download?rep=rep1&type=pdf&doi=10.1.1.179.11.
63. J. Edwards, Y. Whye, T. David, F. Roger, B. M. Maire, and G. Vesom. Making Latin manuscripts searchable using GHMM's. In *Proceedings of the 19th Annual Conference on Neural Information Processing Systems*, pp. 385–392 (2005).
64. J. Chan, C. Ziftci, and D. Forsyth. Searching off-line Arabic documents. In *Proceedings of the International Conference on Computer Vision and Pattern Recognition*, pp. 1455–1462 (2006).
65. A. Kolcz, J. Alspector, and M. Augusteijn, A line-oriented approach to word spotting in handwritten documents, *Pattern Anal. Appl.* **3**(2), 153–168 (2000). URL http://dblp.uni-trier.de/db/journals/paa/paa3.html#KolczAA00.
66. R. Manmatha, C. Han, E. M. Riseman, and W. B. Croft. Indexing handwriting using word matching. In *Proceedings of the First ACM international conference on Digital libraries*, pp. 151–159 (1996).
67. R. Manmatha and T. Rath. Indexing handwritten historical documents - recent progress. In *Proceedings of the Symposium on Document Image Understanding*, pp. 77–85 (2003).

68. Y. Leydier, F. Lebourgeois, and H. Emptoz, Text search for Medieval manuscript images, *Pattern Recognition* **40**(12), 3552–3567 (2007).

69. J. A. Rodríguez-Serrano and F. Perronnin, Handwritten word-spotting using hidden Markov models and universal vocabularies, *Pattern Recognition* **42** (9), 2106–2116 (2009).

70. S. N. Srihari and G. R. Ball, Language independent word spotting in scanned documents, LNCS. Vol. 5362, pp. 134–143 (2008).

71. A. Fischer, A. Keller, V. Frinken, and H. Bunke. HMM-based word spotting in handwritten documents using subword models. In *ICPR*, pp. 3416–3419 (2010).

72. V. Frinken, A. Fischer, R. Manmatha, and H. Bunke, A novel word spotting method based on recurrent neural networks, *IEEE Trans. Pattern Anal. Mach. Intell.* **34**(2), 211–224 (2012).

73. B. Zhang, S. N. Srihari, and C. Huang. Word image retrieval using binary features. In *Document Recognition and Retrieval*, pp. 45–53 (2004).

74. T. Adamek, N. E. O'Connor, and A. F. Smeaton, Word matching using single closed contours for indexing handwritten historical documents, *IJDAR* **9**(2-4), 153–165 (2007).

75. M. Stauffer, A. Fischer, and K. Riesen, Keyword spotting in historical handwritten documents based on graph matching, *Pattern Recognition* **81**, 240–253 (2018). doi: https://doi.org/10.1016/j.patcog.2018.04.001. URL http://www.sciencedirect.com/science/article/pii/S0031320318301274.

76. T. M. Rath and R. Manmatha. Word image matching using dynamic time warping. In *CVPR Conference (2)*, pp. 521–527 (2003).

77. K. Khurshid, C. Faure, and N. Vincent. A novel approach for word spotting using merge-split edit distance. In *CAIP*, LNCS Vol. 5702, pp. 213–220 (2009). URL http://dblp.uni-trier.de/db/conf/caip/caip2009.html#KhurshidFV09.

78. T. Sari and A. Kefali. A search engine for Arabic documents. In *Actes du dixième Colloque International Francophone sur l'Écrit et le Document*, pp. 97–102 (2008).

79. A. Fischer, A. Keller, V. Frinken, and H. Bunke, Lexicon-free handwritten word spotting using character HMMs, *Pattern Recogn. Lett.* **33**(7), 934–942 (2012).

80. A. H. Toselli, E. Vidal, V. Romero, and V. Frinken, Hmm word graph based keyword spotting in handwritten document images, *Information Sciences.* **370-371**, 497–518 (2016). ISSN 0020-0255. doi: https://doi.org/10.1016/j.ins.2016.07.063. URL http://www.sciencedirect.com/science/article/pii/S0020025516305461.

81. M. Khayyat, L. Lam, and C. Y. Suen. Verification of hierarchical classifier results for handwritten Arabic word spotting. In *Proc. 12th International Conference on Document Analysis and Recognition* pp. 572–576, (2013).

82. M. Khayyat, L. Lam, and C. Y. Suen, Learning-based word spotting system for Arabic handwritten documents, *Pattern Recognition* **47**(3), 1021–1030 (2014).

83. M. W. Sagheer, N. Nobile, C. L. He, and C. Y. Suen. A novel handwritten urdu word spotting based on connected components analysis. In *20th International Conference on Pattern Recognition,* pp. 2013–2016 (2010). doi: 10.1109/ICPR.2010.496. URL https://doi.org/10.1109/ICPR.2010.496.
84. S. Sudholt and G. A. Fink, Phocnet: A deep convolutional neural network for word spotting in handwritten documents, *CoRR.* abs/1604.00187 (2016). URL http://arxiv.org/abs/1604.00187.

Chapter 5

A New Roadmap for Evaluating Descriptive Handwritten Answer Script

Palaiahnakote Shivakumara[*], Umapada Pal[†], Tong Lu[‡],
Tapabrata Chakraborti[†] and Michael Blumenstein[§]

*[*]Faculty of Computer Science and Information Technology
University of Malaya, Kuala Lumpur, Malaysia,
hudempsk@yahoo.com
[†]Computer Vision and Pattern Recognition Unit,
Indian Statistical Institute, Kolkata, India,
umapada@isical.ac.in
[‡]Notational Key Lab for Novel Software Technology,
Nanjing University, Nanjing, P. R. China,
lutong@nju.edu.cn
[§]University Technology of Sydney, Australia,
michael.blumenstein@uts.edu.au*

In computational pedagogy, a relatively simple Optical Character Recognizer system can robustly evaluate objective response types automatically without human intervention. This saves time, cost and man-hours. Thus, the next question becomes whether it is possible to develop an automated system for evaluating descriptive handwritten answer types. Recent experiences show that human evaluation of long examination responses is quite subjective and prone to challenges like inexperience, negligence, lack of uniformity in the case of several evaluators, etc. In this work, we present the roadmap for an automated vision system that evaluates descriptive answers based on extracting relevant words and finding the relationship between words according to weights. We introduce context features to handle variations of words written by different users to estimate the final score.

1. Introduction

One of the established systems in document image analysis is the Optical Character Recognizer (OCR) for printed documents, which has achieved more than 98% recognition rate [1] in many scripts. OCR engines are now available in different languages on the market for many applications where digitization is a prerequisite [1]. An open research problem is to achieve the same success for recognizing degraded, historical and handwritten documents. This type of handwritten OCR can be used in several real-life applications, such as postal automation, bank cheque processing, signature verification, etc. However, due to large variations in writing styles (e.g., different persons, paper/ink quality, double-sided writing, and writer's mood), developing an OCR for handwritten texts is considered a challenging task in the field of automated document image analysis [2]. Developing an automated and robust system for descriptive answer evaluation poses further challenges because of its sensitivity to individual writing.

There are existing works that evaluate short answers using stroke-based structural features and classifiers for grading [3, 4]. These methods are suitable for short answers and work well for limited cases. Therefore, descriptive answer evaluation requires a new roadmap in order to develop a working vision system. To the best of our knowledge, there has been no single attempt to develop a comprehensive method towards that direction to-date. The main reasons are: (1) large variations in writing styles, (2) word extraction from answers poses challenges due to non-uniform spacing between words, (3) difficulties in proving that extracted words are relevant to evaluate answers written by different students (one can expect that we have to handle such nuances as synonyms and the different ways of expression due to individual difference in thinking, knowledge, writing ability, vocabulary, etc.), (4) difficulties in deciding degree of the relevance of the answers, (5) difficulties in finding the relationship between relevant words to assign weights or scores, which in turn help in confirming answers, and (6) difficulties in deciding the final score based on weights of words. These are challenges because different students write answers in different ways, which may contain a few words, more words or even no relevant words. Consequently, as the number of students increases, the complexity of the problem increases. Therefore, there is a major challenge to develop a working system that can be scalable for any number of students with the minimum cost and high reliability.

The main objective of the chapter is to provide a roadmap for developing an automated system that can evaluate handwritten descriptive answers without human intervention, such that we have an objective uniform evaluation under one scheme. To achieve this goal, we divide the main objective into sub-objectives, which will be discussed in detail in the proposed methodology section.

2. Related Work

In this section, we review the methods on short answer evaluation as there are no methods currently available for evaluating descriptive answers. Suwanwiwat et al. [5] proposed an off-line restricted set for handwritten word recognition for automated student identification through a short answer question assessment system. The method explores Gaussian grid and modified directional features for recognition. Srivastava and Bhattacharyya [6] proposed a captive short answer evaluator. In this method, the natural language concept is used for recognizing words written by students. Suwanwiwat et al. [7] proposed short answer question examination using an automatic off-line handwriting recognition system. This method combines features obtained by the water reservoir model and Gaussian grid features for word recognition. Duenas et al. [8] proposed automatic prediction of item difficulty for short answer type questions. The method extracts a large number of features and then uses a classifier for prediction. Hasanah et al. [9] proposed an information extraction approach for automatic short answer grading. The method uses several matching techniques such as parse tree matching, regular expression matching, Boolean parse matching, Syntactic parse matching, and Semantic word matching for grading. Suwanwiwat et al. [10] proposed novel combined features for a handwritten short answer assessment system. The method is an extension of their previous method by adding more features and using a classifier for the recognition of texts. Rababah and Taani proposed [11] an automated scoring approach for Arabic short answers to essay questions. This method finds the similarity between answers written by students and predefined model answers (using an answer schema). For finding similarity, the method uses a cosine similarity measure. Based on the degree of similarity, the method assigns a grade for each question. Srihari et al. [3] proposed automatic scoring of short handwritten essays in reading comprehension tests. The method initially segments text lines and words from each document image. It then proposes a fusion of analytic and holistic methods together with contextual processing based on trigrams. Finally, lexicons for recognizing handwritten words are derived from reading passages, the testing prompt, answer rubric and student responses. Srihari and Singer [4] proposed a role for automation in the examination of handwritten items. In this method, integrating developed tools into a unified framework was discussed. They also provided overall advantages, disadvantages and future directions for evaluating essay-type answers. Meena and Raj [12] proposed evaluations on descriptive-type answers using hyperspace analog to language and self-organizing maps. The method explored clusters of Kohonen self-organizing maps for evaluation.

In light of the above discussion, it is noted that none of the methods addressed the issues of descriptive answer type evaluation, except the frameworks suggested in [4] and [12]. This shows that the problem is still an open challenge. Most of the methods used handwriting recognition for evaluating short answer assessment. When we increase the number of student answers and the number of lines such as answers that span full or half pages, these methods may not perform well. Hence, in this proposal, we try to provide a new idea in the form of a roadmap to develop a system to evaluate descriptive answers automatically.

3. Proposed Roadmap

Recent trends suggest the use of deep learning to solve complex tasks across all the problems of machine intelligence [13]. This has inspired the proposed roadmap for solving the complex problem of evaluating descriptive answer types. Based on the proposed roadmap, one can develop vision systems to find viable solutions in the future. It is noted that while writing answers, students usually do some extra rough handwork to remember or recall the concepts, or to calculate intermediate results. As a result, a handwritten page contains many instances of unwanted writing, which is sketchy with an irregular structure. These noisy sketches hinder subsequent steps such as text line segmentation, word segmentation and character recognition because noisy sketches may cause touching lines, lose actual shapes of characters, etc. Therefore, the first step need to be cleaning the handwritten document images.

Generally, due to time constraints and practice, students write answers without worrying about orientations or the spacing between words and text lines. This makes text line segmentation more complex and challenging. As a result, conventional methods that work based on connected component analysis and binarization-based methods may not work well for handwritten document images. So the second step is text line and word segmentation from cleaned handwritten document images.

Extracting relevant words from answers written by different students in different styles without any restrictions of grammar, words and sentences is really challenging for researchers. However, we believe that each question must be associated with a few technical words according to the question. The idea is to spot such technical words, if any, in the descriptive answer. With the help of the words in model answers (schema), it is possible to find the degree of relevancy. Therefore, the next challenge is to spot these words based on the degree of relevance with respect to words in the model answers.

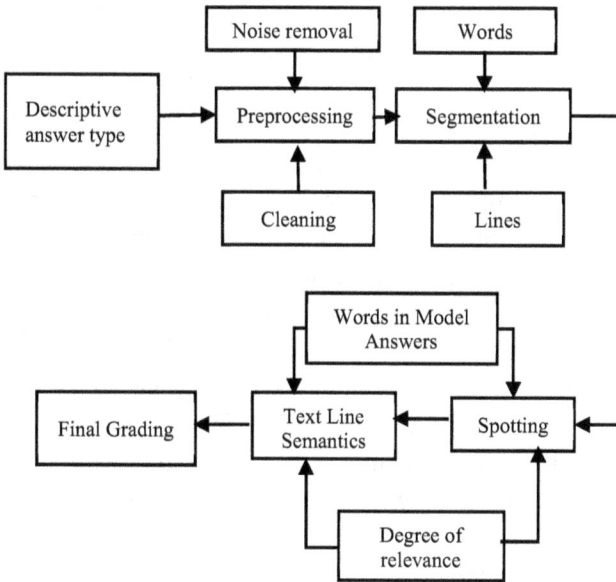

Fig. 1. Framework of the proposed roadmap.

In order to understand descriptive answers, we consider words that have been spotted as the seed words. Then the method finds neighboring words in the text lines of seed words to find the relationship between seed words and neighboring ones semantically based on a dictionary, natural language processing concepts, etc. This results in understanding the sentences of descriptive answers. Based on this understanding, we need to assign weights, which should help us to give grades. Finally, the weight of each sentence is analyzed further to assign the total grade for the full descriptive answers. In other words, the method should find the degree of relevance at the text line level to assign the final grade. The schematic diagram of the proposed roadmap can be seen in Figure 1. The idea to find solutions for each of the above steps is discussed in the subsequent sections.

3.1. *Preprocessing for Cleaning Documents and Removing Struck out Text*

Since our target is to consider descriptive handwritten answers such as essay type answers, one can expect working (handwritten) on the sides of the page, such as intermediate calculations before computing the final calculations, writing a few keywords to recollect answers, and struck-out text while writing the answers. These are the main causes which prevent good accuracies from being achieved in subsequent steps, namely, text line, word segmentation, keyword spotting and estimating the degree of relevance at the word and text line levels. Therefore, it is necessary to remove such noise from raw handwritten document images. Cleaning handwritten documents is not a new problem in the document analysis field [14]. However, most of the methods depend on binarization and structural points, such as end, junction and intersection points appearing in different zones [13]. Since the above cases are not simple to identify as noisy edges or components, it is a requirement to use grayscale images without binarization because these give more details compared to binarize outputs. It is true that directions of pixels of actual text have regular patterns, whereas unconstrained noisy texts have irregular direction patterns. We need to explore such regular direction patterns along with gradient values, which give low values for noisy texts and high values for regular text due to the difference in force and speed in writing regular texts versus noisy texts.

In order to achieve the above distinct direction patterns, we can use simple but effective gradient directional features. This is because of the fact that gradient directions moves perpendicular to the edge direction. For actual edges, we get regular patterns with directions, while for noisy texts, one cannot expect regular patterns due to irregular writing without any constraints. The same directional features can be used for removing struck-out text since a strike-out over text provides a long run in the same direction. This feature can be used to separate directions, which represent texts and strikes. The schematic diagram in Figure 2 illustrates the development of the method to clean handwritten document images.

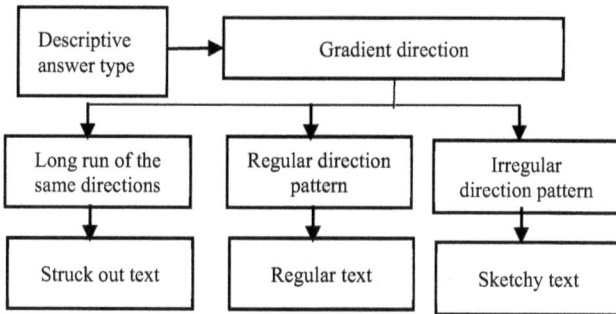

Fig. 2. Schematic diagram for cleaning and removal of struck out text.

3.2. *Text Line and Word Segmentation*

With typing becoming more common, current students are losing the practice of writing. New devices such as smart phones and tablets help us to reduce writing tasks further. As a result, one can expect that writing in an irregular fashion and could become more common with non-uniform spacing between words and/or lines. Thus, segmenting text lines and words is challenging especially from lengthy essays. According to the literature review [15], most of the existing methods use foreground information to segment text lines. However, for documents such as answer scripts where one can come across rulers, which confuse baselines and strokes, it is necessary to use background information along with foreground information in the gray-scale domain.

To achieve good segmentation, one can explore the same gradient directional features as discussed in the previous section. This is because when there is text, gradient directions can form symmetry due to edges [16]. If there is no text, i.e. there is no spacing between lines and words, the gradient direction may not be symmetrical [16]. In addition, when there is text, we can expect high gradient values and when there is no text, we can expect low gradient values. Integration of these two features helps us to identify the space between lines and words. Once we identify the space between text lines, the same symmetry properties can be used for word segmentation. This idea is simple and effective compared to studying the foreground or background with binary information. In addition, this idea is independent of scripts and orientations. The logic is shown in Figure 3, which helps us understand the flow of the steps.

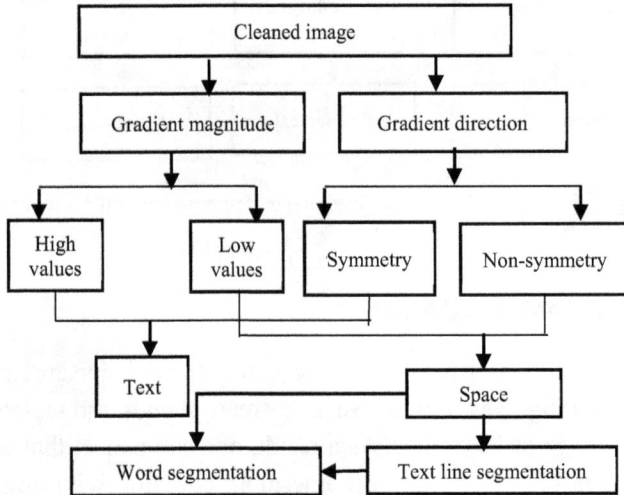

Fig. 3. Logic for text line and word segmentation.

3.3. *Degree of Relevancy for Word Spotting*

The previous steps provide segmented words for the descriptive answer type. The real challenge though is to find relevant words, which can prove that the written answer is relevant to a particular question because each individual can write different words for the same answer. In addition, instead of writing actual key words, they may write some expanded explanations representing the meaning of some technical words. Therefore, we need to find relevant words first to confirm the written answer is related to the correct question. There is a genre of methods in document analysis to search for specific words without recognition, namely, word spotting. The big question, however, is how to estimate relevancy. It is a fact that every question has a general schema to provide keywords and important sentences, which are ingredients for confirming whether the written answer is relevant for efficient grading. This is called the model answers database. The method uses words in the model answer database to estimate the degree of relevancy. Usually, every answer must contain a few technical keywords. Therefore, it is simple to spot the words that have the maximum similarity between the words of the answer and the model answers [17, 18]. This results in seed words, which represent the answers of a particular question.

If an answer does not provide any technical words according to the words in the model answers, we need to find the degree of relevancy with the help of synonyms chosen from a dictionary and other resources. For this situation, we need to explore natural language processing concepts to find relevant meanings of the words, which can match with those in the model answer database. The degree can be estimated based on matching a number of pixels or characters [19, 20]. Based on the degree of relevancy and the words in the model answers, we need to assign grades, which can be used for the final grading. The logic for estimating the degree of relevancy at the word level with the help of model answers (schema) is shown in Figure 4.

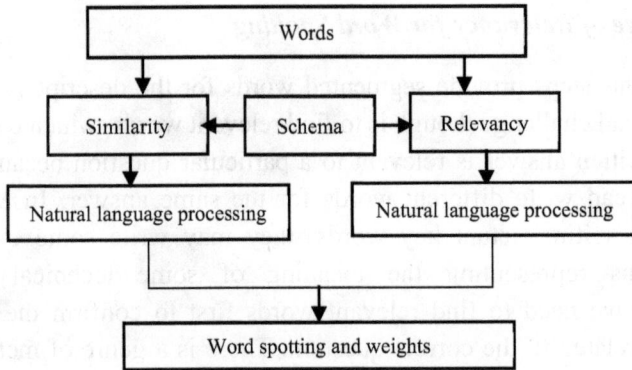

Fig. 4. Degree of relevancy for word spotting.

3.4. Degree of Relevancy at the Text Line Level for Final Grading

The idea presented in the previous section proposes seed words, which represent the correct answers of a particular question. Now, we need to consider seed words as starting words to find the other words of the same sentence in order to understand the meaning of the whole sentence. The method should find the relationship between the words of a sentence with the seed. This is possible by exploring context features between the seed and the other words of the sentence. The context can be defined based on the degree of relevancy of neighbor words with the seed word. With the help of context and the words in model answers, we can predict the meaning of the whole sentence. This process should continue for all the seed words of all the sentences. After confirming correct sentences for the relevant question, the method should assign weights, and this again should be done for all the sentences.

Once the method finds consistency between sentences according to the model answers, the weights of seed words should be revised in order to correct for any mistakes. At the same time, we need to revise the weights at the sentence level before final grading. This is because sometimes, we may not get all the expected words, no words, false words, etc. In this case, we need a relevance feedback mechanism to revisit seed words and weights. Finally, the weights of all the sentences together are considered for the final grading of the answer. The whole idea is shown in Figure 5, where we can see how relevance feedback works for revising weights.

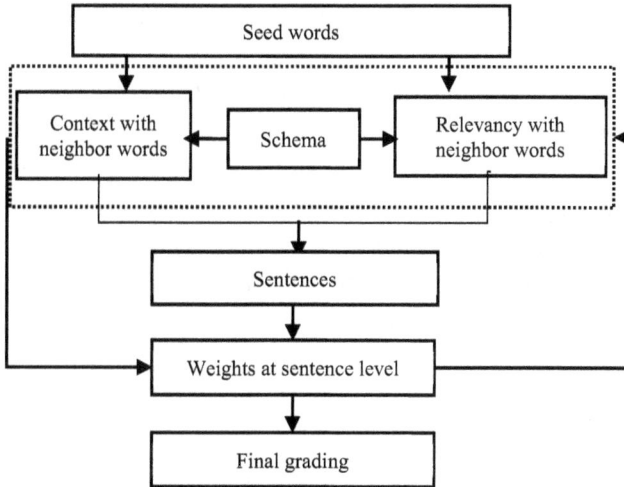

Fig. 5. Degree of relevancy at the text line level for final grading.

4. Experimental Analysis

As evident from the literature survey, there is no existing work for evaluating descriptive answers. Therefore, there is no standard database available in the literature. To evaluate the proposed framework, one would have to collect answer scripts written by various students at different ages, which must include different scripts and documents with varying orientations, noise, sketchy writing, struck-out texts, artifacts, etc. As the number of answer scripts increases, the complexity of a dataset increases as well. To the best of our knowledge, dataset creation and ground-truth generation itself may require a lot of time, especially in a country where we can expect a large population, multiple scripts and a large number of possible variations in writing. Since there are new systems that have the capacity to handle big data, it is easy to solve the complex problem of an automatic descriptive evaluator system.

The proposed framework involves many steps, namely, cleaning, strike-out text removal, text line and word segmentation, keyword spotting, degree of relevancy estimation at the word level and degree of relevancy estimation at the text line level. To evaluate each step of the proposed framework, we need to define measures. For cleaning, it is necessary to calculate recognition rates at the character or word level prior to cleaning and after cleaning. For the other steps, there are standard measures, namely, recall, precision and F-measure. More details for recall, precision and F-measure can be found in [16].

The robustness and effectiveness of the proposed framework are to be tested on a large dataset, which comprises multi-script, multi-oriented images, etc. The results should be compared with human scores for validation. In addition, the proposed system may be compared with short answer evaluations to test their robustness and effectiveness.

5. Conclusions and Future Work

In this chapter, we have proposed a new roadmap for developing an automatic system for evaluating descriptive handwritten answers. We have proposed a new solution for each step of the proposed framework. For instance, a gradient directional pattern for separating noisy texts from actual texts, text lines and word segmentation, degree of estimation for word spotting, degree of relevancy estimation at the word and text line level with the help of model answers and natural language processing concepts. The proposed concepts are script, orientation and writer independent. In addition, the proposed concepts are robust to noise, low resolution and degradation to some extent. The only constraint is that the scope of the work is limited to descriptive answers that have been written in successive order of the questions.

There are many challenges ahead if we consider the possible variations in writing and population of students. Sometimes, students may not follow the order of questions. Instead, they select their own choice or order of questions to write their answers. It is also true that students write answers for different parts of the same question in different places by referring to the question number. Developing generalized systems, which can work at the subject level, college level, university level, etc. has been an open research problem for several decades as it involves an immeasurable number of variations and big data. Therefore, the major question is scalability and accuracy of unified systems. At the same time, collecting datasets and generating ground truth are equally important to judge the ability of such systems.

Acknowledgments

The work described in this chapter was supported by the Natural Science Foundation of China under Grant No. 61672273, No. 61272218 and No. 61321491, the Science Foundation for Distinguished Young Scholars of Jiangsu under Grant No. BK20160021.

References

1. R. Pramanik and S. Bag, Shape decomposition based handwritten compount character recognition, *Journal of Visual Communication and Image Representation*, 50, pp. 123–134 (2018).
2. P. P. Roy, A. K. Bhunia, A. Das, P. Dhar and U. Pal, Keyword spotting in doctor's handwriting on medical prescriptions, *Expert Systems with Applications*, 76, pp. 113–128 (2017).
3. S. Srihari, J. Collins, R. Srihari, H. Srinivasan, S. Shetty and J. B. Griffler, Automatic scoring of short handwritten essays in reading comprenesnion tests, *Artificial Intelligence*, 172, pp. 300–324 (2008).
4. S. N. Srihari and K. Singer, Role of automation in the examination of handwritten items, *Patten Recognition*, 47, pp. 1083–1095 (2014).
5. H. Suwanwiwat, V. Nguyen and M. Blumenstein, Off-line restricted-set handwritten word recognition for student identification in a short answer question automated assessment system, In *Proc. HIS*, pp. 167–172 (2012).
6. V. Srivstava and C. Bhattacharyya, Captivate short answer evaluator, In *Proc. MITE*, pp. 114–119 (2013).
7. H. Suwanwiwat, M. Blumenstein and U. Pal, Short answer question examination using an automatic off-line handwriting recognition system and a novel combined features, In *Proc. IJCNN*, pp. 1–8 (2015).
8. G. Duenas, S. Jimenez and J. Baquero, Automatic prediction of item difficulty for short answer questions, In *Proc. 10CCC*, pp. 478–485 (2015).
9. U. Hasanah, A. E. Permanasari, S. S. Kusumawardani and F. S. Pribadi, A review of an information extraction technique approach for automatic short answer grading, In *Proc. ICITSEE*, pp. 192–196 (2016).

10. H. Suwanwiwat, U. Pal and M. Blumenstein, An investigation of novel combined features for a handwritten short anwer assessment system, In *Proc. ICFHR*, pp. 102–107 (2016).
11. H. Rababah and A. T. A. Taani, An automated scoring approach for Arabic short answers essays questions, In *Proc. ICIT*, pp. 697–702 (2017).
12. K. Meena and L. Raj, Evaluation of the descriptive type answers using hyperspace analog to language and self-organizing map, In *Proc. ICCICR*, pp. 1–5 (2014).
13. R. Sarkhel, N. Das, A. Das, M. Kundu and M. Nasipuri, A multi-scale deep quad tree based feature extraction method for the recognition of isolated hadnwitten characters of popular indic script, *Pattern Recognition*, 71, pp. 78–93 (2017).
14. B. B. Chaudhuri and C. Adak, An approach for detecting and cleaning of struck-out handwritten text, *Pattern Recognition*, 61, pp. 282–294 (2017).
15. V. Papavassiliou, T. Stafylakis, V. Katsouros and G. Carayannis, Handwritten document image segmentation into text lines and words, *Pattern Recognition*, 43, pp. 369–377 (2010).
16. P. Shivakumara, A. Konwer, A. Bhowmick, V. Khare, U. Pal and T. Lu, A new GVF arrow pattern for character segmentation from double line license plate images, In *Proc. ACPR*, pp. 782–787 (2017).
17. A. H. Toselli, E. Vidal, V. Romero and V. Frinken, HMM word graph based keyword spotting in handwritten document images, *Information Sciences*, 370-371, pp. 497–518 (2016).
18. G. Kumar and V. Govindaraju, Bayesian background models for keyword spotting in hadnwritten documents, *Pattern Recognition*, 64, pp. 81–91 (2017).
19. B. Hadjadi, Y. Chibani and H. Nemmour, An efficient open system for offline handwritten signature identification based on curvelet transform and one-class principal component analysis, *Neurocomputing*, 265, pp. 66–77 (2017).
20. Z. Tamen, H. Drias and D. Boughaci, An efficient multiple classifier system for Arabic hadwirtten words recognition, *Pattern Recognition Letters*, 93, pp. 123–132 (2017).

Chapter 6

Improving Chinese Writer Identification by Fusion of Text-dependent and Text-independent Methods

Yu-Jie Xiong[*,†], Li Liu[‡], Patrick S. P. Wang[§] and Yue Lu[†]

*School of Electronic and Electrical Engineering
Shanghai University of Engineering Science
Shanghai 201620, P. R. China*

†*Shanghai Key Laboratory of Multidimensional Information Processing
Department of Computer Science and Technology
East China Normal University, Shanghai 200062, P. R. China*

‡*School of Information Engineering
Nanchang University, Nanchang 330031, P. R. China*

§*Northeastern University, Boston, MA 02115, USA*

*xiong@stu.ecnu.edu.cn, liliu033@ncu.edu.cn
patwang@ieee.org, ylu@cs.ecnu.edu.cn*

A novel method for Chinese writer identification is proposed in this paper, which takes advantage of both text-independent and text-dependent characteristics. The contour-directional features were extracted from a whole image. They were used to calculate the text-independent similarity between the query and reference handwriting images. Meanwhile, character pairs, appearing in both the query and reference handwriting images, were utilized for computing the text-dependent similarity. We propose an effective method to measure the similarity of character pairs. It is rooted from image registration. The displacement field used to align two characters was calculated by the Log-Demons algorithm, and was utilized for a similarity measurement. The final similarity between the query and reference handwriting images is the fusion of text-independent and text-dependent similarities. The best Top-1 accuracy on the HIT-MW and CASIA-2.1 datasets reached 97.1% and 98.3% respectively, which outperformed other previous approaches.

1. Introduction

Writer identification is a method used to identify the authorship of handwritings. It can be generally classified into two categories: text-independent and text-dependent.[1] Text-independent methods are based on the handwritten data with unrestricted text content. They do not focus on particular characters or words, but instead, solve a problem by analyzing the handwriting style. Thus, text-independent methods seem to be more applicable. Furthermore, text-independent methods treat each character of handwriting equally, so all characters contribute to the writing style. However, text-independent methods require a certain minimum amount of text to produce a reliable decision. On the other hand, text-dependent methods require that the text content of the query and reference handwriting images be the same. These methods take advantage of direct comparison between characters of the same text content in both the query and reference handwriting images.

Text-independent methods determine the writer of a handwritten document with unconstrained text content. Zhu et al.[2] adopteded the Gabor filtering technique for text-independent writer identification. Li and Ding[3] proposed the grid microstructure feature (GMF) for Chinese writer identification. However, GMF is sensitive to pen-width variation in practical situations. Xu et al.[4] proposed an inner and inter class variances weighted feature matching method to solve this problem. Wen et al.[5] characterized the frequent structures distribution of edge fragments on multiple scales using edge structure coding. Fiel and Sablatnig[6,7] utilized Scale-Invariant Feature Transform (SIFT) descriptors for both writer identification and writer retrieval. Hu et al.[8] employed SIFT descriptors and presented two coding strategies for feature coding. Wu et al.[9] extracted SIFT descriptors and the scale and orientation information from word regions for writer identification. In our previous work,[10] we employed the modified SIFT descriptor and contour-directional feature to create a two-stage text-independent writer identification system. Meanwhile, with the emergence of deep learning, several approaches also attempted to realize writer identification using Deep Neural Networks (DNNs). Unlike traditional methods, DNNs learn feature mapping from training data directly. Compared with hand-designed feature descriptors, learning-based feature representation can exploit more data-adaptive information from training data. Christlein et al.[11] used Convolutional Neural Networks (CNNs) to learn the activations of the

The query handwriting

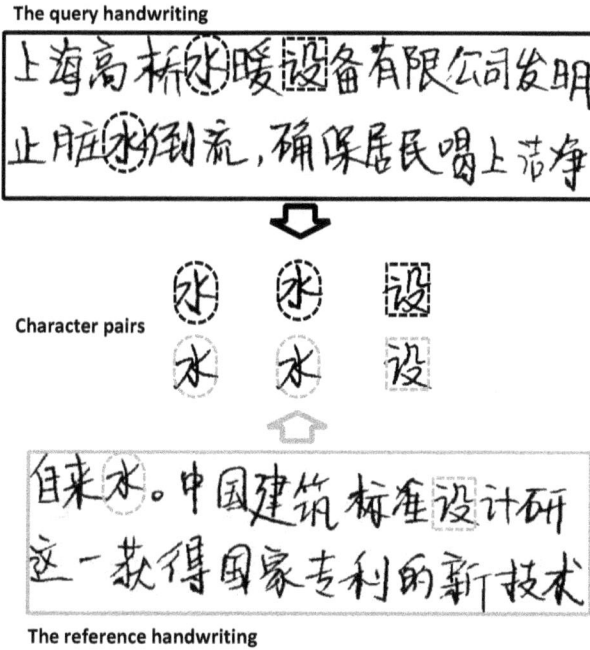

Character pairs

The reference handwriting

Fig. 1. Examples of character pairs appearing in both the query and reference handwritings.

hidden layers and encoded them into feature vectors by GMM supervector encoding for classification. Fiel and Sablatnig[12] used the output of the second-to-last fully connected layer as the feature vector for writer identification. Unlike the above methods, which only use CNNs for feature extraction, Yang et al.[13] proposed an end-to-end writer recognition system which employs CNNs for classification directly.

When we concentrate on the issue of Chinese writer identification, we find that some characters of the same text content appear in both the query and reference handwritten images, in most cases. Two characters containing the same text content in both the query and reference handwriting images are defined as a character pair (as shown in Fig. 1). In this study, our motivation was to improve text-independent Chinese writer identification by utilizing the text-dependent information, i.e, character pairs appearing in both the query and reference handwriting images. The outline of the proposed method is illustrated in Fig. 2. It contains two parts and takes advantages of both text-dependent and

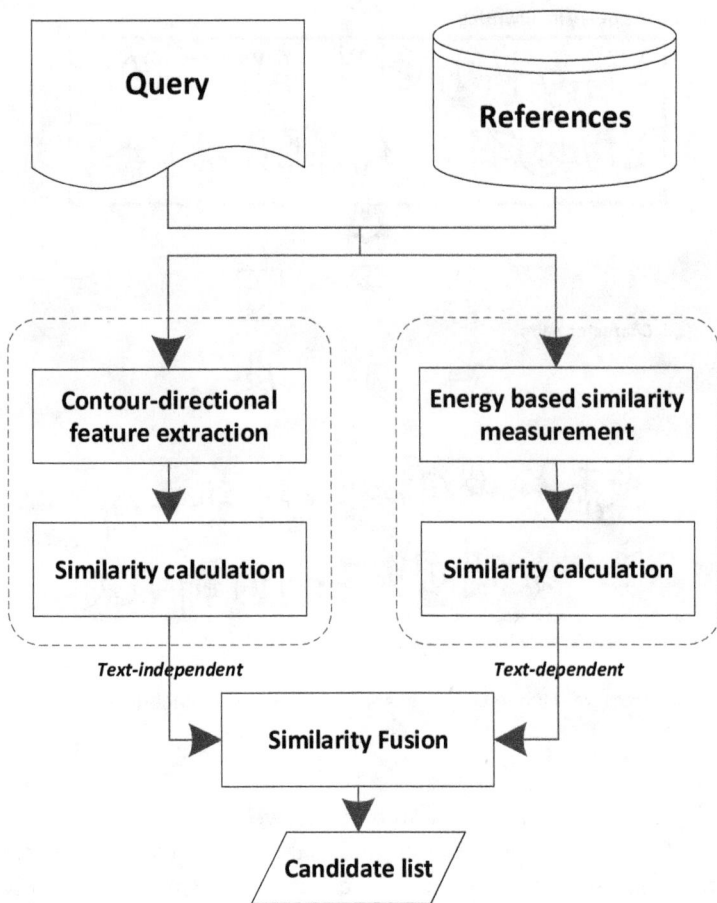

Fig. 2.   Framework of the proposed method.

text-independent methods. In the text-independent part, we extracted the contour-directional feature to represent the handwriting writing style. The weighted Chi-squared metric was used to measure the text-independent similarity between the query and reference handwriting images.   In the text-dependent part, the character images of character pairs were treated as the fixed image and the moving image. Their displacement field was calculated using the Log-Demons algorithm.   The energy of the displacement field was utilized for similarity measurement. Finally, similarities of text-dependent and text-independent methods were fused to generate the final similarity between the query and reference handwriting images. The remainder of the paper is organized as follows: we present the details of the proposed method in Section 2. The experimental results are given in Section 3. We conclude the work in Section 4.

2. The proposed method

The text-independent similarity between the query and reference handwriting images was calculated using contour-directional features. Meanwhile, the text-dependent similarity was calculated by an energy based similarity measurement. Both similarities were fused to obtain the final similarity between the query and reference handwriting images.

2.1. *Text-independent method*

Text-independent writer identification method extracts robust features from the handwriting for pattern representation, which is unrestricted to text content. We utilized the Contour-directional Feature (CDF) presented in our previous work[10,14] to describe the individual writing style of handwriting.

2.1.1. *Contour-directional feature (CDF)*

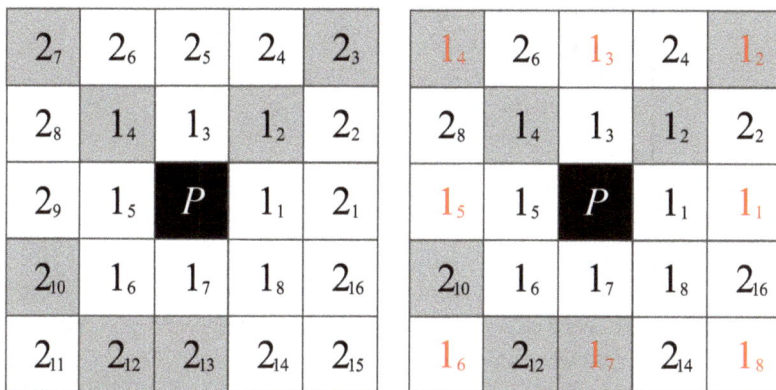

2_7	2_6	2_5	2_4	2_3
2_8	1_4	1_3	1_2	2_2
2_9	1_5	P	1_1	2_1
2_{10}	1_6	1_7	1_8	2_{16}
2_{11}	2_{12}	2_{13}	2_{14}	2_{15}

(a) Find edge pixel pairs.

1_4	2_6	1_3	2_4	1_2
2_8	1_4	1_3	1_2	2_2
1_5	1_5	P	1_1	1_1
2_{10}	1_6	1_7	1_8	2_{16}
1_6	2_{12}	1_7	2_{14}	1_8

(b) Update the symbol of pixels.

Fig. 3. An example of the extraction of the contour-directional feature.

The contour-directional feature utilizes the distribution of pixel pairs based on the directional information to represent the individual trait of the writer.

A contour-directional feature was extracted from a contour image, thus contour detection needed to be performed first. The Sobel operators were employed to generate the contour image from the query handwriting image or reference handwriting image. Then, the distribution of edge pixel pairs in the contour image was recorded as the feature of handwriting. To obtain edge pixel pairs, the contour image was divided into a number of grids of size $n \times n$, and the center of each grid is an edge pixel. A grid of 5×5 is illustrated in Fig. 3(a). The black square is denoted as an edge pixel P, and gray squares are denoted as edge pixels connected to P. Each pixel S in the grid is marked with a symbol $G(S) = D_i$, where D denotes the larger distance in the horizontal and vertical distances between S and P. For each value of D, there are $8 * D$ pixels around the center P and they are assigned from D_1 to D_{8*D}. All the pixel pairs (α, β) which satisfy the following conditions were recorded.

$$\begin{cases} \alpha \text{ and } \beta \text{ are edge pixels,} \\ G(\alpha) = D_i, G(\beta) = D_j, \text{ and } i < j. \\ G(\gamma) = D_k, i < k < j, \text{ and } \gamma \text{ is not an edge pixel.} \end{cases}$$

We define the direction $Dir(S)$ as: $\arctan \frac{S_y - P_y}{S_x - P_x}$, where (S_x, S_y) and (P_x, P_y) are coordinates of S and P. Afterwards, we updated the symbol of each pixel in the grid according to the direction of the pixel. The new symbol of S was denoted as $C(S)$, and rules for updating are listed below:

$$\begin{cases} \text{If } Dir(S_1) \text{ is unique, and } G(S_1) = D_i, \\ \text{then } C(S_1) = G(S_1) = D_i. \\ \text{If } Dir(S_1) = Dir(S_2) = \cdots = Dir(S_n), \\ G(S_1) = D^a{}_i, G(S_2) = D^b{}_j, ..., G(S_n) = D^c{}_k, \\ \text{and } D^a < D^b < \cdots < D^c, \\ \text{then } C(S_1) = \cdots = C(S_n) = G(S_1) = D^a{}_i. \end{cases}$$

As shown in Fig. 3(b), changed symbols are labeled with red color, and the edge pixel pairs $(1_2, 1_4)$, $(1_2, 1_4)$, $(1_4, 2_{10})$, $(2_{10}, 2_{12})$, $(2_{12}, 1_7)$ are recorded as the contour-directional feature. When the center of the $n \times n$ grid has traversed every edge pixel in the contour image, all edge pixel pairs appearing in the grid were also recorded. After normalization, the frequency histogram of edge pixel pairs was generated as the contour-directional feature vector.

2.1.2. Similarity calculation

After the contour-directional features were extracted from the query and reference handwriting images, the weighted Chi-squared metric was used to calculate the similarity. We assume that there were L reference handwriting images, and the query handwriting image and reference handwriting images are denoted by Q and R_i ($1 \leq i \leq L$), respectively. Let CDF_Q ($\{a_1, a_2, ..., a_N\}$) and CDF_R^i ($\{b_1^i, b_2^i, ..., b_N^i\}$) denote their contour-directional features. The distance D_C between Q and R^i is computed by:

$$D_C = \sum_{j=1}^{N} \frac{(a_j - b_j^i)^2}{(a_j + b_j^i) * \sigma_j}, \tag{1}$$

where

$$\sigma_j = \sqrt{\frac{1}{L-1} \sum_{i=1}^{L} (b_j^i - \mu_j)}, \tag{2}$$

and

$$\mu_j = \frac{1}{L} \sum_{i=1}^{L} b_j^i. \tag{3}$$

2.2. Text-dependent method

Text-dependent method is a one-to-one comparison of words or characters. In this study, we propose the geometry based similarity measurement and energy based similarity measurement to calculate the similarity of character pairs appearing in both the query and reference handwriting images.

2.2.1. Energy based similarity measurement (EBSM)

Image registration is the process of transforming different images into the same coordinate system. Many popular approaches[15–19] for image registration are based on Demons algorithm, which is quite efficient and non-parametric. The proposed energy based similarity measurement derives from the idea of image registration, and introduces Log-Demons algorithm[16] into text-dependent writer identification for the first time. First, we give a brief introduction of image registration and the Log-Demons algorithm. Image registration is used find a displacement field, s, which can provide a good alignment of the images C_Q and C_R, and it is usually treated as an optimization problem. A widely used energy function $E(c, s)$[20] for optimizing is defined as:

$$E(c, s) = \frac{1}{\lambda_i^2} \| C_Q - C_R \circ c \|^2 + \frac{1}{\lambda_x^2} \| c - s \|^2 + \frac{1}{\lambda_T^2} \| \nabla s \|^2, \tag{4}$$

where λ_i accounts for the noise on the image intensity, λ_x stands for the spatial uncertainty, and λ_T controls the amount of regularization. The variable c is the exact spatial transformation of s. This function introduces a hidden variable in the registration process: correspondences. This auxiliary variable c is added to decouple the complex minimization into a simple and efficient alternate optimization. The optimization of $E(c, s)$ contains two steps. The first step is to optimize $\frac{1}{\lambda_i^2} \parallel C_Q - C_R \circ s \parallel^2 + \frac{1}{\lambda_x^2} \parallel c - s \parallel^2$, with respect to c and with fixed s. The second step is to optimize $\frac{1}{\lambda_x^2} \parallel c - s \parallel^2 + \frac{1}{\lambda_T^2} \parallel \nabla s \parallel^2$, with respect to s and with fixed c.

Algorithm 1.

Input: The image C_Q, the image C_R and initial displacement field s.
Output: The displacement field s from C_R to C_Q.
   repeat
      compute the update field u with s.
      $u = u * K_{fluid}$ for fluid-like regularization, and the convolution kernel K_{fluid} is a Gaussian kernel.
      $c = s \circ \exp(u)$.
      $s = c * K_{diff}$ for diffusion-like regularization, and the convolution kernel K_{diff} is a Gaussian kernel.
   until convergence

The Log-Demons algorithm is also about the optimization procedure on s. The auxiliary variable u that represents the update displacement field of s is added, and $c = s \circ \exp(u)$. The correspondence energy of u and s is defined as:

$$E_s^{corr}(u) = \parallel C_Q - C_R \circ s \circ \exp(u) \parallel^2 + \frac{\lambda_i^2}{\lambda_x^2} \parallel u \parallel^2, \tag{5}$$

By adapting Gauss-Newton-like approaches, the update field u at each pixel p with the displacement field s is calculated:

$$u(p) = -\frac{C_Q(p) - C_R \circ s(p)}{\parallel J(p) \parallel^2 + \frac{\lambda_i^2}{\lambda_x^2}(p)} J(p)^T, \tag{6}$$

where $J = \nabla^T M \circ s$, and ∇ is the gradient. After that, the value of u obtained was used to update s for iterations. The overview of Log-Demons algorithm is summarized in Alg. 1.

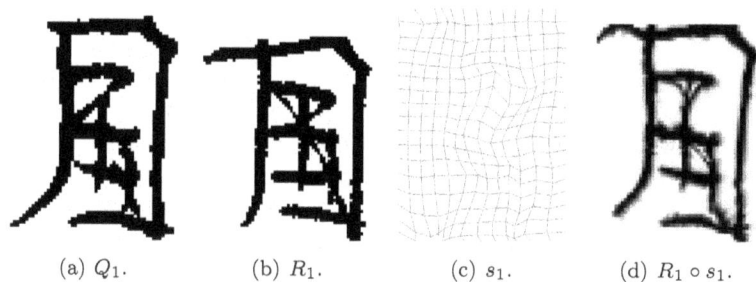

(a) Q_1.   (b) R_1.   (c) s_1.   (d) $R_1 \circ s_1$.

Fig. 4. Image registration result of the character pair (Q_1, R_1) from the identical writer.

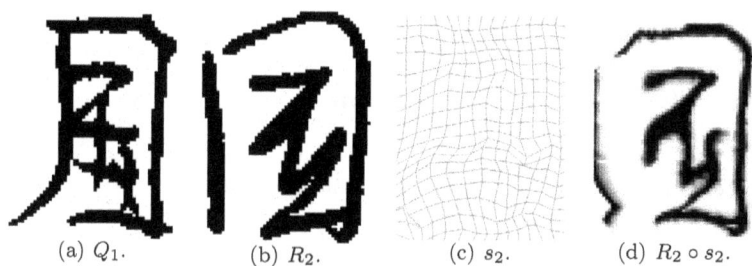

(a) Q_1.   (b) R_2.   (c) s_2.   (d) $R_2 \circ s_2$.

Fig. 5. Image registration result of the character pair (Q_1, R_2) from different writers.

Figures 4 and 5 show the image registration results of character pairs from an identical writer and a different writers. The difference of character pairs from the identical writer was not as significant as that of the character pairs from different writers (Q_1, R_1). As a consequence, the displacement field of character pair from the identical writer is smoother than that of character pair from different writers. For our task of text-dependent writer identification, a character pair (C_Q, C_R) was treated as the fixed image, and the moving image was provided. C_Q is the character image from the query handwriting and C_R is the character image from the reference handwriting. We obtained the best displacement field s, which aligns C_R to C_Q, by the Log-Demons algorithm and calculated the energy score:

$$E(s) = \| C_Q - C_R \circ s \|^2 + \| \nabla s \|^2. \tag{7}$$

It was assumed that the character pair of the identical writer had a lower energy score than the character pair of different writers. In the classification phase, character pairs were ranked in decreasing order of the energy scores. Based on this ranking, we verified whether a character pair had actually been written by the same writer.

2.2.2. *Similarity calculation*

All character pairs of the same text content were used to calculate the similarity. We assumed that there were Num_{cp} character pairs in both the query handwriting image Q and reference handwriting image R, denoted by (C_Q^i, C_R^i). The energy of the displacement field s_i between C_R^i and C_Q^i is denoted as $E(s_i)$. The similarity between Q and R is defined as the average distance and average energy of all Num_{cp} character pairs:

$$D_E = \frac{1}{Num_{cp}} \sum_{i=1}^{Num_{cp}} E(s_i). \tag{8}$$

2.3. *Similarity fusion of text-dependent and text-independent methods*

After text-independent similarity D_C and text-dependent similarity D_E between the query and reference handwriting images were calculated, they were normalized into the interval $[0, 1]$. Then, we summarized D_C and D_E together to measure the final similarity S_Q^R between Q and R:

$$S_Q^R = \delta * D_E + (1 - \delta) * D_C, \tag{9}$$

where $0 < \delta < 1$ is the weight parameter to balance the contribution of text-independent and text-dependent methods, which can be determined by cross-validation.

3. Experimental results

We evaluated the proposed method on the HIT-MW[21] and CASIA-2.1 datasets.[22] The HIT-MW dataset was built for off-line Chinese handwritten text recognition, and contains 853 Chinese handwriting samples. 254 images from 241 writers are labeled with writer information. In our experiments, the handwritings of 240 writers were used in our experiments. We also used another Chinese handwriting database, viz. the CASIA database.[22] This database contains off-line and on-line Chinese handwritings. For the off-line database, there are three sub-datasets. We used one of them, i.e, CASIA-2.1, to evaluate our method and report experimental results. The CASIA-2.1 dataset contains two sub-datasets. We used the larger dataset which contains the handwritings from 240 writers.

Table 1.   Overview of the Experimental Datasets

Dataset	No. of writers	No. of queries	No. of references
Set-A	240	240	240
Set-B	240	240	240

As shown in Table 1, both datasets are divided into the query and reference set, and every writer has only one image in each set. Given a query handwriting image Q, the system sorts all the images in the reference set based on the their similarities compared with Q. Ideally, the reference handwriting image with the minimum distance should be created by the same writer of Q. A ranking list (Top-N) was used to measure the performance of the proposed method. For the Top-N criterion, a correct hit was accumulated when at least one handwriting in the first N place of the ranking list was created by the correct writer. In our experiments, we used the identification accuracy of the Top-1, Top-5, and Top-10 to evaluate the performance of our method. The size of grid for the contour-directional feature extraction was set to 15 × 15. The ground truth of the HIT-MW and CASIA-2.1 datasets was utilized to find character pairs in both the query and reference handwriting images.

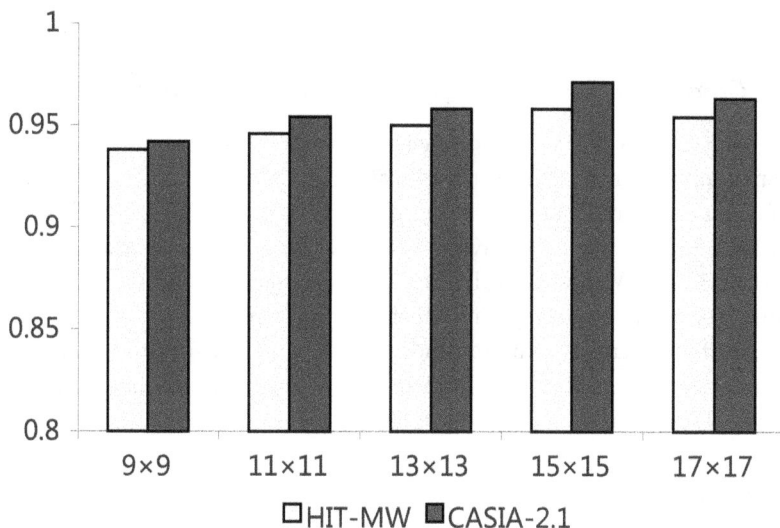

Fig. 6.   The Top-1 accuracy of CDF extracted from different window sizes.

3.1. *The window size of CDF*

The size of window influenced the effectiveness of the CDF. The local structure information was cracked when the size of window was too small, while the stroke information was rough when the window size was too large. A good choice of the window size is related to the character size of the handwriting. We used windows with different sizes to extract CDF from the handwritings and evaluated the performance of obtained features. Fig. 6 gives the Top-1 accuracy of CDF extracted from different window sizes on both datasets. When the size of the window is 15×15, the identification accuracy is the highest. The reason for this phenomenon is that the height of the characters of the two datasets was in the range of $[40, 90]$ pixels. Thus, the size of 15×15 is capable to get both stroke and local structure information of the characters.

3.2. *Weight parameter δ*

We carried out the experiment to find the optimal weight parameter δ of the two datasets. The value of δ was selected from 0 to 1 incrementally. For each value, we evaluated the Top-1 accuracy to investigate its effect on the performance. The optimal weight parameter δ of the HIT-MW dataset was 0.27, and that of the CASIA-2.1 dataset was 0.21.

3.3. *Comparison of the proposed method with others*

We compared the proposed method with other methods of text-independent Chinese writer identification. Tables 2 and 3 show the performance of our method with previous ones on the HIT-MW and CASIA-2.1 datasets, respectively. The best Top-1 identification accuracy on the HIT-MW and CASIA-2.1 datasets reached 97.1% and 98.3% respectively, which outperforms other previous approaches.

This demonstrates that text-independent and text-dependent methods characterize the handwriting from different aspects, and the combination of both characteristics enhance the identification performance.

4. Conclusion

In this paper, we proposed a novel method for Chinese writer identification taking advantage of both text-independent and text-dependent characteristics. In order to exploit text-dependent information, we proposed

Table 2. The accuracy of different methods on the HIT-MW dataset.

Features \ Top-N	Top-1	Top-5	Top-10
Li[3]	95.0%	98.3%	98.8%
Hu[8]	95.4%	98.8%	**99.2%**
CDF[10]	95.9%	98.8%	**99.2%**
CDF+EBSM(ours)	**97.1%**	98.8%	**99.2%**

Table 3. The accuracy of different methods on the CASIA-2.1 dataset.

Features \ Top-N	Top-1	Top-5	Top-10
Li[3]	90.0%	NULL	97.1%
Hu[8]	96.3%	NULL	**99.6%**
CDF[10]	97.1%	98.8%	**99.6%**
CDF+GBSM(ours)	**98.3%**	**99.2%**	**99.6%**

a new strategy to measure the similarity of character pairs appearing in both the query and reference handwriting images. We borrowed the idea from image registration and introduced the Log-Demons algorithm into writer identification for the first time. We calculated the displacement field, which was used to align the character pairs, and utilized the energy of displacement field for similarity measurement. Experimental results show that the proposed method enhances the identification performance of text-independent methods, and outperforms other previous approaches on two public datasets. Although it is only tested on Chinese datasets, the proposed method likely can be extended to other languages. In the future, we will further investigate this issue to make the proposed method more versatile.

References

1. R. Plamondon and G. Lorette, Automatic signature verification and writer identification — the state of the art, *Pattern Recognition.* **22**(2), 107–131 (1989).
2. Y. Zhu, T. N. Tan, and Y. H. Wang. Biometric personal identification based on handwriting. In *Proceedings of the International Conference on Pattern Recognition*, pp. 797–800 (2000).
3. X. Li and X. Q. Ding. Writer identification of Chinese handwriting using grid microstructure feature. In *Proceedings of the International Conference on Biometrics*, pp. 1230–1239 (2009).

4. L. Xu, X. Q. Ding, L. Peng, and X. Li. An improved method based on weighted grid micro-structure feature for text-independent writer recognition. In *Proceedings of the International Conference on Document Analysis and Recognition*, pp. 638–642 (2011).

5. J. Wen, B. Fang, J. L. Chen, Y. Y. Tang, and H. X. Chen, Fragmented edge structure coding for Chinese writer identification, *Neurocomputing*, **86**, 45–51 (2012).

6. S. Fiel and R. Sablatnig. Writer retrieval and writer identification using local features. In *Proceedings of the International Workshop on Document Analysis Systems*, pp. 145–149 (2012).

7. S. Fiel and R. Sablatnig. Writer identification and writer retrieval using the fisher vector on visual vocabularies. In *Proceedings of the International Conference of Document Analysis and Recognition*, pp. 545–549 (2013).

8. Y. J. Hu, W. M. Yang, and Y. B. Chen. Bag of features approach for offline text-independent Chinese writer identification. In *Proceedings of the International Conference on Image Processing*, pp. 2609–2613 (2014).

9. X. Q. Wu, Y. B. Tang, and W. Bu, Off-line text-independent writer identification based on scale invariant feature transform, *IEEE Transactions on Information Forensics and Security*, **9**(3), 526–536 (2014).

10. Y.-J. Xiong, Y. Wen, P. S. Wang, and Y. Lu. Text-independent writer identification using SIFT descriptor and contour-directional feature. In *Proceedings of the International Conference on Document Analysis and Recognition*, pp. 91–95 (2015).

11. V. Christlein, D. Bernecker, A. Maier, and E. Angelopoulou. Off-line writer identification using convolutional neural network activation features. In *Proceedings of the German Conference on Pattern Recognition*, pp. 540–552 (2015).

12. S. Fiel and R. Sablatnig. Writer identification and retrieval using a convolutional neural network. In *Proceedings of the International Conference on Computer Analysis of Images and Patterns*, pp. 26–37 (2015).

13. W. X. Yang, L. W. Jin, and M. F. Liu. Chinese character-level writer identification using path signature feature, dropstroke, and deep CNN. In *Proceedings of the International Conference on Document Analysis and Recognition*, pp. 546–550 (2015).

14. Y.-J. Xiong and Y. Lu. Chinese writer identification using contour-directional feature and character pair similarity measurement. In *Proceedings of the International Conference on Document Analysis and Recognition*, pp. 119–124 (2017).

15. T. Vercauteren, X. Pennec, A. Perchant, and N. Ayache. Symmetric log-domain diffeomorphic registration: A demons-based approach. In *Proceedings of the International Conference on Medical Image Computing and Computer-Assisted Intervention*, pp. 754–761 (2008).

16. T. Vercauteren, X. Pennec, A. Perchant, and N. Ayache, Diffeomorphic demons: efficient non-parametric image registration, *NeuroImage*, **45**(1), 61–72 (2009).

17. B. T. Yeo, M. R. Sabuncu, T. Vercauteren, N. Ayache, B. Fischl, and P. Golland, Spherical demons: fast diffeomorphic landmark-free surface registration, *IEEE Transactions on Medical Imaging*, **29**(3), 650–668 (2010).
18. T. Mansi, X. Pennec, M. Sermesant, H. Delingette, and N. Ayache, ilogdemons: A demons-based registration algorithm for tracking incompressible elastic biological tissues, *International Journal of Computer Vision*, **92**(1), 92–111 (2011).
19. H. Lombaert, L. Grady, X. Pennec, N. Ayache, and F. Cheriet, Spectral log-demons: diffeomorphic image registration with very large deformations, *International Journal of Computer Vision*, **107**(3), 254–271 (2014).
20. P. Cachier, E. Bardinet, D. Dormont, X. Pennec, and N. Ayache, Iconic feature based nonrigid registration: the PASHA algorithm, *Computer Vision and Image Understanding*, **89**(2), 272–298 (2003).
21. T. H. Su, T. W. Zhang, and D. J. Guan, Corpus-based HIT-MW database for off-line recognition of general purpose Chinese handwritten text, *International Journal on Document Analysis Recognition*, **10**(1), 27–38 (2007).
22. C. L. Liu, F. Yin, D. H. Wang, and Q. F. Wang. CASIA online and off-line Chinese handwriting databases. In *Proceedings of the International Conference on Document Analysis and Recognition*, pp. 37–41 (2011).

Chapter 7

Online Handwriting Analysis for the Assessment of Alzheimer's Disease and Parkinson's Disease: Overview and Experimental Investigation

Donato Impedovo* and Giuseppe Pirlo†

Computer Science Department,
University of Bari Aldo Moro, Italy
*donato.impedovo@uniba.it, †giuseppe.pirlo@uniba.it

The relation between handwriting and Alzheimer's Disease (AD) as well as Parkinson's Disease (PD) has been studied so far. However, it is just in the last decade that Computer Aided Diagnosis system have been investigated by the scientific community. This work intends to provide a hands-on description from a pattern recognition perspective: state of the art on online data acquisition, feature extraction and classification is described. Successively experimental evidences are provided on two datasets.

1. Introduction

Cognitive and perceptual-motor tasks are involved in handwriting [1]. Parkinson's Disease (PD) and Alzheimer's Disease (AD) result in changes on handwriting: dysgraphia (i.e. disorganization and degeneration of the various components of handwriting) has been observed in AD patients, micrographia (reduction in writing size) is typically associated with PD [2], [3].

In the online domain, the handwritten trait is represented as a sequence $\{S(n)\}n=0, 1,...,N$, where $S(n)$ is the signal value sampled at time $n\Delta t$ of the writing process ($0 \leq n \leq N$), Δt being the sampling period. The online acquisition gives the possibility to acquire useful dynamics info of the writing process. Studies on motor control in healthy and unhealthy people are available so far [4], but only recently, a growing research interest has arisen towards the possibility to automatically discriminate between impaired subjects and healthy controls (HC) having the aim of developing research in the direction of a Computer Aided Diagnosis (CAD) system [5].

This chapter intends to provide a brief review made from a Pattern Recognition perspective and based on data acquisition, feature extraction ant classification. Successively, experimental evidence of state of the art approaches is provided. Finally, conclusions and future research directions are discussed.

2. Data Acquisition

Data acquisition deals with the acquisition device as well as with the writing/drawing tasks. Many devices can be considered ranging from electronic pens [6] to professional tablets, however since in some situation the use of an electronic pen on a digital screen could be un-usual or unfamiliar to patients, writing with an inking pen on paper fixed to the tablet has been also considered [7], [8]. Raw data acquired depends by the specific device, however typically acquired parameters are:

- (x-y) coordinates,
- time stamps,
- pen orientation (azimuth and altitude),
- pressure,
- button status.

The last parameter (button status) gives the possibility to identify in air movements (when the tip is not in contact with the writing surface) and on-pad movements. Electronic (smart) pen can also acquire pressure of the fingers holding the pen [6].

Another important issue is the one related to the writing/drawing task performed by the user to acquire traits. In general, three kinds of tasks can be considered [5]:

- Simple drawing tasks. Spirals, straight lines, circles and other have been considered for motor skill evaluation [9], [10], [11]. Alternatively, bigram trigram and similar have been used: "eeee", "elel", "l", "le", "lilili", "lll", "lln" [12]. Such characters are easy to be written and minimize the linguistic-comprehension processes.
- Simple writing tasks. Simple words and short sentences have been also adopted [13], [14]. In same situation a sentence containing words having a common "core" have been considered (e.g. "Ein helles grelles Licht" [15] or "The leveler leveled all levels" [4]). In general, a sentence requires a high degree of simultaneous processing, it offers the possibility to evaluate motor-planning activity, hesitations, in air movements (between a word and the other) as well the effect of fatigue during writing [16], [17], [18]. Handwritten signatures have been also considered [19].
- Complex tasks. Motor, cognitive and functional issues are involved. Given a word or a sentence to be written, constrains on time duration [3] and stroke dimension [20] have been considered. In [21], authors requested participants to count the number of heard tone while writing loops. Copying tasks have included the copying of the fields of a bank check [7], [8] as well as addresses, phone number, grocery list, etc. [7], [8], [22].

Complex tasks acquire a relevant importance in the AD casesince AD is primarily characterized by cognitive deficits. For example, the Clock Drawing Test (CDT) [22], [23] is able to reveal visual-spatial deficits: in some case of dementia this deficit is evident since early stages. CDT, as well as many others complex tasks, involves various neuro-psychological functions: auditory perception, auditory memory, abstraction capacity, visual memory, visual perception, visual-space functions, programming and execution capacity. For a more detailed discussion, interested readers can refer to [5]. Figure 1 reports as example of bank check copying performed by an AD patient.

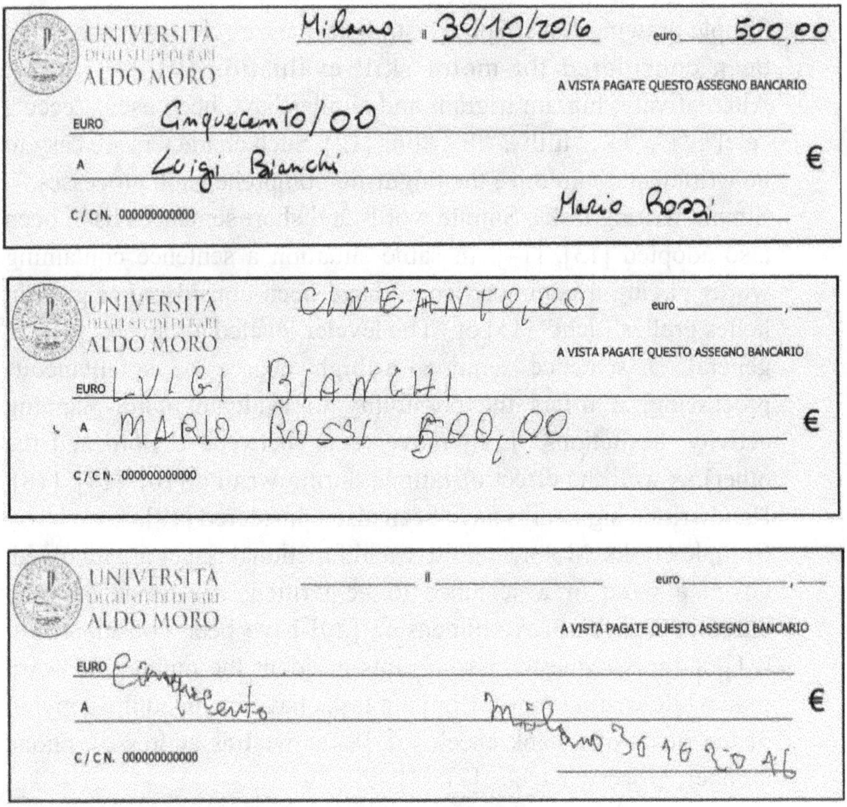

Fig. 1. Template displayed (a). Field copying execution by an AD patient (b)(c).

3. Features

Function and parameter features can be considered. In the first case features are time functions, whereas in the second one they are vector of elements, each one representative of the value of a feature.

3.1. *Function Features*

The most common function features are: (x,y) coordinates, time stamp, button status, pressure, azimuth, altitude, displacement, velocity and acceleration. Some of these features are directly conveyed by the acquisition device whereas others are numerically derived (Table 1). It is not surprising to note that the most used are velocity (often called speed) and acceleration: the first conveys information related to the slowness of PD and AD movements, while changes on the acceleration profile are able to reveal tremor.

In air-based features (coordinates, azimuth, altitude, velocity, acceleration) can be considered. This is a very important aspect since it has been recently demonstrated to convey very useful information [23], [24] since the pen must be hold without a support: tremor and hesitation are much more evident than in the case of the pen on the pad.

Table 1. Function features.

Feature Name	Source	Reference
Position	Device	[6], [7], [8], [16], [17], [18]
Button Status	Device	[7], [8], [16], [17], [18]
Pressure	Device	[7], [16], [17], [18], [22], [25]
Azimuth	Device	[7], [8], [16], [17], [18], [25]
Altitude	Device	[7], [8], [16], [17], [18], [25]
Velocity	Calculated	[2], [8], [11], [12], [13], [14], [15], [19], [22], [26], [27], [28]
Acceleration	Calculated	[9], [12], [15], [22], [29]
Gyroscope	Device	[6]

3.2. Parameter Features

Parameter features are obtained by means of transformations upon the function features (Table 2). Some parameters have been specifically designed with the aim of AD and PD analysis, some others are common within the field of handwriting recognition. Parameter features can be evaluated at global (task level) or even at local level (typically at stroke level). Stroke is considered as a single component of the handwritten trait which is connected and continue: in other words it can be considered as the signal between two consecutive pen-downs. The number of strokes per second can is representative of the handwriting frequency: in AD patients a significantly low writing frequency has been observed.

Jerk (which characterize PD) can be measured in terms of Number of Changes in Acceleration (NCA), it is often taken into account with the Number of Changes in Velocity (NCV). Since jerk/tremor introduces "noise" on the handwriting signal, entropy and energy features have used and valuated starting from the (x,y) coordinates adopting well known Shannon and Rény operators.

Empirical Mode Decomposition has been applied. EMD is able to decompose a signal within finite and small number of components which convey info related to the most oscillating (high-frequency) part of the signal.

Features based on the kinematic theory of rapid human movement have been also considered by adopting the Sigma-Lognormal model to represent the information of both the motor commands and timing properties.

Finally, in order to have statistical representation of the available function features, max, min, means, standard deviation, range and median have been considered too.

Table 2. Parameter features.

Feature Name	Description	Disease	Reference
Task duration	Total time duration of the performed task (e.g. clock drawing)	AD	[8], [11], [30]
		PD	[12], [16], [17]
Dimension	Length and/or height of the trait in terms of samples or pixels both at task and at stroke level	AD	[8]
		PD	[7], [16], [17]
In-air time	Total time of the pen in air movements while performing a task	AD	[8], [11], [30]
		PD	[7]
On-the-pad time	Total time of the pen on pad movements while performing a task	AD	[8], [11], [30]
		PD	[17], [18]
In-air/on-the-pad ratio	Ratio of the total time of the pen in air movements above the on the pad one	AD	[30]
		PD	[17]
Stroke Number	Number of strokes within a task	AD	[11]

NCV	Number of changes of velocity (NCV has been also normalized on the duration of the task/stroke)	AD	[30]
		PD	[12], [16], [17], [18]
NCA	Number of changes of acceleration (NCA has been also normalized on the duration of the task/stroke)	AD	[30]
		PD	[12], [16], [17], [18]
Entropy	Shannon or Rény operators applied on (x,y) coordinates	PD	[16], [17], [31]
Energy	Teager-Kaiser energy or conventional energy	PD	[16], [17]
NLOGnorm	Number of log-normal components within the trait	AD	[14], [19]
EMD	Empirical mode decomposition	PD	[16]

4. Classification

Slowness [4], [13], [20], [27], reduction in amplitude of repeated actions (bradykinesia) and micrografia [10], [21], [29], tremor and rigidity [10], [32], [33] have been observed on PD patients. Moreover, they generally write smaller letters, apply less pressure and require more time than healthy people. It must be underlined that not all the mentioned characteristics have been simultaneously observed under whatsoever task. In fact, micrographia or reduction in letter size has been observed within longer words or within signatures or sentences [29] and not on a sequence of few characters [34]. PD also results in cognition, planning and execution impairments [35]. Complex tasks can be used to reveal such characteristic [4], [21].

The classification problem has been considered, until now, as a binary one: PD patients vs. healthy. Support Vector Machine – SVM [16], [17], [18], Discriminant Analysis [7], Convolutional Neural Network [6] and Naïve Bayes [32] have been adopted. Results are reported in Table 3.

Concerning AD, fine motor control and coordination [30], [36], are impaired at the early stage. Moreover, speed values are almost regular in healthy persons while very different in AD patients [14]. In general, AD

Table 3. PD CAD Systems. Abbreviations: PD = Parkinson's disease patients; EC = elderly controls; T = tablet; ST = sheet of paper fixed on the tablet; EP = electronic pen: AUC = area under the ROC; DA = discriminant analysis; SVM = support vector machines; CNN = convolutional neural networks; NB = Naïve Bayes.

Dataset			Features	Class.	Acc.	Ref.
Users	Device	Tasks				
37 PD 38 EC	T	Spiral drawing, repetition of "*l*", "*le*", "*les*", three words, a sentence	Entropy, signal energy, empirical mode decomposition (on-surface) + feature selections	SVM	88.1%	[16]
			Stroke height/width, duration, writing length, NCP, Entropy, Energy, EMD	SVM	89,09%	[17]
			Kinematic and pressure features + feature selection	SVM	82,5%	[18]
24 PD 20 EC	T	Line drawing	Position, Normalized Velocity Variability, velocity's Standard Deviation, Mean velocity, Entropy	NB	88.63%	[32]
14 PD 21 EC	EP	Spiral and meander drawing	Pressure, grip pressure, refill pressure, tilt and acceleration	CNN	87.14%	[6]
20 PD 20 EC	ST	Name writing, copying an address	On-surface + in-air features	DA	97.5%	[7]

patients result in slower, less smooth, less coordinated, and less consistent handwriting movements than their healthy counterparts [3], [5]. Also, in this case, the classification problems has been considered as a binary one. Discriminant Analysis [8], [22], Logistic Regression [23], [24], and Bagging Cart [19] have been adopted. Results are reported in Table 4.

Table 4. AD CAD Systems. Abbreviations: AD = Alzheimer's disease patients; EC = elderly controls; T = tablet; ST = sheet of paper fixed on the tablet; DA = discriminant analysis, Logistic Regression = LR.

Dataset			Features	Class.	Accuracy	Ref.
Users	Dev.	Tasks				
23 AD 17 EC	ST	Dictated sentence writing, free sentence writing, two and three dimensions drawing, clock drawing	Pressure, time, velocity, acceleration, energy, complexity	DA	from 63.5% to 100% depending on the task	[22]
20 AD 20 EC	T	Three-dimensional house copying	time-in-air, time-on surface, total time	LR	AUC = 0.925	[23]
20 AD 20 EC	T	Clock drawing test	time-in-air, time-on surface, total time	LR	87.2%	[24]
29 AD 30 EC	T	Handwritten Signature	Velocity profiles	Bagging CART	ERR= 3%	[19]
22 AD 41 EC	ST	Copying: a phone number, a grocery list, the details of a check, the alphabet sequence and a paragraph	Size, duration (on-paper time and the in-air), pressure, mean velocity, mean pressure	DA	72%	[8]

5. Experiments

In order to perform experiments, two datasets have been considered. The Parkinson's Disease Handwriting Database (PaHaW) consists of multiple handwriting samples from 37 Parkinsonian patients and 38 age- and gender-matched controls [16]. Tasks include words written in Czech (the native language of the participants). The AD dataset includes handwritten trials collected from 41 people: 12 HC and 29 AD patients. Details of the two datasets are reported in table 5.

The set of features already described and reported in section III has been implemented and extended. More specifically displacement, velocity, acceleration, jerk (derivative of the acceleration) have been computed along the horizontal and vertical directions. In air and on pad strokes dimensions have been also computed. For all the function features and for the parameter features resulting in a vector of elements, the following basic statistical measures have been computed: mean; median; standard deviation; 1st percentile; 99th percentile; 99th percentile – 1st percentile.

Table 5. Datasets.

Dataset Name	Size	Acq. Device	Tasks	Ref.
PaHaW	37 PD 38 ED	Wacom Intuos 4M	Spiral drawing, repetition of *"l"*, *"le"*, *"les"*, *"lektorka"*, *"porovnat"*, *"nepopadnout"*, *"Tramvaj dnes už nepo-jede"*	[17]
ISUNIBA	29 AD 12 ED	Wacom Intuos Touch 5	Repetition of *"Mamma"*	[19]

Two more "new" features (not already used on this specific task) have been also considered based, respectively, on the Maxwell-Boltzmann distribution and on the sigma-lognormal model [37]. The Maxwell-Boltzmann distribution is here used to derive and entropy measure. The second set of parameters are derived by the sigma-Lognormal Kinematic Theory of the handwriting process which *"describes a stroke velocity profile as the output of a system made up of two neuromuscular systems, one agonist (acting in the direction of the movement) and the other antagonist (acting in the opposite direction)"* [37]. The evaluation of the sigma-lognormal results in a feature vector of six elements for each stroke defined as in the above and not to be confused with the prior definition (sequence of points within two consecutive pen-downs.

The amount of data in the PaHaW dataset has allowed feature selection based on Variance Threshold (VT), Random Forest (RF) and Relief (R) [5]. Three different classifiers have been considered: SVM, LDA and LR [5]. Results have been obtained by a 10-fold cross-validation and are reported in table 6. It is worth noting that an accuracy of 89.28% has been obtained when SVM and VT have been adopted. This results strongly improve the current state of the art on the PaHaW dataset, in fact the accuracy of 89.09% reported in [17] has been obtained with a feature selection schema applied on the entire dataset, while here feature selection has been performed only on the training set and adopting 10-fold cross-validation.

Table 6. PD classification results.

Features Selection Schema	Classifier	Accuracy
VT	SVM linear	**89.28%**
RF		86.78%
R		81.25%
VT	LDA	74.82%
RF		84.64%
R		75.89%
VT	LR	80.18%
RF		84.65%
R		88.75%

The AD dataset has permitted a reduced set of consistent experiments, if compared to the previous, since different users have different number of trials. In this case a two-fold cross validation has been adopted, SVM with linear kernel was able to perform 84.71% of accuracy.

Finally, even if many limitations, a multi class test has been also performed on the PaHaW dataset. The PaHaW dataset includes 5 patients at stage 1 of the disease based on the UPDRS catalogation, 18 at stage 2, 6 at stage 2.5, 5 at stage 3, 2 at stage 4 and 1 at stage 1. It is quite clear that the dataset is unbalanced. VT and SVM with linear kernel have been adopted since they provided the best performance in the binary classification problem. Approximatively 70% of dataset was used as training data and 30% for testing. The confusion matrix is reported in table 7. It's quite clear that the multiclass is a hard task which requires further research.

Table 7. PD classification multiclass confusion matrix.

	HC	UPDRS-1	UPDRS-2	UPDRS-2.5	UPDRS-3
HC	0.91	0.09	0	0	0
UPDRS-1	0	0	0.33	0	0.67
UPDRS-2	0	0.09	0.55	0.09	0.27
UPDRS-2.5	0.25	0.25	0.25	0	0.25
UPDRS-3	0	0	0.67	0	0.33

6. Conclusion and Future Work

Handwriting can be successfully used for the assessment of AD and PD. The pattern recognition community has provided an effort in the direction of a CAD system just in the last 5-6 years: there is a call for research still completely open.

First of all the most part of experiment has been led on private datasets. These are different in tasks, size, acquisition device, etc.. Only very few and dataset are currently available [16], [38], [6]. The lack of a big dataset strongly limits the research development. In general task already considered only refers to draw or write: finger taps [39] should also be considered: just think to the daily use of smartphones and the connected potentialities. Many issues can be inspected: segmentation, features, classifiers etc., as well as investigation of non-western languages [40].

Acknowledgments

This work is supported by the Italian Ministry of Education, University and Research within the PRIN2015 - Handwriting Analysis against Neuromuscular Disease - HAND Project under Grant H96J16000820001.

References

1. M.H. Tseng, S.A. Cermak, "The influence of ergonomic factors and perceptual-motor abilities on handwriting performance". American Journal of Occupational Therapy, 47(10), 1993, pp. 919–926.

2. E. Onofri, M. Mercuri, M. Salesi, S. Ferrara, G.M. Troili, C. Simeone, M.R. Ricciardi, S. Ricci, T. Archer, "Dysgraphia in relation to cognitive performance in patients with Alzheimer's disease". Journal of Intellectual Disability-Diagnosis and Treatment, 1(2), 2013, pp. 113–124.

3. C. De Stefano, F. Fontanella. D. Impedovo. G. Pirlo, A. Scotto di Freca, "Handwriting analysis to support neurodegenerative diseases diagnosis: A review", in Pattern Recognition Letters, Vol. 121, 2019, pp. 37–45.

4. A.W. Van Gemmert, H.L. Teulings, G.E. Stelmach, "The influence of mental and motor load on handwriting movements in Parkinsonian patients". Acta psychologica, 100(1), 1998, pp. 161–175.

5. D. Impedovo and G. Pirlo, "Dynamic handwriting analysis for the assessment of neurodegenerative diseases: a pattern recognition perspective," in IEEE Reviews in Biomedical Engineering. vol. 12, 2019, pp. 209–220.

6. C.R. Pereira, S.A. Weber, C. Hook, G.H. Rosa, J.P. Papa, "Deep Learning-Aided Parkinson's Disease Diagnosis from Handwritten Dynamics" In 29th SIBGRAPI Conference on Graphics, Patterns and Images, 2016, pp. 340–346.

7. S. Rosenblum, M. Samuel, S. Zlotnik, I. Erikh, I. Schlesinger, "Handwriting as an objective tool for Parkinson's disease diagnosis". Journal of Neurology, 260(9), 2013, pp.2357–2361.

8. P. Werner, S. Rosenblum, G. Bar-On, J. Heinik, A. Korczyn, "Handwriting process variables discriminating mild Alzheimer's disease and mild cognitive impairment". Journals of Gerontology Series B: Psychological Sciences and Social Sciences, 61(4), 2006, pp. 228–236.

9. T.E. Eichhorn, T. Gasser, N. Mai, C. Marquardt, G. Arnold, J. Schwarz, W.H. Oertel, "Computational analysis of open loop handwriting movements in Parkinson's disease: a rapid method to detect dopaminergic effects". Movement Disorders, 11(3), 1996, pp. 289–297.

10. J.G. Phillips, G.E. Stelmach, N. Teasdale, "What can indices of handwriting quality tell us about Parkinsonian handwriting?". Human Movement Science, 10(2), 1991, pp. 301–314.

11. A. Schröter, R. Mergl, K. Bürger, H. Hampel, H.J. Möller, U. Hegerl, "Kinematic analysis of handwriting movements in patients with Alzheimer's disease, mild cognitive impairment, depression and healthy subjects". Dementia and Geriatric Cognitive Disorders, 15(3), 2003, pp. 132–142.

12. W.G.K. Cobbah, M.C. Fairhurst, "Computer analysis of handwriting dynamics during dopamimetic tests in Parkinson's disease". In Proc. of 26th Euromicro Conference, 2000, pp. 414–418.

13. M.P. Caligiuri, H.L. Teulings, J.V. Filoteo, D. Song, J.B. Lohr, "Quantitative measurement of handwriting in the assessment of drug-induced Parkinsonism". Human Movement Science, 25(4), 2006, pp. 510–522.

14. D. Impedovo, G. Pirlo, F.M. Mangini, D. Barbuzzi, A. Rollo, A. Balestrucci, R. Plamondon, "Writing generation model for health care neuromuscular system investigation". In Proc. of International Meeting on Computational Intelligence Methods for Bioinformatics and Biostatistics, 2013, pp. 137–148.

15. O. Tucha, L. Mecklinger, J. Thome, A. Reiter, G.L. Alders, H. Sartor, K.W. Lange, "Kinematic analysis of dopaminergic effects on skilled handwriting movements in Parkinson's disease". Journal of Neural Transmission, 113(5), 2006, pp. 609–623.

16. P. Drotár, J. Mekyska, I. Rektorová, L. Masarová, Z. Smékal, M. Faundez-Zanuy, "Decision support framework for Parkinson's disease based on novel handwriting markers". IEEE Transactions on Neural Systems and Rehabilitation Engineering, 23(3), 2015, pp. 508–516.

17. P. Drotár, J. Mekyska, I. Rektorová, L. Masarová, Z. Smékal, M. Faundez-Zanuy, "Contribution of different handwriting modalities to differential diagnosis of Parkinson's disease". In Proc. of the IEEE International Symposium on Medical Measurements and Applications, 2015, pp. 344–348.

18. P. Drotár, J. Mekyska, I. Rektorová, L. Masarová, Z. Smékal, M. Faundez-Zanuy, "Evaluation of handwriting kinematics and pressure for differential diagnosis of Parkinson's disease". Artificial Intelligence in Medicine, 67, 2016, pp. 39–46.

19. G. Pirlo, M. M. Diaz-Cabrera, M.A. Ferrer, D. Impedovo, F. Occhionero, U. Zurlo, "Early diagnosis of neurodegenerative diseases by handwritten signature analysis". In: International Conference on Image Analysis and Processing, 2015, pp. 290–297.

20. H.L. Teulings, H.L., Stelmach, G.E.: Control of stroke size, peak acceleration, and stroke duration in Parkinsonian handwriting. Human Movement Science, 10(2), 1991, pp. 315–334.

21. S. Broeder, E. Nackaerts, A. Nieuwboer, B.C. Smits-Engelsman, S.P. Swinnen, E. Heremans, "The effects of dual tasking on handwriting in patients with Parkinson's disease". Neuroscience, 263, 2014, pp.193–202.

22. J. Garre-Olmo, M. Faúndez-Zanuy, K. López de Ipiña, L. Calvó-Perxas, L., O. Turró-Garriga, "Kinematic and pressure features of handwriting and drawing: preliminary results between patients with mild cognitive impairment, Alzheimer disease and healthy controls". Current Alzheimer Research, 14, 2017.

23. S. Müller, O. Preische, P. Heymann, U. Elbing, C. Laske, "Diagnostic value of a tablet-based drawing task for discrimination of patients in the early course of Alzheimer's disease from healthy individuals". Journal of Alzheimer's Disease, 55(4), 2017, pp. 1463–1469.

24. S. Müller, O. Preische, P. Heymann, U. Elbing, C. Laske, "Increased Diagnostic Accuracy of Digital vs. Conventional Clock Drawing Test for Discrimination of Patients in the Early Course of Alzheimer's Disease from Cognitively Healthy Individuals". Frontiers in Aging Neuroscience, 9, 2017. (2017b)

25. A. Ünlü, R. Brause, K. Krakow, "Handwriting analysis for diagnosis and prognosis of parkinson's disease". In International Symposium on Biological and Medical Data Analysis, 2006, pp. 441–450.

26. M. San Luciano, C. Wang, R.A. Ortega, Q. Yu, S. Boschung, J. Soto-Valencia, R. Saunders-Pullman, "Digitized Spiral Drawing: A Possible Biomarker for Early Parkinson's Disease". PloS one, 11(10), 2016, e0162799.

27. D. Impedovo, "Velocity-Based Signal Features for the Assessment of Parkinsonian Handwriting", Signal Processing Letters IEEE, vol. 26, no. 4, 2019, pp. 632–636.

28. N.Y. Yu, S.H. Chang, "Kinematic Analyses of Graphomotor Functions in Individuals with Alzheimer's Disease and Amnestic Mild Cognitive Impairment", Journal of Medical and Biological Engineering, 36(3), 2016, pp. 334–343.

29. A.W. Van Gemmert, H.L. Teulings, G.E. Stelmach, "Parkinsonian patients reduce their stroke size with increased processing demands", Brain and Cognition, 47(3), 2001, pp. 504–512.

30. J.H. Yan, S. Rountree, P. Massman, R.S. Doody, H. Li, "Alzheimer's disease and mild cognitive impairment deteriorate fine movement control". Journal of Psychiatric Research, 42(14), 2008, 1203–1212.

31. K. López de Ipiña K. et al., "Selection of entropy based features for the analysis of the Archimedes' spiral applied to essential tremor," 4th International Work Conference on Bioinspired Intelligence, 2015, pp. 157–162.

32. C. Kotsavasiloglou, N. Kostikis, D. Hristu-Varsakelis, M. Arnaoutoglou, "Machine Learning-based Classification of Simple Drawing Movements in Parkinson's Disease", Biomedical Signal Processing and Control, 31, 2017, pp. 174–180.

33. S. Sveinbjornsdottir, "The clinical symptoms of Parkinson's disease". Journal of Neurochemistry, 139: 2017, pp. 318–324.

34. C. Bidet-Ildei, P. Pollak, S. Kandel, V. Fraix, J.P. Orliaguet, "Handwriting in patients with Parkinson disease: Effect of L-dopa and stimulation of the sub-thalamic nucleus on motor anticipation". Human Movement Science, 30(4), 2011, pp. 783–791.

35. J. Jankovic, "Parkinson's disease: clinical features and diagnosis". Journal of Neurology, Neurosurgery & Psychiatry 2008;79, pp. 368–376.

36. H. Platel, J. Lambert, F. Eustache, B. Cadet, M. Dary, F. Viader, B. Lechevalier, "Characteristics and evolution of writing impairment in Alzheimer's disease". Neuropsychologia, 31(11), 1993, pp. 1147–1158.

37. R. Plamondon, "Handwriting generation: the delta lognormal theory". In Proceedings of the Fourth International Workshop on Frontiers in Handwriting Recognition, 1994.

38. M. Isenkul, B. Sakar, O. Kursun, "Improved spiral test using digitized graphics tablet for monitoring Parkinson's disease". In Proc. of Int'l Conf. on e-Health and Telemedicine, 2014, pp. 171–175.

39. M. Pastorino, J. Cancela, M.T. Arredondo, M. Pansera, L. Pastor-Sanz, F. Villagra, M.A. Pastor, J.A. Marten, "Assessment of bradykinesia in Parkinson's disease patients through a multi-parametric system". In Proc. of International Conference on Engineering in Medicine and Biology Society, 2011, pp. 1810–1813.
40. K. Ubul, G. Tursun, A. Aysa, D. Impedovo, G. Pirlo, T. Yibulayin, "Script Identification of Multi-Script Documents: A Survey," IEEE Access, vol. 5, 2017, pp. 6546–6559.

Chapter 8

Online Analysis of Hand-Drawn Strokes for Geometry Learning

Omar Krichen, Eric Anquetil, Nathalie Girard and Mickaël Renault

Univ Rennes, CNRS, IRISA
F-35000, Rennes, France
firstname.lastname@irisa.fr

This work takes place within the *ACTIF* project, in the context of the *eFran* call for projects that aims for active and collaborative learning promotion. This paper presents a pattern recognition and analysis system for Geometry learning in middle school. The goal is to allow students to draw geometric shapes on a pen-based tablet, given a teacher's instruction. To make the student active, the system have to recognize and analyze on the fly the hand-drawn student's productions in order to produce real-time visual, corrective, and guidance feedback. We base our work on the visual grammar CD-CMG[1] (Context Driven Constraints Multi-set Grammar), to model the domain prior knowledge and interpret the hand-drawn sketches on the fly. Our first contribution lies in adapting this grammar to the Geometry domain to cover the geometric objects taught in middle school curriculum. Although being expressive enough to model this large scope, the original formalism could not cope with the requirement of real-time analysis, given that the multiple interactions between geometric objects generate combinatorial issues. Our second contribution lies in extending the formalism to obtain acceptable performance for a real-time user interaction system. The first experiments on complex geometric figures drawing scenarios show that the proposed approach allows complexity and interpretation time reduction. We present also our result on another application domain, architecture plan sketching, to prove the generecity of our approach.

1. Introduction

Our work is in the context of e-FRAN *ACTIF** project, which aims to use pen-based tablets in an educational context, mainly in French middle schools, to foster active learning.[13] In this paper, we focus on learning Geometry by drawing freely on a touch-tablet. Dynamic Geometry Software products are now an important part of teaching geometry. Their goal is to make geometric concepts understanding easier for the student by graphical construction, manipulation and visualization of figures. To our knowledge, the tools used in middle schools, Geogebra[2] being one of the most widely used ones, rely on a drag-and-drop approach to manipulate geometric objects. Indeed, in order to compose a figure, a student must choose from a graphical panel the object he wants to create then has to place its components in the interface. This tends to limit the creative process of the user. Fiorella and Mayer[12] demonstrate that "generative drawing", *i.e.* learning by drawing, has a positive impact on students learning abilities in the classroom. Kluger and DeNisi[14] show the impact of feedback intervention on learning performance. These two points represent the pedagogical foundation of our project. We propose a pen-based system that simulates the traditional pen and paper figure sketching and enriches it by real-time visual, corrective and guidance feedback. This paper presents the first works done in the project, and focuses on the online recognition method of the system. The method is based on modelling the knowledge domain with a bi-dimensional formalism (CD-CMG grammar). Although the formalism is expressive, it could not cope with complexity of the application domain in terms of the handwritten strokes analysis time. We therefore optimized and extended this formalism have an acceptable performance in the context of real-time user interaction. In the literature several works have been done for hand-drawn sketches recognition, the following Sec. 2 presents an overview of existing approaches. Based on this overview and the application domain, we introduce the formalism in Sec. 3. Section 4 describes the formalism extension and its impact on the analysis process. Section 5 presents our experiments and results while conclusion and perspectives are given in Sec. 6.

---

*ACTIF: Apprentissage et Collaboration sur Tablettes, Interactions et Feedback - Learning and collaboration on digital tablets, interactions and feedback.

2. Related Works

In this work, we are interested in on-line recognition of handwritten structured documents. We distinguish between two types of handwritten documents interpretations methods: lazy[8] and eager[9] (see Fig. 1). **Lazy interpretation** means that the analysis process begins after completion of the user's production. **Eager interpretation** means that the handwritten strokes are analyzed on the fly, which is more relevant to our objective of having real-time corrective and guidance feedback to prevent error propagation.

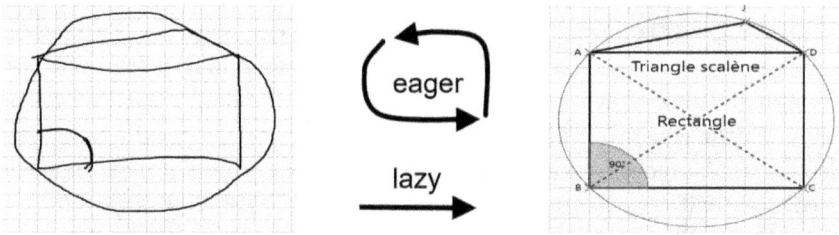

Fig. 1. Difference between eager and lazy interpretation: at left, the handwritten strokes, at right, analysis result and beautification.

There are two major approaches for document analysis: statistical and structural. **Statistical approaches**[3] rely on learning on large labelled databases to discriminate between symbols and are well suited for isolated shapes recognition. However, they do not allow the modelling of the document's structure. Since we are in Geometry context, the system has to recognize not only the geometric shapes, but also the structural relations between the objects. **Structural approaches** consider a symbol in terms of its constituents, the graphical primitives, and the structural relations between them. For instance, a triangle is considered as three segments related by spacial relations. Structural approaches rely on modelling prior domain knowledge by visual grammars. We distinguish between two classes of structural recognition methods. The former is based on **graph grammars**. For example, Zannibi *et al.*[4] use labelled graphs to recognize handwritten mathematical expressions. One problem with graph-based methods is that they are complex to manipulate for the designer, especially if the production rules number is high. The latter is based on **bi-dimensional grammars**. For example, in Hammond and Davis[5] proposed Ladder, a generic description language, and applied it for the interpretation of Truss diagrams in a digital learning context.[6] In[7] a bi-dimensional extension to the Stochastic Context Free Grammar is proposed for handwritten mathematical expressions analysis. In this work, to model the geometry domain knowledge, we prefer to use Context Driven Constraints Multi-set Grammar[1] (**CD-CMG**), a generic formalism for eager interpretation of hand drawn documents. Indeed, in this grammar, the context is explicitly specified in the production rules, which reduces the search space. Moreover, this formalism is the combination between a statistical approach (to locally recognize a shape) and a structural approach (to model the global structure of the document). Finally, CD-CMG has been applied to various types of documents such as architectural plans[10] or electrical sketches.[1] All these features show this formalism is well adapted for our purpose. Thereafter, our contribution lies in twofold: adapting this grammar to the Geometry domain for e-education (see Section 3), and extending this formalism to match the constraint of real-time analysis of geometric productions (see Section 4). Moreover, we have to ensure that our extension of the formalism is coherent with the genericity aspect of CD-CMG, *i.e.* that our optimization not only improve the system's performance in the geometry sketching domain, but also on other applications. In Section 5, we present the impact of the formalism extension on the analysis complexity in two different but related domains: *geometry sketching* and *architecture plan sketching*.

3. Geometry Domain Modelling

In this section, we present the formalism, and illustrate it through its adaptation to the Geometry domain.

3.1. *Context Driven Constraints Multi-Set Grammar*

As an extension of the well-known grammar CMG,[11] CD-CMG is formally defined as follows:

Definition 1. *A CD-CMG is a tuple $G=(V_N, V_T, S, P)$ with:*

- V_N: *the set of non terminal symbols = symbol classes;*
- V_T: *the alphabet, here $V_T = \{stroke\}$;*
- *S: the first symbol, or axiom;*
- *P: the set of production rules.*

And where a production rule $p \in P$ is composed of three blocks allowing different levels of vision on the document. The **precondition** and the

postcondition blocks stand for the global vision of the document while the **constraint** block stands for the local vision of the analyzed strokes. Therefore, a production rule p is denoted as follows:

$$\alpha \to \beta \left\{ \begin{array}{l} \text{Preconditions} \\ \text{Constraints} \\ \text{Postconditions} \end{array} \right\} \mid \alpha \in {V_N}^+, \beta \in (V_T \cup V_N)^+$$

Preconditions and postconditions are based on the concept of *Document Structural Context*, which models a zone in the document and the awaited elements in it, defined as follows:

Definition 2. *A DSC is defined by* (λ)*[position]*(γ)*[part] where:*

- λ *is a set of reference elements;*
- *position is a zone (i.e. a position) related to* λ*;*
- γ *is a set of awaited symbols in this zone;*
- *part is a part of the awaited symbol that has to intersect the zone.*

The **preconditions** are a set of DSC that have to be satisfied and represent the context in which β can be replaced by α. The **postconditions** are a set of DSC that represent the objects that can be created from the new reduced elements α. This formalization enables to drive the analysis process by the context. Indeed, the preconditions represent the **verification step** while the postconditions represent the **prediction step**. The **constraints** model a local vision on the analyzed elements β. They have two purposes: checking that the shape of β is consistent with the production, and decide if it is pertinent to reduce β into α.

3.2. *Adaptation of CD-CMG to Geometry*

We consider the main geometric objects taught in French middle schools: segments, arcs, circles, angles, all the types of triangles and quadrilaterals. We defined around 20 productions rules to model these objects productions as well as the interactions between them (*e.g.* intersection and orthogonality). Let's illustrate this with two production rules.

Figure 2 presents a part of a **segment production rule**, while Fig. 3 and Fig. 4 illustrate a segment composition. In this example, the red stroke in Fig. 3 is transformed into a segment if the **precondition** block and the **constraint** block are satisfied. The first postcondition DSC in the PostConditions block (green rectangle in Fig. 2) models the fact that a bisector production rule will be triggered if a straight d intersects the center zone of the new created segment (res).

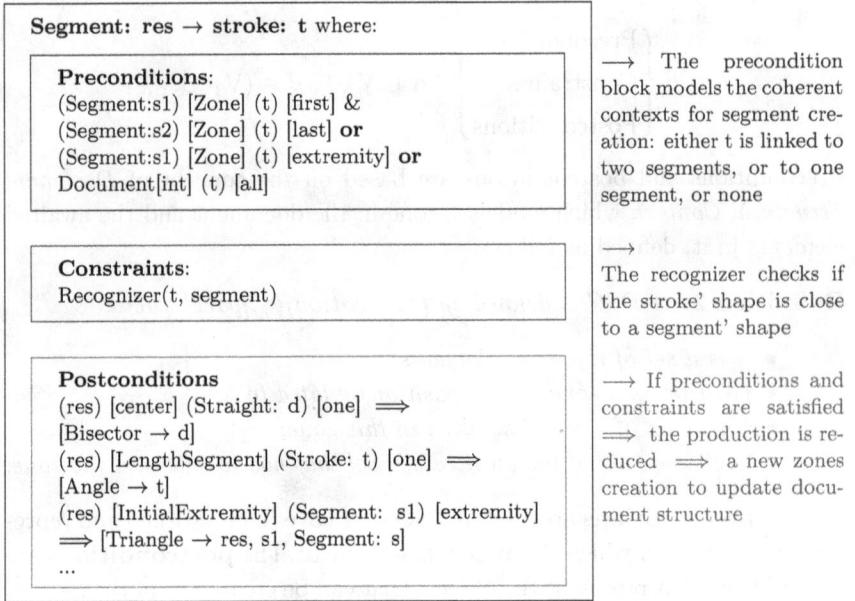

Segment: res → stroke: t where:

Preconditions:
(Segment:s1) [Zone] (t) [first] &
(Segment:s2) [Zone] (t) [last] **or**
(Segment:s1) [Zone] (t) [extremity] **or**
Document[int] (t) [all]

⟶ The precondition block models the coherent contexts for segment creation: either t is linked to two segments, or to one segment, or none

Constraints:
Recognizer(t, segment)

⟶
The recognizer checks if the stroke' shape is close to a segment' shape

Postconditions
(res) [center] (Straight: d) [one] ⟹
[Bisector → d]
(res) [LengthSegment] (Stroke: t) [one] ⟹
[Angle → t]
(res) [InitialExtremity] (Segment: s1) [extremity]
⟹ [Triangle → res, s1, Segment: s]
...

⟶ If preconditions and constraints are satisfied ⟹ the production is reduced ⟹ a new zones creation to update document structure

Fig. 2. Segment production rule in CD-CMG.

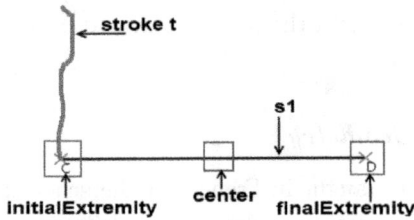

Fig. 3. Drawn stroke (in red).

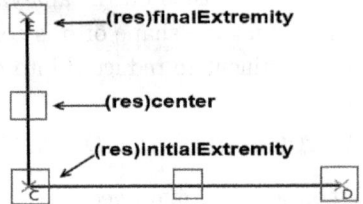

Fig. 4. Interpreted segment.

Figure 5 illustrates **the production rule of a scalene triangle**. The precondition block is composed of one precondition which is a conjunction of three DSC modelling the fact that each segment intersects a zone related to the other two. The constraint here is structural, such that it verifies that the three segments are linked by their extremities. Since the structural context is the same for all types of triangles (and quadrilaterals as well),

---

Triangle: res → segment: s1, s2, s3 with:
Preconditions:
(S1) [Zone] (s2) [one] & (S2) [Zone] (s3) [one] & (S3) [Zone] (s1) [one]
Constraints:
LinkedSegments(s1, s2, s3)
Postconditions:
(res)[TriangleZone] (Circle: c) [All] ⟹ [Inscribed-Circle → c]

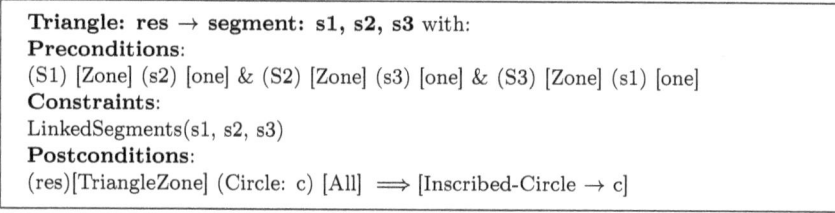

Fig. 5. Triangle production rule.

we established a hierarchy between production rules, from general to specific, in order to prune the search space and speed up the analysis process. For example, a triangle can be reduced into an isosceles triangle if two of its sides are equal.

3.3. *Analysis process associated to CD-CMG*

The analysis process, extensively explained in,[1] is a combination of a bottom-up strategy (guided by the reduced elements) and a top-down strategy (guided by the postconditions DSCs). For each new element, the parser searches the DSC it satisfies and vice versa. Consequently, a production is triggered if its β elements contain at least a new element and its precondition block contains at least a new DSC. Let's consider the scene illustrated in Fig. 6 composed of a new stroke t (in red) and three segments (s1, s2, s3).

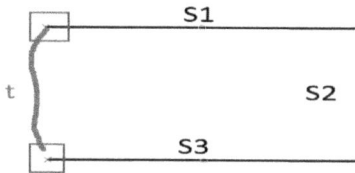

Fig. 6. Stroke analysis process.

The analysis of t leads to the construction of the analysis (or derivation) tree presented in Fig. 7. The root represents the stroke t. The nodes and the leaves represent the triggered rules, while the blue path is the sequence of reduced production rules, *i.e.* the analysis result. As shown in Fig. 7, t is first reduced into a segment, denoted thereafter *s4*. Then, several rules are tested among which the production rules that led to the correct interpretation of the user's drawing. The exploration strategy is explicit for each rule. *For basic shape creation*, the strategy is **breadth-first**, *i.e.* the analyzer checks if the stroke is either an arc, an angle, a segment, a circle, or a point. Each production rule is associated with a score, depending on the adequacy with the preconditions and the constraints. If there are more than one possible interpretation (two applicable productions at the same analysis level for example), the analyzer expands the analysis tree, and chooses the sequence of productions with the highest score. For other productions, such as triangle creation, the exploration strategy is **depth-first**, such as the first applicable rule is reduced without considering the other alternatives. This allows to reduce the search space.

3.4. *Limits of CD-CMG in geometry*

As we can see in Fig. 7, the triangle production rule is triggered three times for each possible combination of segments: (s4, s1, s2), (s4, s1, s3) and (s4, s2, s3), even if there is no coherent context for creating a triangle in this scene. This is due to the fact that these productions contain a new element (s4) and one of their preconditions DSC is satisfied (c.f. Fig. 6). Only the precondition block is checked in this case, since not all DSC are satisfied. The impact on the combinatorics is not important here, but when the document is complex, the analysis becomes costly. Even though the formalism is generic and expressive enough to model the prior geometry knowledge, the multiple possible interactions between geometric objects, *e.g.* creating sub-figures from existing ones (c.f. Fig. 8), also generate combinatorial problems in the analysis process.

Let's consider the triangle production rule (c.f. Fig. 5). A direct conse-

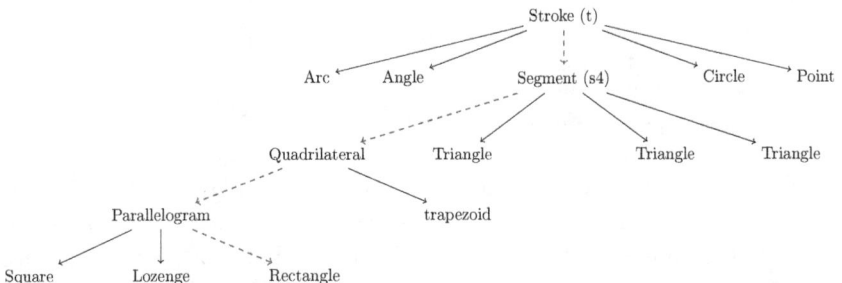

Fig. 7. Analysis tree.

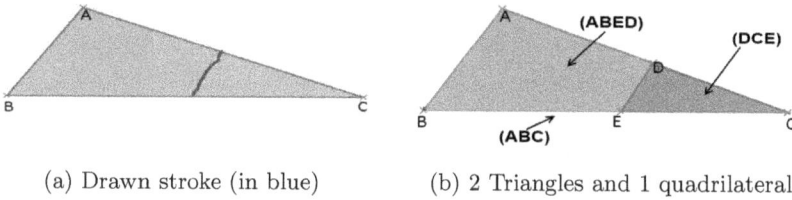

(a) Drawn stroke (in blue)   (b) 2 Triangles and 1 quadrilateral

Fig. 8. Sub-figures creation.

quence of adapting CD-GMC to the geometry domain is that the β elements (here the 3 segments) are not really replaced by the α elements (here the triangle). They contribute to create the triangle but they remain considered in the analysis process in order to create other new elements. This has a big impact on the applicable rules search space size. We identify two factors producing the combinatorial explosions: **the format of the DSCs,** and **the computation of equivalent interpretations.** We will explicit these factors and our proposed solutions in the next section.

4. Revision and Formalism Extension

In this section, we present the problems we faced in terms of analysis process complexity and our proposed solutions.

4.1. *The DSC problematic*

The expressivity of the formalism in terms of describing the document structure with the DSC allows to formalize that all the components of a polygon are linked by their extremities. Unfortunately, as we have seen in Section 3.C, the fact that a production can be triggered even if only one of its preconditions DSC is validated generates a combinatorial problem. Indeed, the more segments a polygon contains, the more DSC there are in the polygon production. Figure 9 illustrates the composition of a new stroke t in the context of three already interpreted segments. t will be recognized as a new segment called thereafter s2. The fact that s2 is linked to [AB] (blue zone in Fig. 9) will activate the DSC:

[AB] [InitialExtremity] s2 [one] $\implies$ *triangle* $\rightarrow$ *[AB],s2,s3.*

     The parser will search the third segment (*i.e.* s3) that completes the triangle rule with [AB] and s2. There is no contextual information in this DSC about the segment [BC] that completes the triangle since it is not concerned by the zone [AB] [InitialExtremity]. In consequence, for this scene composed of 3 segments besides [AB] and s2, the triangle production rule will be tested three times (for s3=[BC], s3=[ED] and s3=[EF]) instead of once. Thus, the analysis time can be very long, especially if the document is complex. In fact, this issue relies on a CD-CMG limitation. The formalism does not allow to have more than one zone in a DSC, which would enable positioning many awaited elements in relation to one reference element.

To resolve this problem, we propose to **refine the constraints on the zones** such that a zone can cover all the awaited symbols in the same DSC.

The DSC related to the triangle production rules will then be:
[AB] [TotalLengthSegment] s2, s3 [one],
where *TotalLengthSegment* is the zone that covers the length of [AB] (in blue in Fig. 10). This formulation allows to have a contextual information on all the segments composing a triangle. The loss in focus of the zone (from covering an extremity to covering all the segment) is balanced in the *Constraint* block by verifying that the segments are structurally linked by their extremities. For the scene illustrated in Fig. 10, the triangle production rule is triggered only once, which reduces the analysis complexity.

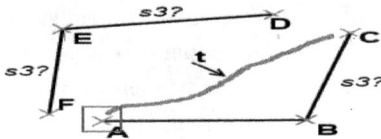

Fig. 9. Strict DSC.   Fig. 10. Refined DSC.

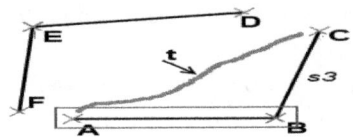

Segment: res → stroke t with:
Preconditions:
FirstPrecondition:
(Segment:S1) [Zone] (t) [first]& (Segment:S2) [Zone] (t) [last] **or**
(Segment: S1) [Zone] (t) [extremity] **or**
(Document) [in] (t) [all]
...

Fig. 11. Precondition block for segment production.

4.2. *Problem of equivalent interpretations and formalism extension*

Since we are in Geometry learning context, it is important to know the dependency links between the elements, *e.g.* the connections between several segments. These links are modeled in the preconditions DSCs. Figure 11 presents a focus on the precondition block of the segment production rule. It is composed of a disjunction of three preconditions. They model the fact that there are three possible contexts for a segment creation. The stroke can be linked to two existing segments by their extremities, or linked to the extremity of only one segment, or not linked to anything (in the document). The *FirstPrecondition* operator, introduced in Ref. 10 establishes an order between the preconditions, e.g. from specific to general, and forces the parser to stop the context research at the first valid precondition.

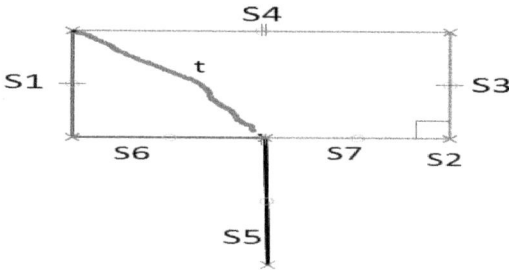

Fig. 12. FirstPrecondition limits.

Figure 12 illustrates a scene in which a stroke t is recognized as a segment. *FirstPrecondition* forces the parser to consider the stroke as linked to two segments, *considering* only the first precondition. Without this operator, the three preconditions, which are valid in this case, will be tested as hypotheses. The parser will expand the analysis tree in a breadth-first manner then choose the interpretation with the highest score.

A limit to this operator is that the verification of the first precondition can also be complex. Indeed, in this example, there are six contextually valid hypotheses: t can be linked to the couples (s1, s5), (s1,s6), (s1, s7), (s4, s5), (s4, s6), (s4, s7). Hence, six equivalent branches will be created in the analysis tree multiplying the analysis complexity by six. The issue is that the existing grammar does not include alternative strategies to deal with these hypotheses. The context search will then be exhaustive, generating in consequence combinatorial problems, where in fact the six hypotheses mentioned above are equivalent. To tackle this problem, we propose to extend the formalism by creating a new operator $FirstContext$. This operator forces the parser not only to stop the research at the first valid precondition, but also **at the first valid context** within a precondition. It means that the search is stopped when the first reference elements that are coherent with the precondition are found. In the example (Fig. 12), the parser will choose the first couple of segments that satisfies the DSCs of the preconditions, *e.g.* it will choose the couple (s1, s7) without considering the other combinations. This means we have an alternative exploration strategy enabling to reduce the search space. This will drastically reduce complexity, without losing information about connections. In use, we have noticed a limit to this new operator, which occurs when the segments are not exactly connected, but have overlapping zones (see the example in Fig. 13). Without the $FirstContext$ operator, the system computes the mem-

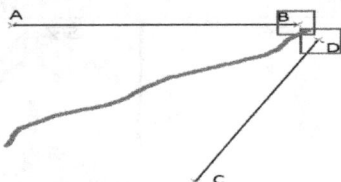

Fig. 13. Zone overlap problem.

bership degree of the stroke's extremity in each zone of the segments to choose the best possible interpretation. With $FirstContext$ operator, it has to choose the first valid interpretation, which is not necessarily the best. However, the robustness of this extension lies in the interaction with the user since he has the possibility to implicitly validate the interpretation by continuing his drawings, or to delete the segment and redraw it more precisely. This is a trade-off between interpretation precision and analysis process. We will detail the impact of our contributions in the next section.

5. Experiments and Results

5.1. *Quantitative study on Geometry domain*

To evaluate the impact of our contributions on the system performance, we established several criteria:

- Iterations: number of reduced productions rules
- Interpretations: number of branches in the analysis tree
- Time: Analysis time
- Triggered: Number of triggered rules

The evaluation is realized on one complex drawing benchmark, illustrated in Fig. 14.

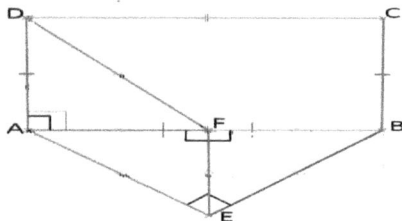

Fig. 14. Benchmark.

We study the impact of our contributions on three critical steps of the drawing scenario of this figure, illustrated in Fig. 15, Fig. 16, and Fig. 17. We compare the performance of our system with the existing CD-CMG grammar and its associated parser. In the following, the term *ZoneOpt* refers to the constraints refinement on the zones while *FirstContext* refers to the formalism extension by the addition of the new operator.

5.1.1. *First step of the scenario*

The scene (Fig. 15) illustrates a drawn stroke that will produce an analysis process. The stroke will be first interpreted as segment [AD]. This segments will trigger the production of a rectangle.

Table 1 presents the analysis results for this step.

Since the document is still simple, the performance is good (around 0.20 seconds). However, our contributions have no real impact on the analysis time. With *ZoneOpt*, the number of triggered rules decreases from 43

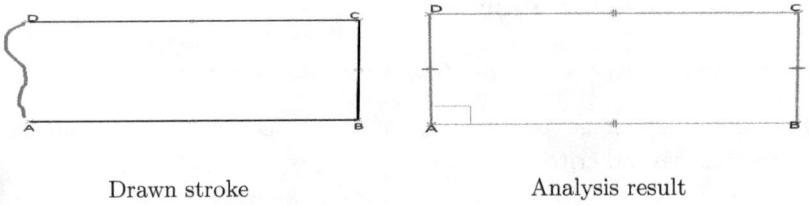

Drawn stroke   Analysis result

Fig. 15. First step of the scenario.

Table 1. First step analysis result.

Approach	Iterations	Interpretations	Time	Triggered
DALI	4	1	0.23 s	43
ZoneOpt	4	1	0.20 s	**23**
FirstContext	4	1	0.20 s	43
ZoneOpt+ *FirstContext*	4	1	0.19 s	23

to 23. *FirstContext* operator has no effect since there is no equivalent interpretations to consider.

5.1.2. *Second step of the scenario*

The scene (Fig. 16) illustrates a more complex production. The drawn stroke will be first interpreted as segment [EB]. This segments will trigger the production of two triangles, one being isosceles and the other rectangle.

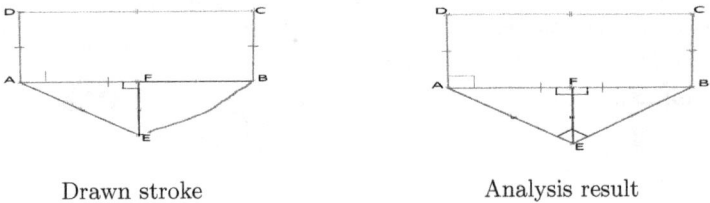

Drawn stroke   Analysis result

Fig. 16. Second step of the scenario.

The impact of our contributions on this step is illustrated in Table 2.

With the existing formalism, the performance is not acceptable since analysis time takes 6.4 seconds. This is due to the number of triggered rules (1057) and equivalent interpretations (3). By modifying the format of the DSCs, *ZoneOpt* improves the analysis time (2s) by reducing the number

Table 2. Second step analysis results.

Approach	Iterations	Interpretations	Time	Triggered
CD-CMG	15	3	6.4 s	1057
ZoneOpt	15	3	2 s	330
FirstContext	5	1	4.2 s	356
ZoneOpt + *FirstContext*	5	1	**0.62 s**	113

of triggered rules. *FirstContext* operator forces the parser to consider only one interpretation. In consequence, the number of triggered rules decreases from 1057 to 356, and the analysis time is down to 4.2 seconds, which is still not acceptable in a context of real-time interaction with a user. However, the coupling of Opt1 and Opt2 enables to have an analysis time of 0.62 which is acceptable.

5.1.3. *Third step of the scenario*

In this final step of the scenario (illustrated in Fig. 17), the drawn stroke will be first interpreted as segment [DF]. This segment will trigger the production of right-angled triangle, a trapezoid and a parallelogram.

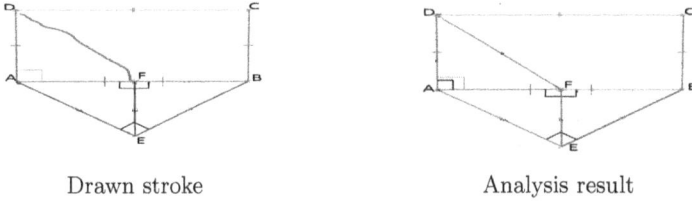

Drawn stroke   Analysis result

Fig. 17. Third step of the scenario.

For this step of the scenario, the coupling of *ZoneOpt* and *FirstContext* enables to decrease the analysis time from 30 seconds to only 1.5 seconds. As we can see from Table 2 and Table 3, the more complex the scene gets,

Table 3. Third step analysis results.

Approach	Interpretations	Analysis time	Triggered rules
CD-CMG	6	30 s	2472
Extended zones	6	7 s	962
FirstContext	1	5 s	412
Extended zones + *FirstContext*	1	**1.5 s**	**167**

the greater the impact of our contributions on the performance gets. Thus, taking into account the desired **real-time user interaction**, the proposed optimization allow the design of a system with acceptable performance.

5.2. *Quantitative study on Architecture domain*

To prove the genericity of our approach, we adapt our extension of CD-CMG to **the Architecture sketching domain**. The previous version of the formalism was already applied in this domain as mentioned before in Section 2. The elements are walls, editable doors and windows. We add the possibility to recognize rooms, which are modelled by polygons. This adds another layer of complexity which wasn't incorporated until now. Moreover, the analysis engine is not only capable of detecting newly created rooms, but also to create what we call "implicit rooms" (elements that are not displayed), which are determined by the combinations of all the connected rooms in the scene (c.f. Fig. 18). This is an important functionality because

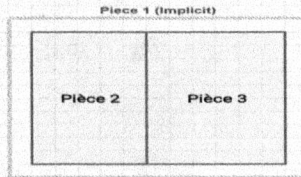

Fig. 18. Explicit rooms (piece 2 and piece 3), one implicit room (piece 1).

we want to be able to maintain the notion of a created room, even after deleting a wall connecting two adjacent rooms. As we can see in Fig. 19, after the deletion of "chamber 4", "couloir" (corridor in French), and "salle a manger" (dining room), the implicit room "pièce 14" becomes explicit and is displayed in the scene. We study the impact of our formalism extension (mainly the *FirstContext* operator) on a complex drawing scenario illustrated in Fig. 20. The red stroke will lead to the creation of segment, which will lead to the creation of 29 "implicit" rooms, and one visible room ("chambre 1"). We study the impact of our optimization using the same criteria as in Geometry sketching domain. We can see from Table 4 that the extension of the formalism with the *FirstContext* operator, enabling to choose alternative strategies for context search, has the consequence of dividing nearly by 10 the analysis time, from 2.09 to 0.22 seconds. We can

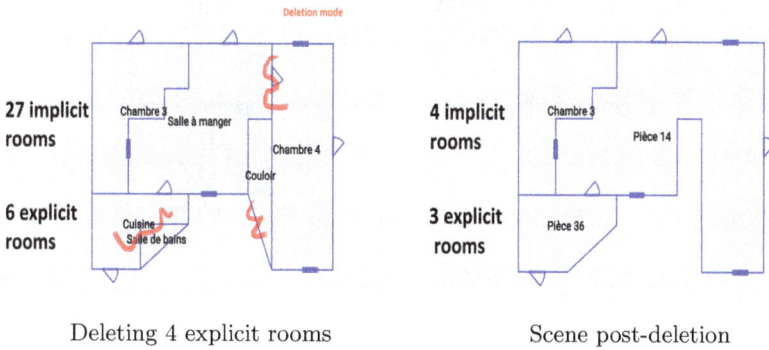

Deleting 4 explicit rooms   Scene post-deletion

Fig. 19. Complexity of architecture domain.

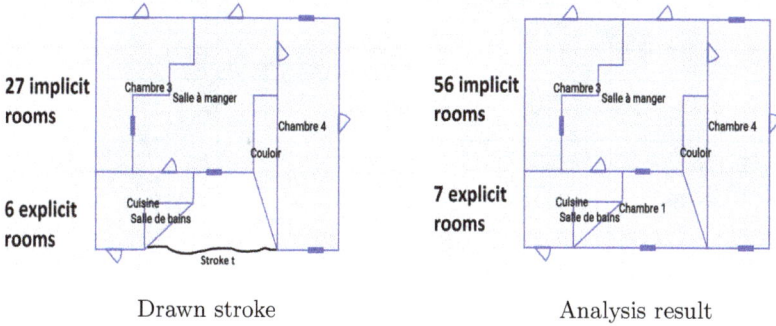

Drawn stroke   Analysis result

Fig. 20. Drawing scenario for architecture plans domain.

Table 4. Third step analysis results

Approach	Interpretations	Analysis time	Triggered rules
CD-CMG	9	2.09 s	760
Extended formalism	**1**	**0.22 s**	**92**

then say that **our extension is coherent with the generic aspect of the formalism**.

5.3. *Qualitative study*

As shown in Fig. 21, we have implemented a pen-based prototype for the composition of geometric sketches. The real-time analysis of the user's composition allows to give visual feedback, which are signs that the system has correctly interpreted the hand-drawn figures (see angle recognition in green in Fig. 21).

To respect to continuum with pen and paper habits, the system has to be flexible enough in order to make the exercise execution as intuitive for the child as possible. For example, the construction of a parallelogram needs a level of precision that can interfere with our free drawing objective. Therefore, we integrated an edition mode to our system to facilitate the drawing process.

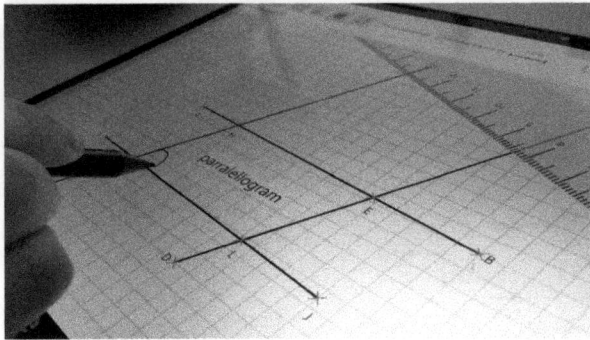

Fig. 21. Prototype interface.

5.3.1. *Edition mode*

We propose edition functions for the user, such as the ability to modify angles, force segments equality and manage parallelism and orthogonality, plus a protractor and compass tools. These features are important in the context of geometric figure composition, such as drawing a parallelogram with certain constraints on segments length and angles. Orthogonality and equality symbols are integrated in the grammars, whereas the tools are unrelated from the formalism, and are for creating arcs, circles or angles with the desired precision. Figure 22 represents the production rule for equality coding (two equality signs drawn on two segments to modify the length of the last one), while Fig. 23 illustrates the drawing process and the analysis result.

Segment: res → segment: s1, EqualitySign: eq1, EqualitySign: eq2 with:
Preconditions:
(s1) [Zone] (eq1) [one] &
(s2) [Zone] (eq2) [one]
Constraints:
OrderBetweenSegments(s1, s2)
Postconditions:

Fig. 22. Equality coding production rule.

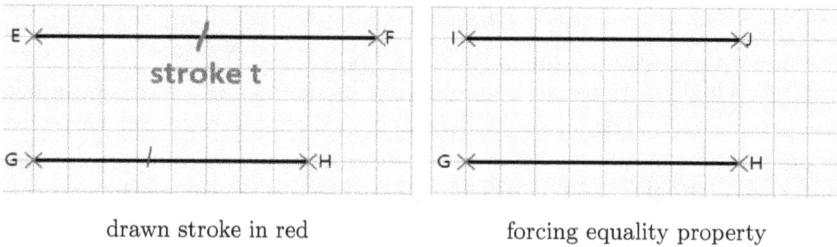

drawn stroke in red   forcing equality property

Fig. 23. Including geometry codes in CD-CMG.

5.4. *First user experiments*

We work closely with our partners in ergonomics and usages (Loustic, LP3C), in our user-centered design. They conducted the first user experiments on a beta version of the system, with 12 volunteer children from a Brittany region middle-school. The objective was to perform a simple exercise in a short time (5 minutes, after 5 minutes of training). Even if some children encountered difficulties in completing the task, due to some system imperfections and lack of training time, the post-test questionnaire showed a prevailing feeling of satisfaction from the pupils and the teachers towards our application and its potential.

6. Conclusion and Perspectives

In this paper, we propose a pen-based system that interprets in real-time geometric figures, based on the modelling of the prior domain knowledge with a bi-dimensional grammar. We optimize and extend the CD-CMG formalism to adapt it to the geometry domain. Our formalism extension is coherent with the genericity aspect of the grammar, as we has proven when adapting CD-CMG to the architecture domain. Our contributions have a consequent impact on the system performance which is now acceptable for real-time user-interaction. Our future work consist in improving even more the analysis time, one possible solution being the modification of the analysis process in terms of triggering rules. Given that there multiple layers of interpretation (basic shapes, polygons, etc), the idea would be to extend the grammar to include the notion of hierarchy between production rules. We will also work on the semantic interpretation of the child's drawing. The goal is to enable the teacher to create customized exercises. The system will be generate automatically the solver procedure from the teacher's drawings. Given that there are more than one possible solution for solving the exercise, we will have to generate all the alternative solutions as sequence of actions. The goal is for the system to detect in real-time from the child's actions the solution that he intends to realize and guide him accordingly. The successive versions of our prototype will be tested in pilot middle schools to validate our approach, and we will benefit from the studies of LP3C and LOUSTIC laboratories in usage psychology and ergonomics to be aware of the users needs and preferences in terms of visual and corrective feedback, and other features such as virtual manipulable tools.

Acknowledgments

"ACTIF" is funded by the region of Brittany and the French state call for projects e-FRAN, operated by the "Caisse des Dépôts". The project is supported by the LabCom « ScriptAndLabs » (n° ANR-16-LVC2-0008-01). The authors would like to tank the academic partners, the LP3C and LOUSTIC.

References

1. S. Macé, E. Anquetil, "Eager interpretation of on-line hand-drawn structured documents: The DALI methodology", *Pattern Recognition* 42, 2009, pp. 3202–3214.
2. K. Bhagat, C-Y. Chang, "Incorporating GeoGebra into geometry learning – A lesson from India", *Eurasia Journal of Mathematics, Science & Technology Education*, 11 (1), 2015, pp. 77–86
3. A. Delaye, E. Anquetil. "Hbf49 feature set : A first unified baseline for online symbol recognition", *Pattern Recognition* 46(1), 2013, pp. 117-130.
4. R. Zanibbi, H. Mouchère, C. Viard-Gaudin, "Evaluating structural pattern recognition for handwritten math via primitive label graphs", *Document Recognition and Retrieval XX*, 2013, pp. 1–11.

5. T. Hammond, R. Davis, "LADDER, A Sketching Language for User Interface Developers", *Computers & Graphics* 29, 2005, pp. 518-532.
6. O. Atilola, S. Valentine, H. H. Kim, D. Turner, E. McTigue, T. Hammond, J. Linsey, "Mechanix: A natural sketch interface tool for teaching truss analysis and free-body diagrams", *Artificial Intelligence for Engineering Design, Analysis and Manufacturing*, 28, 2014, pp. 169-192.
7. Á. Muñoz, F. S. Peiró, J. B. Ruiz, "Recognition of on-line handwritten mathematical expressions using 2D stochastic context-free grammars 48 and hidden Markov models", *Pattern Recognition Letters* 35, 2014, pp. 58-67.
8. A. Ghorbel, A. Lemaître, E. Anquetil, S. Fleury, E. Jamet, "Interactive interpretation of structured documents: Application to the recognition of handwritten architectural plans", *Pattern Recognition*, 48(8), 2015, pp. 2446-2458.
9. E. Lank, J. Thorley, S. Chen, D. Blostein, "On-line recognition of UML diagrams", *Proc. Sixth International Conference on Document Analysis and Recognition*, 2001, pp. 356–360.
10. M. Pecot, S. Macé, E. Anquetil, "Interprétation interactive de plans d'architecture composés à main levée", *Actes du XIème Colloque International Francophone sur l'Ecrit et le Document*, 2010, pp. 185-200.
11. K. Marriott, "Constraint multiset grammars", in *Proceedings of the IEEE Symposium on Visual Languages*, 1994, pp. 118–125.
12. L. Fiorella, R.E Mayer, *Learning as a Generative Activity: Eight learning strategies that promote understanding*, Cambridge University Press, 2015.
13. A. W. Chickering, S. C. Ehrmann. "Implementing the seven principles: Technology as lever", *AAHE Bulletin*, 49, 1996, pp. 3–6.
14. A. N. Kluger, A. DeNisi, "The effects of feedback interventions on performance: A historical review, a meta-analysis, and a preliminary feedback intervention theory", *Psychological Bulletin*, 119, 1996, pp. 254-284.

Chapter 9

Automatic Detection of Counterfeit Coins by Visual Measurements

Ke Sun* and Ching Y. Suen[†]

Centre for Pattern Recognition and Machine Intelligence (CENPARMI)
Computer Science and Software Engineering Department
Concordia University, Montreal, Canada
*pincessrr@gmail.com, [†]suen@encs.concordia.ca

Detection of counterfeit coins is a meaningful yet challenging topic due to their small physical size and quick improving forging quality. In this paper, we present a visual measurement methodology on automatic counterfeit coin detection. This system consists of lettering extraction, lettering matching, feature measurement and counterfeit detection. For validation, we tested 3 sets of samples, and the results demonstrate almost perfect accuracy.

1. Background

The circulation of counterfeit coins is becoming a big concern nowadays. Traditionally, it is common to forge antique coins. But during the past decade, proofs show that there is an emerging trend for modern high-value coin to be forged for circulation [1]. The latter will bring in loss to even wider spread of victims and have harmful impact to our society.

With modern manufacturing capability, massive production of counterfeit coins is becoming possible. In the meantime, the quality has also improved dramatically. Common old fake characteristics include unmatched design and date, overly shiny or dim brightness, misaligned orientation of the front and the reverse side. More technical and finer properties of today's coins include but not limit to poorly defined milled edge, uneven letterings in depth, dislocated letterings or image pattern, etc. [2, 3] Fake coins falling in the first category can be easily spotted with

151

strong evidence, whereas those correspond to the second category are elusive to detect. Nevertheless, even if one fake coin of such kind is noticed, it usually lacks confidence to claim that it is fake.

The lack of proofs is mainly due to the small physical size of the coins. Accurate measurement on letterings or image patterns is hard to carry out. There is yet no known measurement method or theory so far. Most facilities used in industry like vendor machines and banks are focused on physical qualities like weight, radius, etc. [4, 5, 6], which are far from being sufficient to detect exquisitely forged fake coins. In response, images are always deployed to enlarge details. A comprehensive study on how images can help coin recognition can be found in [7].

In response, we propose a visual measurement system that focuses on the fine details in the topography of the surface of the coin, in particular the letterings. Image processing techniques are introduced to facilitate the visual measurement and feature extraction. To begin with, letterings are segmented from the background image. To enable automatic feature comparison, lettering alignment is applied afterwards. Next new features with regard to letterings are introduced. Last but not the least, a hierarchical clustering method – max-spacing K-clustering – is applied to detect fake coins.

This paper is arranged as follows. In the second section, a brief description of the employed database is provided. Next in the section Methodology, image-processing techniques are summarized to illustrate the lettering segmentation, letterings matching and feature measurement. In section 4 Experiment, three sets of coins are trained and tested, including 123 Danish Coins of years 1990, 114 coins of year 1991, and 60 coins of year 1996. Section 5 will draw conclusions on our results so far. The main contributions of this thesis as well as future research directions will be presented.

2. Database

The database consists of 3 sets of Danish coins, namely 20 Kroners of years 1990, 1991 and 1996, as listed in Figure 1. Coins to the left are genuine, and to the right are counterfeits. It is noticeable that fake coins of years 1990 and 1991 appear very similar to their genuine counterparts. This corresponds to the high-quality forging mentioned beforehand. Whereas in contrast, fake coins of year 1996 have severe worn-out effects, compared to the real coins. Also note that the images are not aligned in the database.

a. Genuine coin of 1990   b. Counterfeit coin of 1990

c. Genuine coin of 1991   d. Counterfeit coin of 1991

e. Genuine coin of 1996   f. Counterfeit coin of 1996

Fig. 1. Samples from the database.

20 Kroner is a high-value coin, which is worth of 2.91 U.S. dollars (2015). The diameter, thickness and mass of 20 Kroners are respectively 27mm, 2.35mm and 9.3g respectively. All the coins selected in the database are within reasonable tolerance in physical measurements.

In response to the small physical size, 3D sensors are used to capture the topography of the metallic surface, as shown in Figure 1. The sensors are optimized based on the patented nonlinear photometric stereo method. Its depth resolution is in the micron size range and lateral resolution is 7.7 microns per pixel. For topography images, information of the coin's depth is coded and represented in intensity value. Table 1 records the coin samples in the database.

Table 1. Inventory of database.

	Genuine	Counterfeit
1990	100	23
1991	100	14
1996	50	10

3. Methodology

The visual image of coin provides information such as letterings, texture and images. Lettering includes letters, characters, digits and other symbols on the coin surface. It is the most important component of a currency since it conveys massive cognitive information. Revolving around the letterings, four sub-steps are developed in this section, including lettering extraction, lettering matching, feature measurement, and counterfeit detection.

3.1. Lettering Extraction

Figures 2 and 3 demonstrate the process of lettering extraction. Firstly, since our focus of interest is concentrated in a ring surrounding the centroid of the coin, a ring-shape mask is applied on top of the image to segment the letterings; next in Figure 3b a local adaptive thresholding method by Niblack [8] is applied to binarize the letterings; then connected components are detected in Figure 3b, and the area of block is used to filter out the irrelevant components, a cleaned result is given in Figure 3c. Figure 3c is prepared for both lettering matching and feature measurement in Sections 3.2 and 3.3.

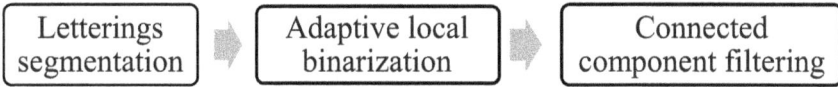

Fig. 2. The workflow of lettering extraction.

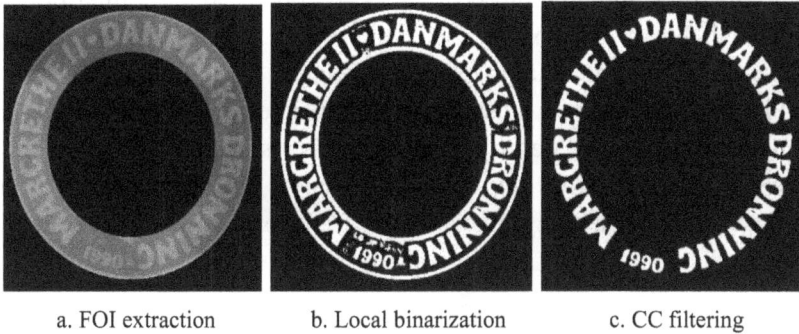

a. FOI extraction   b. Local binarization   c. CC filtering

Fig. 3. The process of lettering extraction.

3.2. Lettering Matching

There are 32 symbols on a complete coin surface. While the letterings of two coins are compared, it should be assured that only symbols at the same location be compared. For example, the features of letter 'A' on one coin are not comparable to the features of letter 'N' from another coin. Thus the lettering features should be organized in such an order that applies to all coin images from the same group. Thus the matching of letterings is necessary and the output can affect the final accuracy.

We have explored two ways to align letters. In the first algorithm, the well-known shape descriptor feature [9, 10] is exploited, whereas the second algorithm defines a new shape feature for alignment.

Shape context descriptor based alignment

Shape context is a rich local descriptor defined for each contour point. It describes the relative distribution of the remaining contour points in terms of distance and angle. Corresponding points on two similar shapes will have close shape contexts.

For the purpose of alignment, first of all, a template coin is selected to provide 32 shape prototypes, as there are 32 letterings in a complete coin image. These prototypes are used to compare against the letters from all the query coins. Secondly, each letter's contour is approximated and points on the contour are sampled. Next, point-wise correspondences between a shape and the 32 stored prototype shapes are found and the similarities are calculated. Lastly, by sorting the similarity vector, the query shape is assigned to the one that has the shortest distance.

Figure 4 and Figure 5 illustrate an alignment example. In Figure 4, the result of shape context descriptor matching is visualized. The red marker shows a letter 'R' from the template, whereas the blue marker is the extracted 'R' from a query image. Ninety five correspondences are found between these two letters and their shape context matching score is 0.284.

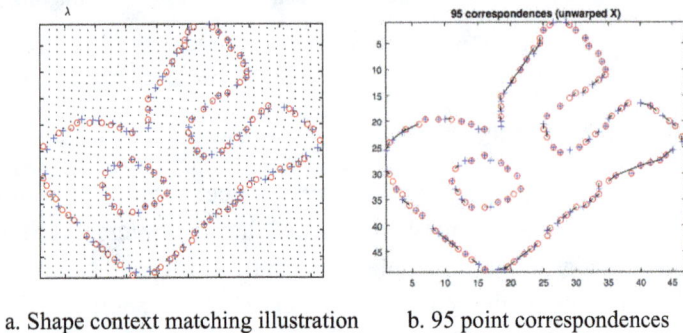

a. Shape context matching illustration   b. 95 point correspondences

Fig. 4. Shape context descriptor based point correspondences.

Figure 5 illustrates the character alignment result between two coin images. As is shown 24 of 27 characters are matched with their corresponding letters correctly.

Fig. 5. Shape context based lettering alignment.

Angle vector ψ based alignment

This algorithm consists of two steps, namely (a) obtain misalignment angle, and (b) match letters. There are plenty ways to get the misalignment angle. For example, M. Reisert etc. [11, 12] defined a correlation function based on normalized gradient images and applied Fourier Transform to expedite the calculation. M. Nolle etc. [13] deployed a fast correlation method based on the edge images restricted to the inner area of the coin. However, both methods are time-consuming and cannot be ideally applied due to the high resolution of our images. Instead, we extract an angle vector as elaborated below.

Based on the segmented lettering image in Figure 3c, a circle is generated from the centroid, as illustrated in Figure 6. The pixel value of each angle ranging from 1 to 360 is recorded. In return, an angle vector ψ of size 360*1 is produced to represent each coin.

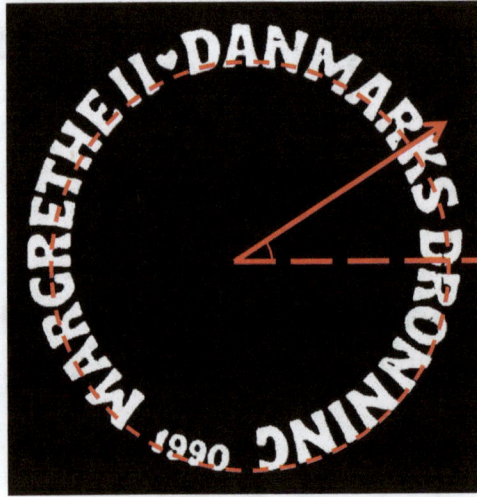

Fig. 6. Angle vector extraction.

To find the misalignment between two coins, we used the average Euclidean distance. Suppose the angle vectors for two samples are ψ and ψ' respectively. $g\psi,\psi'$ is denoted as the function of misalignment between ψ and ψ', as shown in Equation (1).

$$g(\psi, \psi') = arg \min_{\alpha} \sqrt{\frac{(\psi(\alpha)-\psi')^T(\psi(\alpha)-\psi')}{length(\psi)}} \qquad (1)$$

For the purpose of lettering matching, a template is selected from each group, which is used to compare against the remaining data marked as the query coins. A template is used as a standard, as to provide information below.

Angle vector as explained above;
Centroid of each letterings used for matching.

a. Template with centroids   b. Query with centroids   c. Aligned centroids

Fig. 7. Lettering alignment.

Figure 7 illustrates how to match letters given the misalignment angle. Figure 7a shows the template, where the red markers denote the centroids of each letter; likewise, Figure 7b is a query coin with all letters' centroids marked. In Figure 7c, the red markers are centroids from Figure 7a, the green one are centroids from Figure 7b, whereas the markers in the blue channel are rotated centroids of Figure 7b, whose rotation angle is the misalignment angle. It can be easily noted that the red markers almost overlap with the blue ones. Thus, for each letter in the template, it is matched to the letter with the closest centroid after rotation.

3.3. Feature Measurement Equation

In this section, five features are proposed, including stroke width, roughness, relative distance, height and width.

Stroke width is the letter's thickness of the stroke. This attribute specifies the width of the outline of the letters. We have adopted a heuristic algorithm to obtain stroke width of a binary letter. To begin with, the image is scanned column-by-column and row-by-row, while the distance between every pair of crossing points of a stroke is recorded; next, use a normal distribution to fit the records and filter out the values lying outside 3 times of the standard deviation. Repeat the filtering until the value diverges, which is used as the stroke width.

The property of roughness is inspired by the sharp contrast between contours of genuine and fakes coins as shown in Figure 8. A bumpy contour will add extra length, yet the area usually changes more severely. Therefore, it is defined as the ratio of enclosed area to the contour length.

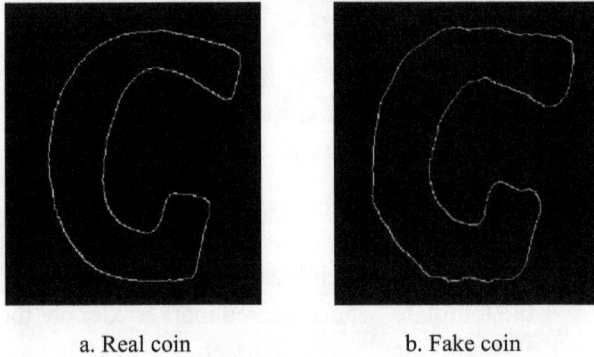

a. Real coin   b. Fake coin

Fig. 8. Contour roughness comparison.

As depicted in Figure 9, relative position is a cross-lettering feature, which records the distance between every pair of adjacent letters. This feature uncovers the displacement property of letters and symbols.

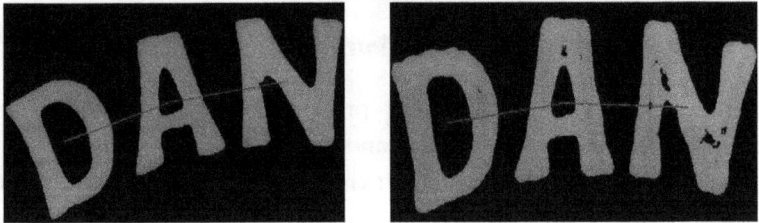

a. Real coin   b. Fake coin

Fig. 9. Relative position comparison.

Last but not least, letter's height and width are inspected. To measure these two dimensions, we bring in the concept of minimum bounding box [14]. It is a rectangle with the smallest measure — area in this case — which encloses the whole shape or point set.

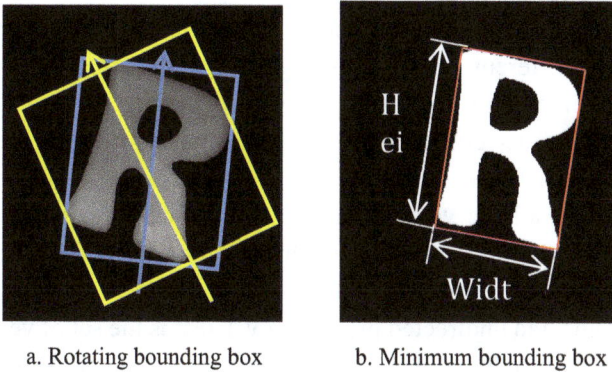

a. Rotating bounding box   b. Minimum bounding box

Fig. 10. Height and width measurement.

Since the lettering to be checked is standard, its minimum bounding box is subject to the constraint that the edges are parallel to the letter's principal axis. Accordingly, moment theory [15] is applied firstly to obtain the letter's principal axis. In practice, its result is used as an estimation of the letter's orientation. Starting from this approximation, the bounding box is rotated as demonstrated in Figure 10. The yellow and blue rectangles depict two bounding boxes imposed on the letter, in two directions. When its size reaches the minima during rotation, it is selected as the minimum bounding box. Its length and width are also used as the measures of the lettering.

3.4. Counterfeit Detection

In the real world, the numbers of genuine coins and counterfeits are severely biased, as is the case reflected in our database. Since real coins trace back to the same authority source, in the high-dimensional space, genuine samples shall locate cohesively close to one kernel. On the contrary, counterfeit coins are supposed to scatter separately in a wide outer space.

To explore this space distribution property, we investigated a hierarchical clustering method – max-spacing K-clustering. It follows an agglomerative pattern, that pairs of clusters are merged as one while moving up the hierarchy. The optimization goal of max-spacing K-clustering is achieved only when the minimum distance among any pair of samples from different clusters should be the maximum.

The implementation of Max-spacing K-clustering can be reduced from another well-known graph problem — minimum spanning tree (MST) construction [16, 17]. A spanning tree is an acyclic sub-graph of a graph G that contains all the vertices in G. The minimum spanning tree of a weighted graph is the minimum-weight spanning tree of that graph [18]. A formal definition is provided below.

For a connected undirected graph $G=(V,E)$, V is the set of vertices, and E is the set of edges. A weight $w(u,v)$ is assigned to each edge $\{u,v \in E | u,v \in V\}$. The minimum spanning tree is an acyclic subset $T \in E$ that connects all of the vertices, yet the total weight $wT=(u,v) \in Tw(u,v)$ is minimized.

In this application, the edge weight is calculated as the Euclidean distance in the feature space. Once the MST is established, depending on whether k is given, there are two ways to produce a set of clusters [17, 18]. If the number of clusters k is known ahead, then one shall sort the edges of the minimum spanning tree in non-increasing order according to their weights. And all samples are clustered based on the connection from the first k-1 edges. Otherwise, a threshold on edge's weight shall be given in advance; all edges that exceed the threshold are removed from the tree. The results are clusters connected by edges shorter than the given threshold. In implementation, we used Union-Find data structure.

To best generalize the real world scenario, we suppose that counterfeit coins are from varying sources, thus they do not necessarily belong to one cluster in the feature space. Therefore, the second method is chosen, i.e. query coins are detected based on a threshold. If the minimum distance between the query and genuine samples is larger than the threshold, it is detected as a counterfeit; otherwise, it is genuine.

4. Experiment

We examined the performance of the proposed method using the coin dataset from Section 2. The experiment consists of two phases, feature extraction and counterfeit detection. For the purpose of validation, half of the fake coins are randomly selected as testing data.

4.1. Feature Extraction

Among the five features mentioned beforehand, letterings height and width are employed. They are proved to be the two most effective features in previous research [19, 20]. As for alignment, we deployed angle feature based algorithm. To extract features, there are three steps.

1. A template is selected from each coin group, and its angle feature and centroids of all letterings are recorded. To generate the best effects, the template must be of high quality and free of indents, stains, bumps, etc.
2. All training and testing coins are binarized and aligned to the template. Their letterings on the surface are extracted.
3. Calculate the height and width for each letter in the aligned order. Table 2 records the feature extraction results.

Table 2. Lettering alignment and feature extraction results.

Group	Template Code	Samples in database		Used samples		Success Ratio	Alignment Accuracy
		+	-	+	-		
1990	90_01	100	23	97	22	96.7%	100%
1991	91_01	100	14	96	11	93.9%	100%
1996	96_01	50	10	48	7	91.7%	100%

The symbols '+' and '-' represent the genuine and counterfeit coins respectively. Take the group 1990 as an example: out of the100 positive samples originally in the database, 97 are binarized and used for further experiment; 22 fake coins out of 23 are adopted. The failed coins have problems with their images. Figure 11 shows the three main reasons. Figure 11a has ghosting effects that are caused by problem with patches stitching; Figure 11b is overly shiny that results that the adaptive binarization cannot work properly; Figure 11c is fake, i.e. its stroke and distribution exhibit large differences from the template.

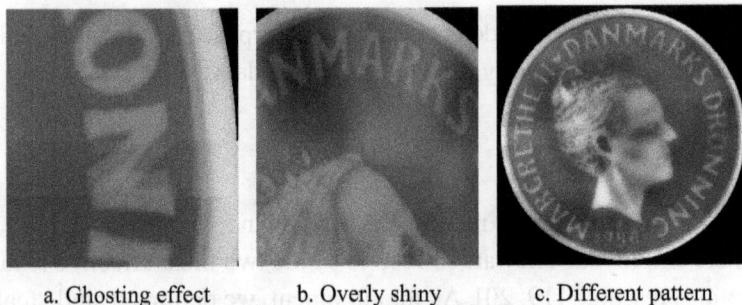

a. Ghosting effect   b. Overly shiny   c. Different pattern

Fig. 11. Failed examples.

Table 3 and Table 4 list the lettering features from experiment. Table 3 includes features of stroke width, roughness, height and width, which are extracted independently. Table 4 has one inter-letter feature distance exclusively. Considering the massive amount of data, three letters, 'R', 'N', 'G', are given as examples in Table 3. Likewise, three letter pairs – 'R-O', 'N-G', 'A-R' – are selected and their distances are given in Table 4. The numbers 1, 2, 3, 4 in both tables are adopted to denote four coins respectively, among which, 1 and 2 represent two genuine coins and 3 and 4 fake coins.

Table 3. Examples of independent features.

Feature in Pixels	Coin	Letter R	Letter N	Letter G
Stroke Width	1	61.67	68.92	59.94
	2	65.34	61.45	63.93
	3	67.03	84.65	72.64
	4	68.67	79.92	76.41
Roughness	1	22.55	25.71	23.56
	2	22.51	23.01	24.19
	3	24.81	29.38	26.24
	4	24.65	28.87	26.70
Height	1	273.85	265.83	282.36
	2	273.47	268.96	284.99
	3	288.31	280.26	305.89
	4	288.51	285.36	312.69
Width	1	210.59	273.12	200.79

	2	213.06	270.12	200.47
	3	224.53	294.45	216.86
	4	224.52	296.00	216.95

Table 4. Feature Distance examples showing letter pairs.

Coins/Letter pairs	R-O	N-G	A-R
1	273.94	276.95	272.27
2	274.51	276.58	272.81
3	284.80	288.11	268.92
4	284.97	288.14	270.72

4.2. Counterfeit Detection

In order to validate the feature and detection model, the data are split into two parts. In the training phase, the data consists of all the genuine coins and half of the counterfeit coins. Two values will be generated using the max-spacing K-clustering model: they are the maximum link among genuine coins denoted as δ, $\delta=\max \{d_{a,b}: a \in A, b \in A\}$; and the minimum link between genuine coin and fake coin as Δ, $\Delta=\min \{d_{a,b}: a \in A, b \in B\}$. A and B denote the genuine and counterfeit classes; a and b mean samples.

The value δ represents how close are the real samples distributed in the feature space, and it ideally should be as small as possible; the latter Δ reflects the sensitiveness of the features, and the larger the value, the better the detection results. A threshold τ is generated based on those two values. For an effective detection model, Δ is supposed to be larger than δ.

As for testing, if the query coin's closest sample in the genuine cluster is farther than τ, it is detected as a counterfeit; otherwise it is a genuine coin. Table 5 records the detection results.

Three conclusions can be drawn from Table 5.

1. Both the features and the classifier model are effective.

In the training result, it should be noted that δ is smaller than Δ. This means our proposed model can distinguish genuine coins from fake coins entirely. Any value within the interval (δ, Δ) can be selected as the threshold τ. Here the medium value is adopted as τ.

Table 5. Counterfeit detection validation result.

Group	Training data		Training Results			Testing data	Accuracy
	Genuine	Counterfeit	δ	Δ	τ		
1990	97	11	3.99	4.79	4.39	11	100%
1991	96	5	3.63	3.99	3.81	6	100%
1996	48	3	3.88	17.56	10.72	4	100%

If δ is larger than Δ, it means either some genuine coins are located far from the genuine cluster in feature space, or certain fake coins are too similar to the genuine coins.

2. Group '1996' has the best detection result.

For group 1996, the gap between δ and Δ is the largest among the three groups. This coincides with the database. As is mentioned in Figure 1, fake coins of years 1990 and 1991 have similar looking to the real ones, yet those of year 1996 are very different from their genuine counterpart.

3. All testing data have been successfully detected.

5. Conclusion

In this paper, we have presented an automatic counterfeit coin detection system. There are three features worth mentioning.

1. Unlike the traditional detecting methods by weight, dimension, or human expert, we have proposed a novel visual measurement system to detect fake coins;

2. From image processing, feature extraction to classification, this system provides a complete solution for counterfeit detection;

3. The features and classification model selected can provide a very high (>91.7%) accuracy.

Further research will be carried out to improve two aspects.

1. This method can be applied to detect coins from different countries, and
2. Visual measurement depends on high resolution and good quality of images. In future research, we hope to reduce this dependency.

Acknowledgments

The generous support from the Natural Sciences and Engineering Research Council of Canada is much appreciated.

References

1. Reid Goldsborough, Counterfeit Coin Detection, http://rg.ancients.info/guide/counterfeits.html. 2013.
2. The telegraph, How Can I Spot A Fake $1 Coin? http://www.telegraph.co.uk/finance/personalfinance/10707540/How-can-I-spot-a-fake-1-coin.html.
3. Martin, J.P., Detecting Counterfeit and Altered U.S. Coins: An ANA Correspondence Course, American Numismatics Association. 1st ed. 1996.
4. Carlosena, A., López-Martin, A.J., Arizti, F., Martínez-de-Guerenu, A., Pina-Insausti, J.L., García-Sayés, J.L., Sensing in Coin Discriminators, *Proceedings of IEEE Sensors Applications Symposium*, pp. 1–6, 2007.
5. Davidsson, P. Coin Classification Using A Novel Technique for Learning Characteristic Decision Trees by Controlling the Degree of Generalization. In *Proceedings of International Conference on Industrial & Engineering Applications of Artificial Intelligence & Expert Systems*, pp. 403–412, 1996.
6. Passeraub, P.A., Besse, P.-A., Raad, C.de, Dezuari, O., Quinet, F., Popovic, R.S., Metallic Profile and Coin Imaging Using an Inductive Proximity Sensor Microsystem. *Sensors and Actuators A — Physical*, vol. 66, pp. 225–230, 1998.
7. Feng, B.-Y., Sun, K., Atughechian, P., Suen, C.Y. Computer Recognition and Evaluation of Coins, in press. *Handbook of Pattern Recognition and Computer Vision, 5th Edition*, pp. 141–158, 2016.
8. Niblack, W., *An Introduction to Digital Image Processing*, Strandberg Publishing, 1985.
9. Belongie, S., Malik, J., Puzicha, J., Shape Context: A New Descriptor for Shape Matching and Object Recognition, pp. 831–837, 2000.

10. Belongie, S., Malik, J., Puzicha, J. Shape Matching and Object Recognition Using Shape Contexts. *IEEE Transactions on Pattern and Machine Intelligence*, vol. 24, pp. 509–522, April, 2002.

11. Reisert, M., Ronneberger, O., Burkhardt, H., An Efficient Gradient Based Registration Technique for Coin Recognition. *Proceedings of the MUSCLE CIS Coin Competition Workshop*, pp. 19–31, 2006.

12. Reisert, M., Ronneberger, O., Burkhardt, H. A Fast and Reliable Coin Recognition System. Pattern Recognition, *29th DAGM Symposium*, vol. 4713, pp. 415–424, 2007.

13. Nolle, M., Penz, H., Rubik, M., Konrad M., Igor H., & Reinhard G., Dagobert— A New Coin Recognition and Sorting System. In Proceedings of 7th Digital Image Computing: Techniques and Applications, pp. 329–338, 2003.

14. Freeman, H. and Shapira, R. Determining the Minimum-Area Encasing Rectangle for An Arbitrary Closed Curve", *Comm. ACM*, vol. 18, pp. 409–413, July 1975.

15. Hu, M. K. Visual Pattern Recognition by Moment Invariants, *IRE Trans. Info. Theory*, vol. IT-8, pp.179–187, 1962.

16. Preparata, F., Shamos, M. *Computational Geometry: An Introduction,* Springer-Verlag, 1985.

17. Zahn, C.T. Graph-theoretical Methods for Detecting and Describing Gestalt Clusters. *IEEE Transactions on Computers*, vol. C-20, pp. 68–86, 1971.

18. Cormen, T.H., Leiserson, C., Rivest, R.L., Stein, C. *Introduction to Algorithms, 3rd edition.* The MIT Press, 2009.

19. Sun, K. Studies on the Detection of Counterfeit Coins and Assessment on Coin Qualities. Master Thesis, Concordia University, Montreal, Canada, 2015.

20. Sun, K., Feng, B.-Y., Atighechian P., Levesque, S., Sinnott, B., Suen, C.Y. Detection of Counterfeit Coins Based on Shape and Lettering Features. In *Proceedings of 28th International Conference on Computer Applications in Industry and Engineering*, pp. 165–170, 2015.

21. Hmood, A. K., Dittimi, T. V., and Suen, C. Y. Counterfeit coin detection using stamp features and convolutional neural network, *Proc. Int. Conf. on Pattern Recognition and AI*, pp. 273–278, 2018.

22. Rad, M. S., Khazaee, S., and Suen, C. Y. Counterfeit coin detection based on image content by fuzzy association rules mining. *Ibid.*, pp. 285–289.

23. Liu, L., Lu, Y., and C. Y. Suen, Visual detection of fake coins using Fisher vectors. *Ibid.*, pp. 296–301.

24. Khazaee, S., Rad, M. S., and Suen, C. Y. Restoring height-map images of shiny coins using spline approximation to detect counterfeit coins. *Ibid.*, pp. 383–387.

Chapter 10

An Ensemble of Character Features and Fine-Tuned Convolutional Neural Network for Spurious Coin Detection

Ali K. Hmood and Ching Y. Suen

Centre for Pattern Recognition and Machine Intelligence (CENPARMI)
Computer Science and Software Engineering Department
Concordia University, Montreal, Canada
{a_alfraj, suen}@encs.concordia.ca

This chapter proposes a robust counterfeit coin detection method to tackle the advancements and sophistications of modern forgery methods. The proposed method uses transfer learning by fine-tuning a pre-trained convolutional neural network (CNN) and then analyzes the features and measures of characters on the coin surface. The fine-tuning process customizes the general image features from the original images used for training the CNN i.e. natural image into modified features that are suitable for coins. On the other hand, characters represent one of the two major parts of the coin stamp and is the one used mainly by human vision system to recognize and authenticate coins. The ensemble method combines the classification results of two classifiers trained by features from convolutional layers and a third classifier trained on character features e.g. distances between characters, stroke width, height and depth of characters. The ensemble method achieved a precision rate as high as 85.1% demonstrating the reliability of combining fine-tuned CNN classification results and the classification results of another classifier based on hand crafted features from characters to authenticate coins. The method is evaluated on a real life dataset of Danish coins as part of collaborative research with Danish authorities.

1. Introduction

Counterfeit coins have always been a concern to law enforcement authorities throughout the years. In addition to highly valuable collectable and ancient coins, there are large numbers of spurious coins in circulation around the world and that number is increasing yearly. A few solutions have been discussed in the literature on coin authentication with promising results. Yet, the coin authentication research field is still immature and the demands of a reliable and efficient method are increasing. Recently, a coin collector, Mike Marshall, informed Canadian authorities about spurious collectable Canadian coins available for sale on eBay's website.[1] While, several governmental reports suggested that the currently circulated coins are susceptible to forgery and there are around 14 million spurious Pound coins in the UK circulated between 2003 and 2004.[2] While more than 47 million spurious £1 coins in 2014 as the Royal Mint estimation reported. Most recently in 2017, Royal Mint found approximately one in thirty £1 coins in circulation is a counterfeit before they decide to replace the current coin by a new one. Therefore, governments are seeking solid solutions to overcome the counterfeiting problem. While, coin recognition aims to classify coins based on their actual age, value, denomination, and minting country.[3] In contrast, coin authentication works on differentiating genuine coins from spurious ones.[4]

Traditionally, the coin authentication is carried out by human experts and the authentication is based on their personal experience. Over time several physical characteristics have been utilized such as the coin weight or diameter. These approaches have proved its lack of accuracy due to advancements in methods used by forgers to counterfeit coins. Therefore, the use of image processing for coin recognition and authentication is more accurate and promising. Unlike counterfeit detection system in other applications, coins are (1) subject to severe degradation due to circulation in our daily use; (2) no prior knowledge of coin orientation; (3) the salient height of characters minted on the coin's surface varies which affect the stroke sharpness and width; (4) different lighting sources highly affect the character appearance due to highlight and shadow variation; (5) different languages used for coins; (6) identical color of the characters and the background.

In this chapter, a new coin authentication method is proposed using the state-of-the-art deep learning method for image classification (CNN) along with several other security features extracted from characters on the coin. CNN is a well-established image classification technique that extracts and trains an optimal image feature set for a given classification task. CNN requires a very large training set even with transfer learning technique in order to achieve a high accuracy. In counterfeit coins research, such a large number of counterfeit coins for training CNN is not available due to security reasons. Therefore, the proposed method uses a fine-tuned pre-trained CNN to classify and extract features to train another classifier while combines other features from characters that are minted on the surface to achieve a higher precision. Figure 1 represents the general framework of the proposed method. Since the method focuses also on extracting features from characters, therefore, the outer circle of the coin is located and transformed into rectangular shape to overcome the orientation problem. Then a set of morphological operations is performed to find the vertical and horizontal profiles, and then the adaptive mask is applied to initialize the height and width of characters. The mask is dynamic in terms of its size based on the relative height and width of each character. The character features along with the classification results of convolutional layer features have produced promising results in detecting counterfeit coins accurately.

2. Related Work

Several studies have been discussed in the literature to authenticate coins. Most existing studies authenticate coins based on physical characteristics such as metal features, thickness, diameter, size, weight, conductivity, electromagnetic field properties, and piezoelectric characteristics.[4] However, new technologies have made it easier for forgers to duplicate a coin with the same physical characteristics.[4] Moreover, other researchers utilized sound and light to authenticate coins such as Ref. 5 that used frequencies obtained to discriminate spurious from genuine coins. However, these frequencies rely mainly on the type of metal. Thus, if the same metal has been used for the spurious coins, it will pass this test.

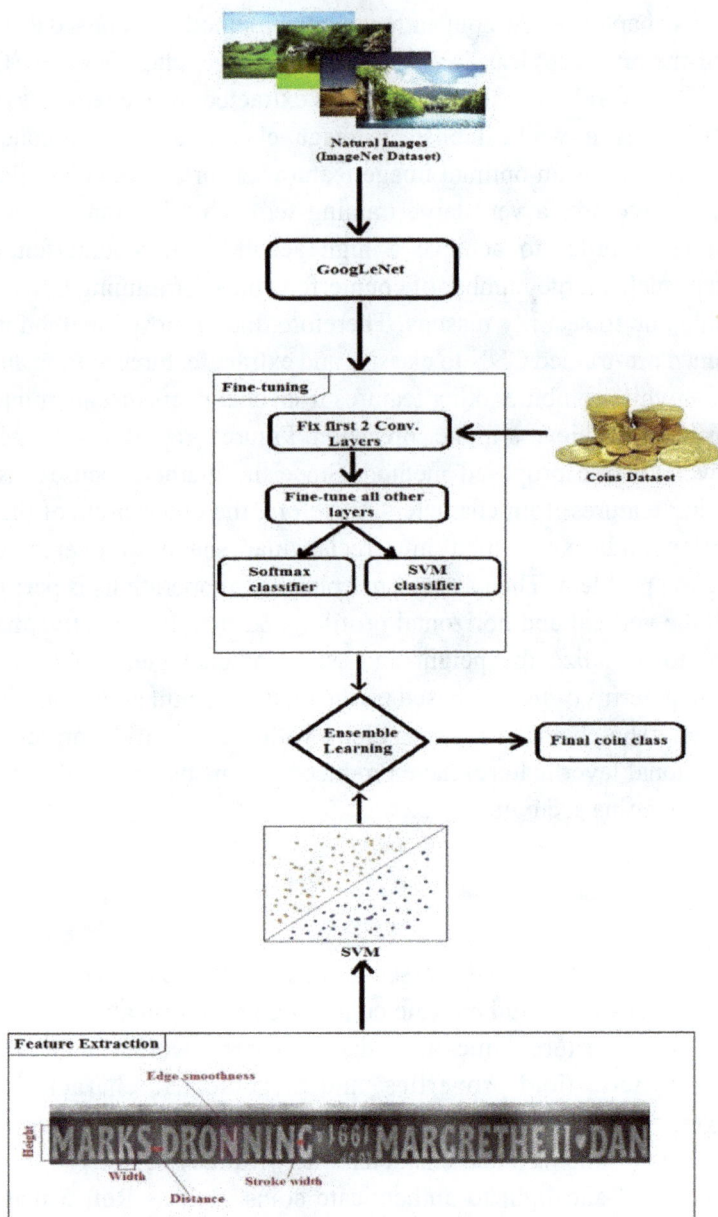

Fig. 1. Framework of the proposed method.

On the other hand, other methods based on X-ray fluorescence have been proposed.[4] X-ray methods are harmful by nature and the use of X-ray fluorescence is impractical and expensive.[4] In addition, these methods are also based on characteristics of metal type.

Therefore, the use of image processing and pattern recognition in coin authentication is introduced and revealed more accurate and promising results. According to the literature, much research has been conducted on coin recognition and proposed different image processing techniques and those methods are mostly applied to *coin extraction, feature extraction,* and *decision*. Generally, there are two main methods for *coin extraction*: the edge-based method and Hough transformation,[6] the latter is also used after edge-based methods to find the center and the radius of coins to separate the coin from its background.

Feature extraction is the most crucial step in coin recognition systems where several methods studying many feature sets were proposed such as *Edge-based statistical features* in,[6] *local image features*[7,8] e.g. *SIFT*[7,8] and *SURF*,[8,9] and *texture features*.[10,11] The last step in a coin recognition system, *decision*, it decides where each coin belongs. Image processing techniques[10] and machine learning[4,6,7] are used to classify the set of features and recognize coins.

However, most of the computer-aided methods described above are designed to recognize and classify the coins into their actual age, political background, denomination, and minting country[6,7,8] while there are very few studies on coins authentication.[4,12,13] Generally, coin authentication methods employ similar image processing, pattern recognition, and machine learning techniques as the ones used for coin recognition.

Sun *et al.*[12] proposed a counterfeit coin detection algorithm based on the character properties such as the stroke width, height and width of the character, relative distances and angles between characters, as well as, local image features. However, the researchers conducted the experimental work on a dataset of 13 coins only and the method claims no guarantee to fit other coins due to the very limited experimental dataset.

Khazaee *et al.*[13] have presented a counterfeit coin detection for 3D coin images. They examined the outer circle of the coin where all characters and numbers occur using the height and depth information obtained by the 3D scanner to identify genuine coins. The method has shown a promising result when images from a specialized 3D scanner are obtained. The access to such scanner is not feasible in daily life and it requires expertise to obtain 3D images of coins.

Recently, Liu *et al.*[4] proposed an image-based counterfeit coin detection system. The proposed system compares the local image features (keypoints) between the test coin and a set of predefined coins. The DOG detector is used to detect the keypoints which are described using the SIFT descriptor. Each comparison between the test image and the predefined image is stored as a vector in dissimilarity space. Finally, the SVM is used to classify the coins into genuine or fake class.

Convolutional neural networks (CNNs) have been the topic of interest to many researchers for its classification results and optimization. CNNs are a deep learning method that implicitly extract features from images and learn more comprehensive data from the image.[14] Training CNNs from scratch to perform optimal feature extraction and training to classify images requires a large amount of images (tens of thousands if not millions) which is not feasible in our study. Hence, many researchers with limited dataset have used a pre-trained CNNs on different image datasets i.e. natural images and transfer learning from those CNNs to the new dataset. The transfer learning methods in other domains such as face recognition or medical image classification reported the state-of-the-art results.

In this research, we used the fine-tuning process to transfer learning from GoogLeNet architecture introduced by Szegady *et al.*[15] to fit our coins dataset. However, the feature sets from GoogLeNet used to train the CNN with softmax activation function and SVM classifiers. In addition, the classification results of GoogLeNet are combined with another SVM classification results of other features extracted from characters i.e. stroke width, character height and width, spaces between characters, and edge smoothness to further classify images accurately. In order to extract features from characters, we transform the coin from circular into rectangular shape and then perform morphological operations to compute the vertical and horizontal projection profiles and apply dynamic adaptive mask.

3. Method Details

The growing needs for coin authentication system have received the attention of researchers to develop an efficient and cost-effective methods. The previous methods based on physical characteristics and features of coins e.g. weight and size are naïve compared to the new methods used by forgers nowadays. Therefore, this chapter proposes a new counterfeit coin detection based on combining convolutional neural networks and other features mainly considered by human experts. Like coin recognition systems, the proposed method starts by coin scaling (extraction) where the goal is to scale the coin to fit the whole image and remove the unnecessary background and marginal information.

The GoogLeNet architecture is then used to fine-tune the features to better extract features from coins. The features from convolution layers are used to train two classifiers, the fully connected layer with softmax and SVM. On the other hand, we used another SVM classifier trained on a set of character features from the coin i.e. characters height, width, stroke size, edge smoothness, spaces between characters, and distances of characters from top and bottom. A dynamic adaptive mask is used to handle the measures of each character separately. The dynamicity of the adaptive mask is achieved through finding the height and width of each character and then decide the mask size w.r.t. character size. Those features are extracted only after applying the straightening algorithm which aims at transforming the circular shape of coin into rectangular shape. Here to mention that only part of the coin image where the text appears is transformed, see Fig. 2(c). The posterior probabilities of softmax and two SVM classifiers are used to determine the actual class of the coins.

3.1. *Preprocessing*

Most of coin recognition, grading, and authentication systems start with coin scaling which is an essential step to remove marginal and unwanted background pixels. Some of the proposed coin recognition solutions in the literature used a simple threshold to discriminate the coin pixels from other marginal pixels. However, this is not always applicable and it only fits images with high variances between coin and marginal pixels. In this research, all edges E from image $I(x, y)$ are detected using Canny edge detection and morphological structuring elements i.e. circular shape is applied to the edge image I_E. one to many circular shapes are presented then, and the method starts to identify a set of center points $p(x, y)$ from $I_E(x, y)$ also a set of radius point $r(x, y)$ corresponding to each circle whose center is $p(x, y)$. The largest circle c_i with $p_i(x, y)$ and $r_i(x, y)$ is selected as a candidate circular shape of the coin. An adaptive mask is then placed over the coin w.r.t. the coin size and the image is cropped to fit the circular shape of the coin. There are still some noisy background pixels appearing on the image due to the circular shape of the coin, hence, all pixels occurring outside the margins of the adaptive mask are blacked out as shown in Fig. 2(b).

(a) Original coin image   (b) Scaled coin image

(c) Image from the straightening algorithm

Fig. 2. Original Danish coin image with preprocessing image result (scaling) and straightening algorithm image result.

3.2. *Convolutional Neural Network*

Convolutional neural network (CNN) is the new era in machine learning. CNNs are a machine learning technique that uses deeper networks to implicitly extract features from images. Deep networks comprise different layers to extract more sophisticated information to better understand the image and need no engineering methods to extract features. CNN has four main operations that can be used in different orders in different architectures. *Convolution, Non Linearity (Rectified Linear Unit), Pooling or Sub Sampling*, and *Classification (Fully Connected Layer)* are the four operations.

Convolution: convolutional layer is the prime layer to extract features from images. It extracts features using small sliding window throughout the whole image. The weight of the sliding window is the same in each convolutional layer. Different numbers of sliding window sizes are often used in single CNN architecture. Figure 3 illustrates the convolutional layer process using a 3x3 sliding window. The stride is a setting of the number of pixels to slide the window over the image. If stride is set to 1, the window slides 1 pixel every time as shown in Fig. 3. Convolutional neural networks consist of multiple layers to improve the feature extraction and to build a better representation of these features. The initial layers learn generic features such as color and edges information while the later layers focus on learning image specific features.

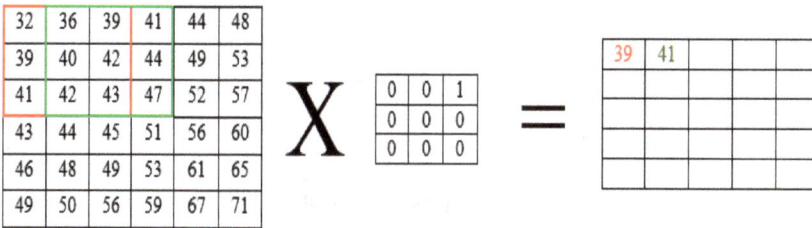

Fig. 3. Convolutional layer concept.

The sliding window is called feature detector, kernel, or commonly known as filter. The filter is sliding through the image w.r.t. the stride setting and the output of every slide is the element wise multiplication of pixel values by the filter values. The output of this process is written into a new matrix called the convolved feature or the feature map.

Rectified Linear Unit (ReLU): is a nonlinear operation whose goal is to transfer all negative value of pixels by zero in the features map. The output of the ReLU layer is that $\forall \rho \in feature\ map;\ \rho = max(zero, \rho)$ where ρ is the pixel value. However, this operation has not been used in several CNN architectures.

Pooling or Sub Sampling: the goal of performing the pooling process is to reduce the dimensionality of the feature map while maintaining the most valuable and unique features. There are several pooling methods that can be used e.g. max, average, and sum. In max pooling for example another sliding window is defined to slide through the feature map and in every position the maximum number from the feature values in the sliding window is returned in a reduced feature map. The same thing for average pooling where the average of the feature values is returned or sum pooling that returns the sum of feature values in the sliding window. However, max pooling is the most widely used method due to its experimentally proven better results. The pooling operation also uses stride to define the number of pixels to slide over and it can be different than the stride setting for convolutional process. Figure 4 shows the concept of max pooling operation using a 2x2 window and the stride is set to 1.

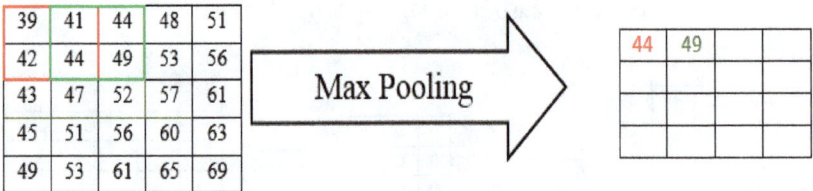

Fig. 4. Max pooling illustration.

Fully Connected Layer: the fully connected (FC) layer is the classification layer and it uses the softmax activation function. This layer can be replaced by other classifiers such as SVM. By definition, the fully connected layer refers to connecting every neuron in one layer to every neuron in the next layer. Fully connected layer is usually placed after the convolutional and pooling layers where the output of these layers is the input to the fully connected layers. The softmax is the activation function used with the fully connected layer to determine the probabilities of assigning each neuron to a class where the sum of all probabilities is 1.

Different architectures have been discussed in the literature w.r.t. number of layers and their distribution. GoogLeNet is one of those architectures introduced by Szegady *et al.*[15] in 2015 and it has outperformed all other architectures for the ImageNet Large-Scale Visual Recognition Challenge (ILSVRC) in 2014. GoogLeNet architecture introduced a network-within-network concept by using a new module *"Inception"* that is a subnetwork containing a number of convolutional filters of different sizes and dimensions working in parallel and concatenating their outputs. GoogLeNet has two convolutional layers, three pooling layers, and nine *"Inception"* layers where each *"Inception"* layer comprises 6 convolution layers and 1 pooling layer which makes it a very deep network. Figure 5 illustrates the GoogLeNet convolution, pooling, and inception layers. The input image dimension of GoogLeNet is 224 × 224. The CNN architecture works on capturing a sparse representation of image information while gradually reducing dimensionality. GoogLeNets have shown better results to other CNN architectures while need fewer trainable weights.

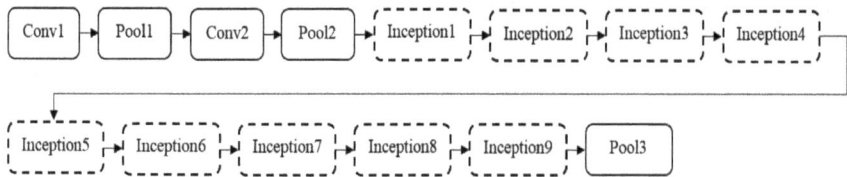

(a) GoogLeNet consisting of two conv, three pooling, and nine inception layers

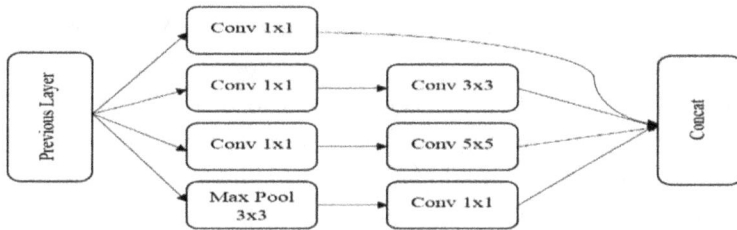

(b) Sample inception layer (Inception5) representation

Fig. 5. Representation of GoogLeNet CNN architecture.

GoogLeNet has originally trained to extract features and classify natural images into 1000 classes. The filter weights are optimized to extract features from ImageNet dataset of natural images. Fine-tuning process continues the backpropagation to optimize the filter weights according to the new image dataset. The fine-tuning process that is used to transfer learning in this research keeps the first two convolution layers fixed, as those layers extract generic type of features i.e. edges, and fine-tune all intermediate layers. Replacing the last fully connected (FC) layer intended is for the 1000 classes of the original dataset used to train GoogLeNet into a new FC layer of two classes to fit our dataset of genuine and counterfeit classes. The original filter weights of natural image are fine-tuned to optimize weights of the coin dataset through backpropagation and stochastic gradient descent to find optimal weights. On the other hand, the feature vectors from the fine-tuned layers are also used to train SVM classifier beside the new FC layer.

Assume that coin dataset D of x images, fine-tuning is an iterative process to update the filter weights w to reach the minimum error rate. As suggested in the literature, we reduced the learning rate and the best results achieved a learning rate $l = 6 * 10^{-4}$ for our dataset. Given that the original filter weights of pre-trained CNN are reasonably good and achieved a good classification results on the original dataset, the fine-tuning process uses lower learning rate to improve and update the filter weights reliably.

3.3. *Extraction of Character Features*

Characters represent a major part of the coin and they form the main part used by humans to recognize coins and by experts to authenticate them. The most common method to forge a coin is to strike a coin using a fake die that is in return molded (designed) from original coin stamp. This method yield in a small variation in salient width which is reflected as the edges in a coin image. In addition, extracting features from characters is influenced by the findings from the literature where some counterfeit coin detection methods proposed the use of features from characters as part of the methods. To extract features from characters accurately, we have used the same work we proposed for character extraction in Ref. 3 to locate coin but not extracting them, as shown in Fig. 6(a).

After characters are located on the coin a set of features are extracted and used to classify the coins. The stroke width, edge smoothness, character height and width, number of pixels, and spaces between characters. Stroke width calculation is inspired by the stroke width transformation method[16] where for every edge boundary pixel i, the algorithm traces the neighboring pixels until it reaches another edge boundary pixel j Fig. 6(b). However, the proposed technique works on reading the pixels horizontally and not vertically; also we consider the other gradient direction other than the actual stroke width such as the line between pixels l and m in Fig. 6(b). The number of pixels between edge boundary pixels is stored as stroke width. The character height and width is specified by the horizontal and vertical profiles that specify the size of the dynamic adaptive mask around each character.

(a) Danish coin image after applying the adaptive mask to locate characters.

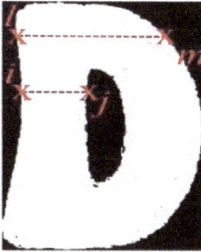

(b) Measuring the stroke width of characters

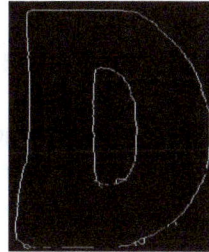

(c) After applying the thinning algorithm

(d) Calculating the distances between characters

Fig. 6. Feature extraction techniques from characters.

On the other hand, the total number of edge pixels (stroke pixels) is calculated as there is deviation in character sizes between characters of the genuine and counterfeit coins. In addition, the spaces between characters are calculated by taking the distance between the centers of every two immediate adaptive masks, see Fig. 6(d). Finally, the edge smoothness is found by first applying a thinning algorithm to produce one pixel edges of the character stroke as shown in Fig. 6(c). Then the number of pixels (that are forming the edge) is calculated as well as the pixels contained within the enclosed area between the edges.

The sets of those features are then used for training a linear support vector machine (SVM) since we have only genuine and counterfeit classes. SVM works on finding a hyperplane separation with maximal margins between two classes. We employed the linear SVM with radial basis function (RBF) kernel to authenticate coins.

3.4. *Ensemble Learning*

The classification results along with their posterior probabilities of the three classifiers are used to decide the class of a coin image. The feature sets from fine-tuned GoogLeNet are used to 1) train the FC layer and the softmax function which discriminates classes based on the largest values in each feature vector while suppressing the less significant values, 2) train a one-vs-one SVM classifier. Additionally, the character feature sets are used to train another one-vs-one SVM classifier. The posterior probabilities for both SVM classifiers are estimated and used with probabilities of softmax function to improve the final classification results using $\hat{c} = \frac{\sum_1^k P_{i,k}(c)}{k}$, where c is the classification result of classifier k for image i. $P_{i,k}(c)$ is the posterior probability of c for image i given by classifier k. $\hat{c}$ to produce the final classification results given to image i.

4. Experimental Results and Discussions

The proposed method was evaluated on different datasets that contain genuine and counterfeit Danish coins. The Danish coin datasets comprise the obverse side of Denmark 20 Korner of different years as shown in

Table 1. The datasets are randomly partitioned into non-overlapped training, validation and test sets. The training set is used to train each classifier while the evaluation of classifiers is conducted using the testing set. In addition, the validation set is used to test and fix the parameter settings. In addition, the impact of using any single classification results and the parameters involved in achieving the proposed method is considered in the evaluation process.

We evaluated the three classifier results and the ensemble methods proposed in this chapter. The fine-tuned GoogLeNet with softmax (FTmax), fine-tuned GoogLeNet with SVM (FTsvm), and character features with SVM (CFsvm) are the three classification methods based on different feature sets where the first two are FTmax and the FTsvm based on the convolutional layer feature sets while the latter is the SVM classifier based on character feature sets.

Table 1. Danish Coin Datasets.

Datasets	Training Set		Validation Set		Testing Set	
	Genuine	Counterfeit	Genuine	Counterfeit	Genuine	Counterfeit
Danish 1990	1144	1097	383	367	383	367
Danish 1991	1144	1097	383	367	383	367
Danish 1996	1144	1097	383	367	383	367
Danish 2008	1144	1097	383	367	383	367

On the other hand, the proposed method (PM) of ensemble classification probabilities of the three classifiers is shown to improve the prediction of counterfeit coins as illustrated below. Fig. 7 illustrates the precision results of the three classifiers and the proposed ensemble method. The figure depicts the precision results of the four datasets used in evaluation of the three classification method separately and the result of ensemble method proposed in this chapter. The character feature sets are classified using binary SVM and are shown to return the lowest precision rate among other methods. The reported lower results can be seen as due to the lower number features than convolutional layer features, as well as, confirm the findings from literature of convolutional layers that have better representation of image features.

A. K. Hmood & C. Y. Suen

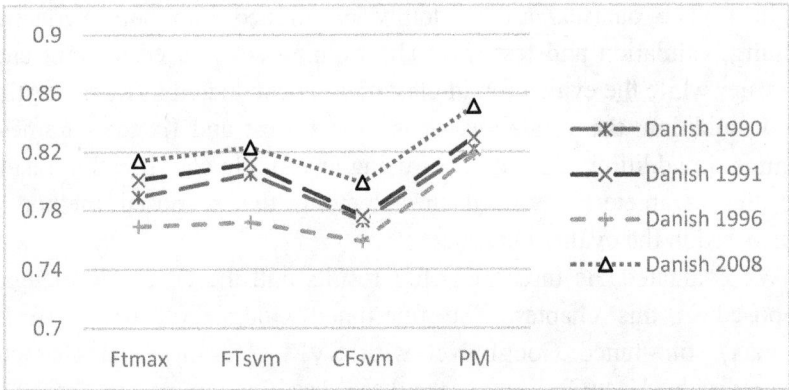

Fig. 7. Precision rates of the three classification results and the proposed method.

The second lowest rates were obtained from the fine-tuned GoogLeNet feature set with softmax function that showed 1% - 3.3% precision rates improvement when compared to SVM results of character features. Yet, both the fine-tuned GoogLeNet with softmax function and character features with SVM were below the precision results of fine-tuned GoogLeNet with SVM where the latter shows the best classification results among the other two methods and showed average improvement of 0.97% over FTmax results. Our ensemble model has returned as high as 85.1% precision rate for Danish 2008 dataset.

We have also evaluated the number of correctly classified images using different combination of two methods among the four methods. Figure 8 illustrates the normalized results of correctly classified coin images by a pair of methods.

The results suggest combing any two methods improves the classification results. The fine-tuned GoogLeNet with softmax and fine-tuned GoogLeNet with SVM combination showed better classification results than using any single method, as well as, showed 1.49% higher true positives than a combination of fine-tuned GoogLeNet with softmax and character features with SVM.

On the other hand, the proposed method achieved the highest number of correctly classified images than any combined two methods while combining the proposed method with the fine-tuned GoogLeNet with

SVM showed the highest normalized number of correctly classified coins rate of 0.843.

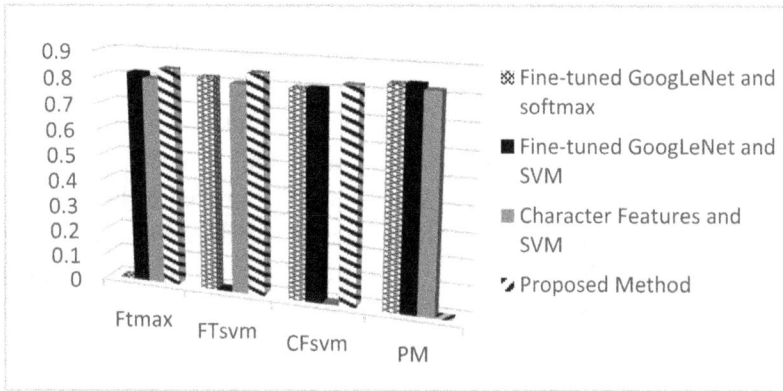

Fig. 8. Normalized number of correctly classified coins by a combination of two methods.

Additionally, we compare the proposed method to those methods discussed in the literature. Unlike previous work [17], the evaluation of this work has been conducted on non-overlapping training, validation, and testing sets. The proposed solution achieved promising results of using convolutional neural network for counterfeit coin detection. The character feature sets in this work were influenced by the results of [12] in the literature that achieved a high precision based on character features. However, the use of the entire coin image to fine-tune the convolutional layers of pretrained CNN has achieved a higher precision than features from characters only. In addition, the proposed ensemble method of combining the results of three classifiers achieved better precision rates and was capable of discriminating counterfeit coins from genuine with less equipment requirements as it was proposed by Ref. 13 using 3D image information.

5. Conclusions

In this chapter, we studied the problem of counterfeit coin detection and proposed an ensemble method of three classification results. The proposed method used a fine-tune process to optimize feature extractors of pretrained CNN and transfer learning to improve feature extraction from our coin dataset. The extracted features from fine-tuned GoogLeNet were used to train two classifiers, softmax and SVM, and define the posture probability of their classification results. In addition, sets of features were extracted from characters minted on the coin and these sets were used to train another SVM classifier. The proposed solution was evaluated on different coin datasets that comprise genuine and counterfeit coins. The proposed ensemble method was experimentally proved to be capable of correctly classify majority of coin images. Experimental results suggest the use of ensemble method can better represent the image information and distinguish between coin images of different classes.

Acknowledgments

The research is supported in part by the Natural Sciences and Engineering Research Council of Canada (NSERC). The authors sincerely acknowledge the support of Ultra Forensic Technology firm in Montreal for providing the dataset and facilitating access to their scanning equipment.

References

1. J. Robitaille, "Counterfeit coins cause for concern among Canadian collectors," *Canadiancoinnews.com,* March 31.2015. [Online]. Available: http://canadiancoinnews.com/counterfeit-coins-cause-concern-among-canadian-collectors/. [Accessed 15 October 2017].
2. C. R. Gagg and P. R. Lewis, Counterfeit coin of the realm–Review and case study analysis, *Engineering Failure Analysis,* 14(6), 1144–1152 (2007).
3. A. K. Hmood, T. V. Dittimi, and Ching Y. Suen. Scale and rotation invariant character segmentation from coins. In *Proc. 14th International Conference on Image Analysis and Recognition,* pp. 153–163, Montreal, Canada (2017).
4. L. Liu, Y. Lu, and C. Y. Suen, An Image-Based Approach to Detection of Fake Coins, *IEEE Trans. on Information Forensics and Security.* 12(5), 1227–1239 (2017).
5. A. Gavrijaseva, O. Martens and R. Land, Acoustic Spectrum Analysis of Genuine and Counterfeit Euro Coins, *Elektronika Ir Elektrotechnika.* 21(3), 54–57 (2015).

6. L. van der Maaten and P. Poon. Coin-o-matic: A fast system for reliable coin classification. In *Proc. Muscle CIS Coin Competition Workshop*, pp. 7–18 (2006).

7. L. Shen, S. Jia, Z. Ji and W.-S. Chen, Extracting local texture features for image-based coin recognition, *IET Image Processing*, 5(5), 394–401 (2011).

8. M. Kampel, R. Huber-Mork and M. Zaharieva, Image-based retrieval and identification of ancient coins, *IEEE Intelligent Systems*, 24(2), 26–34 (2009).

9. M. Kampel and M. Zaharieva. Recognizing ancient coins based on local features. In *Proc. International Symposium on Visual Computing*, pp. 11–22 (2008).

10. C. Xu, Research of Coin Recognition Based on Bayesian Network Classifier, *Advances in Information Sciences and Service Sciences*, 4(18), 395–402 (2012).

11. L. Shen, S. Jia, Z. Ji and W.-S. Chen. Statistics of Gabor features for coin recognition, In *Proc. International Workshop on Imaging Systems and Techniques*, pp. 295–298 (2009).

12. K. Sun, B.-Y. Feng, P. Atighechian, S. Levesque, B. Sinnott, and C. Y. Suen, Detection of Counterfeit Coins Based on Shape and Letterings Features. In *Proc. International Conference on Computer Applications in Industry and Engineering*, pp. 165–170 (2015).

13. S. Khazaee, M. Sharifi Rad and Ching Y. Suen. Detection of Counterfeit Coins Based on Modeling and Restoration of 3D Images. In *Proc. 5th International Symposium CompIMAGE*, pp. 178–193 (2016).

14. Y. LeCun, Y. Bengio, and G. Hinton, Deep Learning, *Nature*, 521(7553), 436–444 (2015).

15. C. Szegedy, W. Liu, Y. Jia, P. Sermanet, S. Reed, D. Anguelov, D. Erhan, V. Vanhoucke, and A. Rabinovich. Going deeper with convolutions. In *Proc. IEEE Conference on Computer Vision and Pattern Recognition*, pp. 1–9 (2015).

16. B. Epshtein, E. Ofek, and Y. Wexler. Detecting text in natural scenes with stroke width transform. In *Proc. IEEE Conference on Computer Vision and Pattern Recognition*, pp. 2963–2970 (2010).

17. Ali K. Hmood, T. V. Dittimi and Ching Y. Suen. Counterfeit Coin Detection Using Stamp Features and Convolutional Neural Network. In *Proc. International Conference on Pattern Recognition and Artificial Intelligence*, pp. 273–278 (2018).

Chapter 11

Cardiac Murmur Classification in Phonocardiograms Using Deep Recurrent-Convolutional Neural Networks

Pengcheng Xi*,†, Rafik Goubran* and Chang Shu†

*Carleton University
†National Research Council Canada
Ottawa, Ontario, Canada
pengcheng.xi@nrc-cnrc.gc.ca

Cardiac murmurs are the first signs of pathological changes in heart valves. Their subtle presence poses great challenges for detection through auscultation or phonocardiograms (PCGs); therefore computer-aided detection (CAD) of heart murmurs has medical significance in assisting health care professionals. Traditional CAD approaches, relying on engineered features, are prone to changes in environmental noise and data collection methods. Deep Convolutional Neural Networks (CNN) have shown robustness in advancing the performance of computer vision tasks through automatic feature learning from large amount of data. Meanwhile, deep Recurrent Neural networks (RNN) have demonstrated state-of-the-art performance on processing sequence data in areas such as speech recognition and natural language processing. With a limited set of labelled PCG recordings, this work first transforms PCGs to topology-preserving spectral images, conducts data augmentation and successfully tunes latest deep CNN architectures with transfer learning. Experimental results indicate that the fine-tuned deep CNNs are effective in classifying cardiac murmurs from PCG recordings without segmentation. Moreover, the deep CNNs gained a further performance boost from learning the dynamics in temporal sequences after being plugged into an RNN model. In summary, the proposed deep recurrent-convolutional neural network approach captured spectral, temporal and spatial features. It achieved an overall accuracy of 94.01% for automatic cardiac murmur detections in phonocardiograms.

1. Introduction

According to the World Health Organization (WHO), cardiovascular disease (CVD) is the leading cause of mortality worldwide.[1] The majority of the problems found in CVD are related to heart valves, in which cardiac murmurs are the first signs of pathological changes. Therefore, classic auscultation and phonocardiography (PCG) play essential roles in early detection of CVDs, providing a guide for further examinations.

Cardiac valve problems include mitral valve prolapse, mitral valve or aortic stenosis, aortic sclerosis and stenosis, and mitral or aortic regurgitation, etc. Stenosis leads to the heart working harder in order to pump blood to the rest of the human body. Regurgitation means the blood is going the wrong way through the valves, resulting in the heart working harder to force the blood through the damaged valves. Both can wear out the heart and lead to heart failure.

Cardiac murmur is the sound of blood flowing through a problematic heart valve. It may also be a condition which makes the heart beat faster and forces the heart to handle more blood quicker than normal. Most heart murmurs are innocent and do not require treatment; however murmurs linked to damaged or overworked heart valves need surgery or treatment. Some murmurs are congenital and others are a part of ageing or from other heart problems.

The evaluation of cardiac murmurs is based on its timing, shape, location, intensity, and duration in the cardiac cycle (S1, systolic, S2, and diastolic). They can be categorized into systolic or diastolic murmurs. In each situation, the murmur takes a particular shape, e.g., crescendo-decrescendo shape for aortic stenosis, decrescendo shape for aortic regurgitation, plat shape for mitral regurgitation or tricuspid regurgitation. This implies that visual representations of heart recordings (in time and frequency domains) can be utilized for detecting cardiac murmurs.

Because of the medical significance of cardiac murmurs, there has been considerable effort on developing computer-aided detection (CAD) approaches.[2-4] Conventional approaches follow three steps: segmentation, feature extraction, and classification. The features used in CAD are selected in three domains: time, frequency, and time-frequency. While the manual features work in certain cases, they are prone to changes in environmental noise and data recording instruments measurement errors.

Recent advances in deep neural networks have enabled automatic feature learning from large amount of training data, providing an end-to-end solution from feature extraction to classifier building. Moreover the learning scheme contributes to the robustness of deep neural networks to dataset noise, making them suitable for solving the cardiac murmur classification problem.

Among deep neural networks, Convolutional Neural Networks (CNN) are especially effective in processing visual data. Therefore, deep CNNs are ideal candidates for cardiac murmur classifications because of the following reasons. First, with minimum information loss, PCGs can be transformed to spectrograms, a visual form that can then be processed through deep CNNs for extracting spatial and spectral features. Second, deep CNNs learn hierarchical features automatically from data. Therefore, they provide a powerhouse for feature learning in order to distinguish cardiac murmur recordings from normal ones.

Likewise, Recurrent Neural Networks (RNN) have demonstrated state-of-the-art performance on applications such as speech recognition and natural language processing. Therefore, RNNs are a natural fit for analysing PCGs or the transformed spectrogram "movies" in order to capture the dynamics in temporal sequences for detecting cardiac murmurs.

This work addresses the following questions: i) how deep CNNs will learn from a limited amount of labelled PCG recordings, ii) whether deep CNNs are robust in classifying PCGs without segmentation, iii) whether the fine-tuned models gain the same performance boost as they achieved in ImageNet Large-Scale Visual Recognition Challenge (ILSVRC),[5] and iv) whether the incorporation of temporal features through RNNs helps improving the performance on cardiac murmur classification.

To address the limited training data problem, we employ data augmentation and transfer the learning to fine-tune state-of-the-art deep CNN architectures. To address the other questions, we compare two approaches: i) we train and test deep CNNs on sampled spectrogram patches, and ii) after applying the deep CNNs for feature extraction, we train a Long Short-Term Memory neural network (LSTM) to account for temporal features in the sequence data.

Experimental results show that the best performing model in the first approach reaches an overall accuracy at 90.26%, which is further pushed to 94.01% after the inclusion of temporal features. This indicates that the proposed approach is promising for solving the problem of classifying cardiac murmurs in phonocardiograms automatically.

In summary, our approach enables the extraction of features for identifying the subtle and challenging differences between cardiac murmur and normal PCGs without segmentation. Our contributions are three-fold:

- Significantly leveraged deep CNNs' hierarchical feature extraction capabilities through transfer learning.
- Successfully tuned deep CNNs on a small training dataset without overfitting through data augmentation.
- Successfully captured spectral, temporal and spatial features in PCG recordings for detecting cardiac murmurs through the integration of deep CNNs and RNNs.

2. Related Work

In this section, we first review the top three results on classifying normal and abnormal heart sound recordings in the PhysioNet/CinC challenge 2016.[6] What is common among the winning methods is the use of shallow neural networks. In contrast, our work attempts to use deep neural networks because of their demonstrated advantage over traditional methods in many computer vision tasks. However, one of the challenges in training deep neural networks with limited data is to avoid overfitting. Therefore, we discuss the many techniques for dealing with the problem. In addition, we discuss recent work on applying deep recurrent and convolutional neural networks on sequence data.

Potes et al.[7] proposed an approach of using ensemble of feature-based and deep learning-based classifiers for the detection of abnormal heart sounds. The classifier ensemble approach obtained the highest score in the competition. Their classifier trained CNNs using PCGs decomposed into four frequency bands. Each of the CNNs consists of three layers: the input layer followed by two convolution layers.

Zabihi et al.[8] used ensemble of neural networks without segmentation and achieved the second best score in the PhysioNet/CinC Challenge 2016. They used 20 feed-forward neural networks — two hidden layers in each network and 25 hidden neurons in each layer. A combination rule is then applied to identify the quality and abnormality of each input.

Kay and Agarwal[9] built a fully-connected two-hidden-layer neural network trained by error back-propagation, and regularized with DropConnect to classify heart sounds as normal or abnormal.

The above approaches all use shallow neural networks as part of their solution mainly due to the limited amount of training data. Other factors that may affect their performance include the manually decided thresholds used in the combination rules[8] and the decomposition of frequency bands.[7]

Limited amount of training data leads to overfitting in deep neural networks. Solutions include dropout, batch normalization and transfer learning.[10] Among all, the simplest solution is to add a regularization term on the connection weights. Dropout works by removing neurons or connections from the network probabilistically during training.[11] Batch normalization works by normalizing layer inputs. It allows the use of much higher learning rates and results in less sensitivity to weight initialization.[12] In addition, Yosinski et al.[13] proposed a transfer learning approach that makes use of a neural network which had been pre-trained on large amount of data and fine-tuning on some of the layers. Other transfer learning approaches include learning from unlabeled data with stacked auto-encoders and then transferring the knowledge to a labeled dataset.[14]

Data augmentation is another way to avoid overfitting in deep learning. It works by increasing the amount of training data from the existing training set. In image processing, this includes operations such as cropping, flipping and rotating the original images. It has been proved effective to avoiding overfitting.

Because of the success from recurrent neural networks on sequence data, there has been recent work on using deep CNNs and RNNs to detect features in electroencephalograms (EEG).[15,16] Bashivan et al.[16] demonstrated a technique on learning representations from EEG data that are invariant to inter- and intra-subject differences in the context of mental load classification task. They transformed EEG activities into a sequence of topology-preserving multi-spectral images and trained a deep recurrent-convolutional network to learn representations from the sequence of images. While VGGNet was used in their work, a recent study by Xi et al.[17] indicates that AlexNet shows better performance in processing PCG data.

Another recent work on using deep CNNs and RNNs comes from Thodoroff et al.[15] They followed a similar approach on the learning spatial, spectral, and temporal structure of EEG signals for automatic seizure detection. Transfer learning was used to deal with limited data problem and for cross-patient detection of seizures.

3. Methodology Using Deep Convolutional Neural Networks

3.1. *Data Selection*

To study heart sound problems, there are four publicly available heart sound databases: (i) the PhysioNet/CinC Challenge 2016,[6] (ii) the PAS-CAL Heart Sounds Challenge 2011,[18] (iii) the Michigan heart sound and murmur database (MHSDB) and (iv) the Cardiac Auscultation of Heart Murmurs database (eGeneralMedical). The PhysioNet/CinC dataset is by far the largest dataset with heart sound recordings labelled as normal and abnormal; however no further labels on murmurs are available. The MHSDB and eGeneralMedical datasets have very limited data. Ultimately the PASCAL dataset is selected for this work as it comprises at-scale heart sound recordings labelled as normal or murmur.

From PASCAL dataset, we selected a subset which was collected from a clinical trial in hospitals using a digital stethoscope. Within the dataset, 66 murmur recordings and 200 normal recordings were used for this study. All the recordings were sampled to 4,000 Hz and their lengths varied from 1 to 30 seconds.

3.2. *Data Pre-processing*

To take advantage of the automatic feature extraction capabilities of deep CNNs, PCGs were first transformed to spectrograms. According to Ranganathan et al.,[19] most cardiovascular murmurs show a frequency range extending from almost zero to 700 Hz. To compute spectrograms, we applied a 512-point Hamming window with 75% overlapping for computing Fast Fourier Transform (FFT) of size 512. A plot of the spectrograms computed on one murmur PCG and one normal PCG is shown in Fig. 1, in which limits of the color axis for spectrograms were set between -120db and -40db.

Our motivation is to conduct automatic feature extraction and classification from data. While traditional approaches segment PCGs into S1, systole, S2, and diastole, this work performed feature extraction and classification without segmentation.

3.3. *Data Augmentation*

An observation on the PCGs and computed spectrograms shows that most cardiac cycles last no more than 1.5 seconds. Therefore, to prepare training

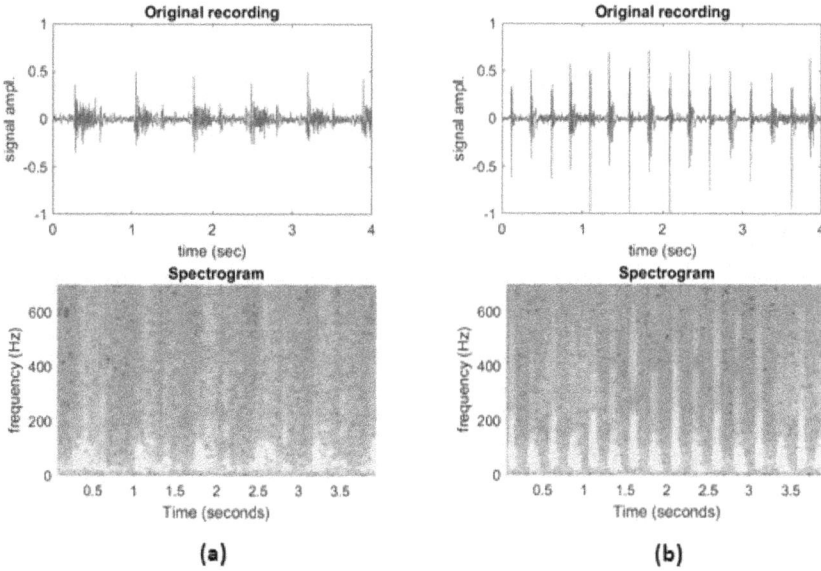

Fig. 1. PCG recordings and spectrograms computed for (a) a murmur subject and (b) a normal subject.

images for deep CNNs, a sliding window of 1.5 seconds was used to extract image patches from spectrograms with an initial step size of 500 samples. As a result, those heart recordings with a length shorter than 1.5 seconds are excluded from this study, leaving the final number of training subjects for murmur and normal categories to be 64 and 180 respectively.

All the windowed image patches are put into two categories, i.e., murmur or normal, and a pre-trained deep CNN is modified to classify two classes at the output. Sample image patches from the two categories are plotted with Fig. 2.

We conducted five-fold cross validations on the training dataset. For each fold, an independent testing set of 12 subjects were set aside for the murmur category and a testing set of 35 subjects were used for the normal category. The remaining subjects within each category were used to extract image patches for training purpose. The grouped image patches were used to fine-tune deep CNNs.

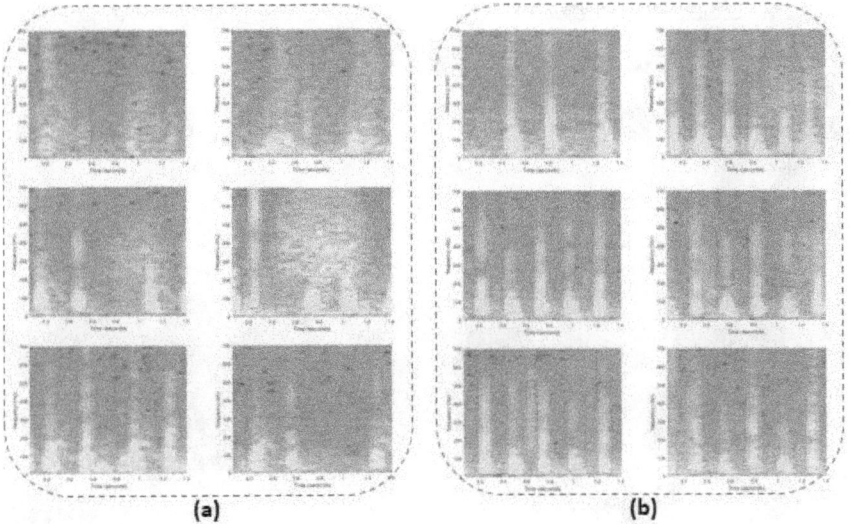

Fig. 2. Sample image patches extracted from spectrograms within (a) murmur and (b) normal categories.

3.4. *Feature Extraction and Model Building*

Following one of the transfer learning approaches, we fed the image patches from both categories into the modified deep CNNs for fine-tuning. The first part of each model was frozen, leaving the last layers actively tuned for high performance.

To test the trained deep CNN models, we applied the same sliding window approach (same width and step size as those used for extracting training image patches) to consecutively extract image patches along a spectrogram. Each patch was fed into the trained deep CNN to predict a label. The predicted labels were then agglomerated to a voting scheme for creating a final prediction. The approach is illustrated in Fig 3.

3.5. *Architectures of Deep CNN*

In visual computing, tremendous progress has been made in object classification and recognition thanks to the availability of large scale annotated datasets such as ImageNet Large Scale Visual Recognition Competition (ILSVRC).[5] The ImageNet dataset contains over 15 million annotated images from a total of over 22, 000 categories.

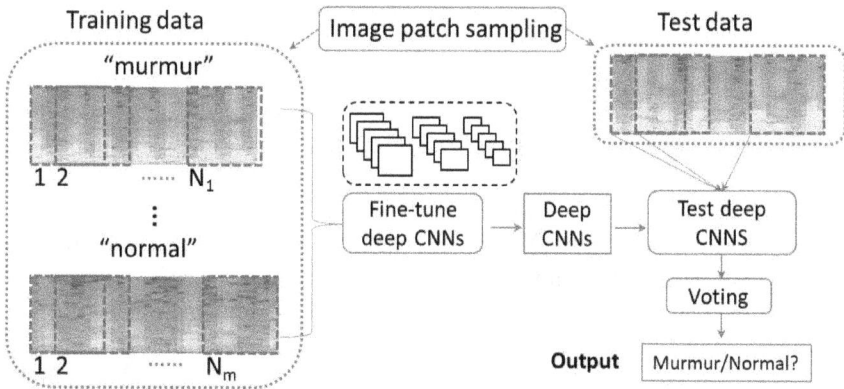

Fig. 3. Diagram of a murmur detection approach using deep CNNs.

Recent years witnessed great performance advancement on ILSVRC using deep CNNs. Comparing to hand-crafted image features, deep CNNs automatically extract features from a large dataset for tasks they are trained for. In this work, we experiment on modifying four of the best-performing models in recent ImageNet challenges and compare their performance on classifying normal and murmur PCGs.

- AlexNet - in 2012, Krizhevsky et al.[20] applied a deep CNN to ImageNet ILSVRC and achieved a top-5 test error rate of 15.3%, compared to 26.2% achieved by the second-best entry. The network was made up of five (5) conv layers, max-pooling layers, dropout layers, and three (3) fully connected layers. This work led to a series of deep CNN variants in following years which consistently improved the state-of-the-art in the benchmark tasks.
- VGGNet - in 2014, Simonyan and Zisserman[21] introduced a deeper 19-layer CNN and achieved top result in the localization task of ImageNet ILSVRC. The network used very small 3x3 convolutional filters and showed significant improvement. This influential work indicated that CNNs needed to have a deep network of layers in order for the hierarchical feature representations to work.
- GoogLeNet - in 2014, Szegedy et al.[22] introduced a deeper CNN to ILSVRC and achieved top-5 error rate of 6.7%. Instead of sequentially stacking layers, this network was one of the first CNNs that used parallel structures in its architecture (nine (9) Inception

modules with over 100 layers in total).

- ResNet - in 2015, He et al.[23] introduced a new 152-layer network architecture and set new records in ILSVRC. ResNet achieved 3.57% error rate in the classification task. The residual learning framework was eight (8) times deeper than VGGNet but still has lower complexity.

All of the above deep CNN architectures were designed for a 1000-class classification task. To adapt them to this task, the last three layers were removed from each network. Three new layers (fully connected layer, softmax layer and classification layer) were appended to the remaining structure of each network. Higher learning rates were set for the newly added fully connected layers so that the first part of each network remained relatively unchanged during training and the newly added layers were fine-tuned on the PCG dataset. Cross validation was then used to test the robustness of the fine-tuned deep CNN.

4. Methodology Using Deep Recurrent-Convolutional Neural Networks

Deep convolutional neural networks have demonstrated good performance on extracting spectral and spatial features automatically from visual data. Essentially, PCG signals are sequence data and therefore temporal features need be learned to be combined with the visual features for detecting cardiac murmurs. Because of the recent successes on applying recurrent-convolutional neural networks on EEG signals,[15,16] we propose an approach on combining the deep convolutional neural networks with recurrent neural networks for the detection of cardiac murmurs in PCG signals.

To learn the temporal features, we select the long short-term memory (LSTM) network,[24] a type of recurrent neural network (RNN) for studying sequence and time-series data. An LSTM network uses memory cells and gated inputs/outputs to learn long-term dependencies between time steps of a sequence. LSTM networks can study the sequence in forward directions or in both forward and backward directions (bi-directional).

4.1. *Data Selection*

We used the same dataset as those used for training deep CNNs. To recall, the number of sequences for murmur and normal classes are 66 and 200, respectively.

4.2. Feature Extraction and Model Building

This approach is illustrated in Figure 4. PCG signals were first transformed to spectrograms using Fast Fourier Transform (FFT), from which a sliding window was used to sample image patches (step size = 100 samples). Selecting one of the fine-tuned deep CNNs from Section 3, we computed, for each image patch, a feature vector. This captured spatial and spectral patterns. After feeding the feature vectors into a bi-directional LSTM network, a classifier was trained to learn the temporal pattern. As a result, a deep recurrent-convolutional neural network based cardiac murmur detector was built.

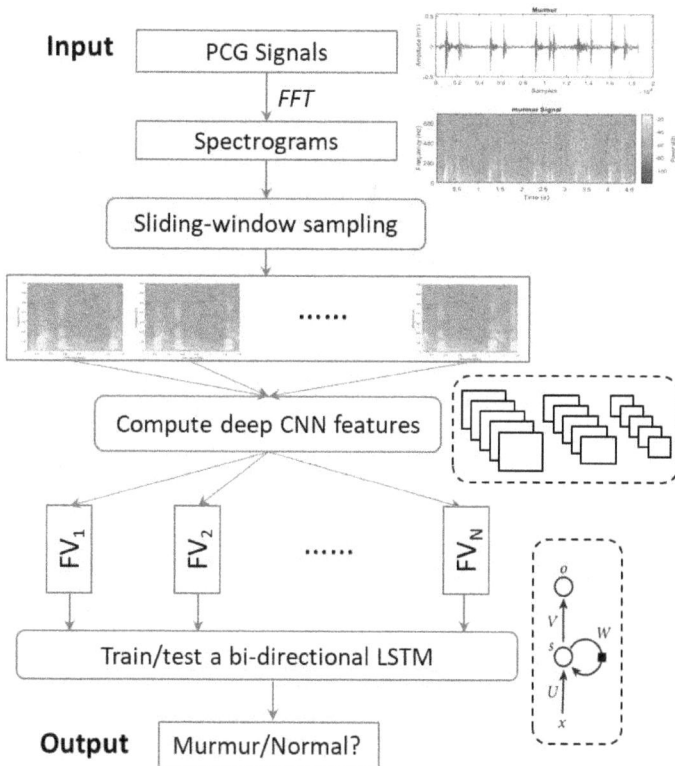

Fig. 4. Diagram of a murmur detection approach using deep recurrent CNNs (FFT - Fast Fourier Transform; FV - Feature Vectors).

The following settings were used to design the architecture of the bidirectional LSTM neural network. The input sequence layer size was set as the length of the feature vector computed from the deep CNN. A bidirectional LSTM layer was added with an output size of 100. The output of the LSTM was defined at the last unit, followed by a fully connected layer of size two (a two-class classifier), a softmax layer, and a classification layer.

5. Experiments with Deep Convolutional Neural Networks

5.1. *Comparison on Results from Deep CNN Architectures*

We applied the following parameter settings for training each modified deep CNN: Stochastic Gradient Descent with Momentum (SGDM) as the optimization algorithm, batch size of 10, initial learning rate as $1e-4$, and the learning rate for the last fully connected layer as 20.0. Each network stops from further training if the mean accuracy on the fifty most recent batches reaches 99.5%. On average, the training takes between 20 and 40 minutes to complete on an NVIDIA GeForce GTX TITAN X GPU (20 minutes for AlexNet, 40 minutes for VGGNet, and 30 minutes for both GoogLeNet and ResNet). The final size of fine-tuned VGGNet is about 20 times that of GoogLeNet, with in-between sizes for AlexNet and ResNet.

The voting strategy during testing on a spectrogram was as follows. If over 20% of the image patches extracted from a spectrogram were classified as murmur, the corresponding PCG was then classified as murmur, otherwise as normal. For each deep CNN, we computed the average accuracies (sensitivity, specificity and overall accuracy) from the five-fold cross validations in Table 1. Varying the percentage threshold used in voting made small updates to the accuracies and they were not big enough in changing the difference among the methods. As an example, increasing the threshold to 60% led to overall accuracies for the four models being 86.36%, 84.38%, 83.02%, and 60.86%, respectively.

Table 1.   Classification Accuracies of Deep CNNs (step size = 500).

Model	Sensitivity	Specificity	Overall accuracy
AlexNet	85.00%	90.86%	87.93%
VGGNet	81.67%	89.14%	85.40%
GoogLeNet	95.00%	46.29%	70.64%
ResNet	93.33%	22.29%	57.81%

One natural question is how data augmentation will affect the classification performance of different models. Keeping the remaining parameter settings the same, we reduced the window step size from 500 to 100 in order to create more training image patches for both categories of murmur and normal. Because different folds contained PCG recordings at different lengths, we counted the average number of murmur and normal training images. The averages increased from (6,633, 9,345) to (13,240, 18,617) after a step size change. Feeding the larger dataset to the four deep CNNs for training and then testing with five-fold cross validations led to updated performance in Table 2.

Table 2.   Classification Accuracies of Deep CNNs (step size = 100).

Model	Sensitivity	Specificity	Overall accuracy
AlexNet	81.67%	98.86%	**90.26%**
VGGNet	76.67%	97.71%	87.19%
GoogleNet	98.33%	45.14%	71.74%
ResNet	76.67%	56.57%	66.62%

5.2. *Prediction on Spectrograms using AlexNet and ResNet*

We further analysed the performance of different deep CNN models on classifying individual image patches extracted from two spectrograms (one from murmur PCG and the other from normal PCG). In particular, we selected AlexNet and ResNet as they represent the best and worst performing models in overall prediction accuracy. We randomly selected two spectrograms (one murmur and the other normal) from the independent test set and ran classifications with the fine-tuned deep CNNs, which were also randomly selected from one of the five-fold models trained with each architecture.

The first set of prediction results in Fig. 5 are the outputs from deep CNNs trained on image patches extracted at 500 samples apart. In each prediction plot, we used '1' for output class 'murmur' and '0' for 'normal'. Their location in the plots matches the center of each sliding window. These plots helped to identify the area of the spectrogram that was correctly classified or mis-classified. The left column from top to bottom is the spectrogram for a murmur PCG, prediction results from one of the five-fold AlexNet models, and results from one of the five-fold ResNet Models.

The right column of Fig. 5 is the prediction results on a normal PCG.

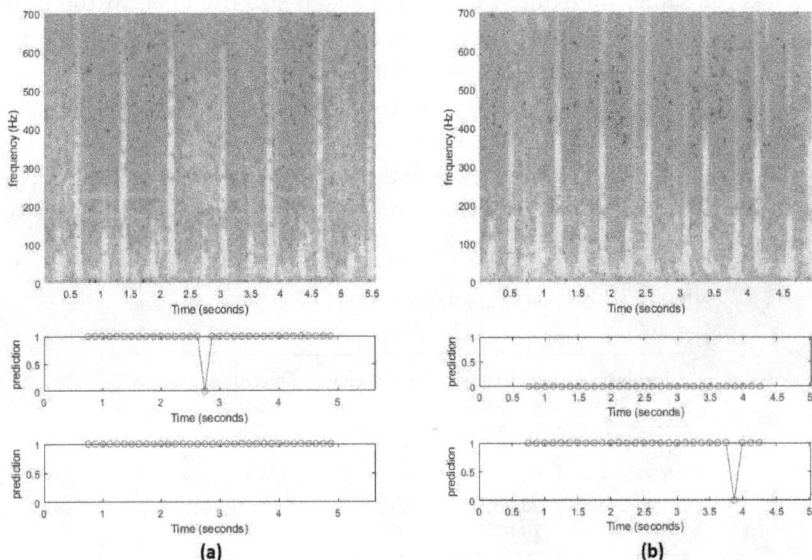

Fig. 5. Predictions on consecutive image patches extracted from spectrograms computed on (a) a murmur PCG and (b) a normal PCG (step size for training image window = 500). From top to bottom: spectrogram, prediction from a AlexNet model, and prediction from a ResNet model.

Figure 5 indicates that both networks gave accurate predictions for the murmur spectrogram, while ResNet predicted poorly on the normal spectrogram (lower right sub-plot in Fig. 5).

Figure 6 lists the second set of prediction results from deep CNNs trained on image patches extracted at 100 samples apart. Parameter setting for testing remained the same. It indicates that, after data augmentation and model re-tuning, ResNet improved its prediction performance on the same normal spectrogram (lower right sub-plot in Fig. 6).

5.3. *Prediction on Spectrograms using VGGNet and GoogLeNet*

Using the same test examples as previous experiments, we conduct classification experiments on consecutive spectrogram image patches using the fine-tuned VGGNet and GoogLeNet. The classification output results are

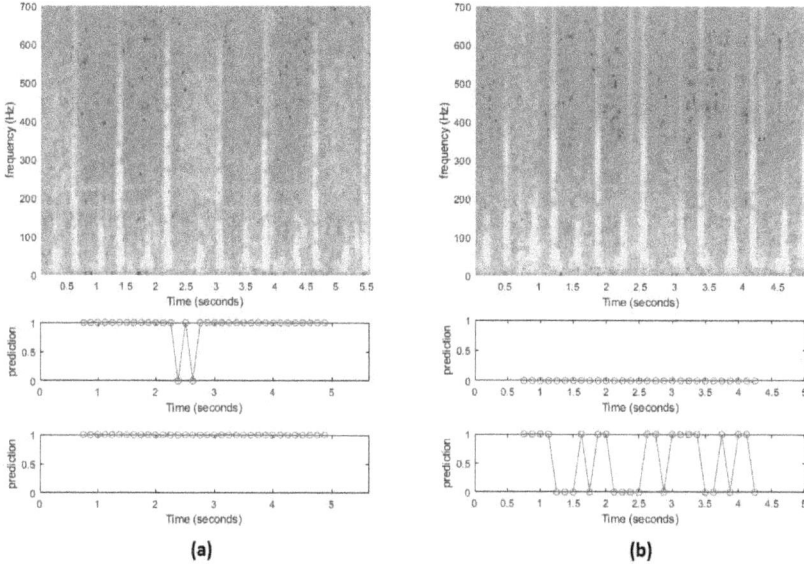

Fig. 6. Predictions on consecutive image patches extracted from spectrograms computed on (a) a murmur PCG and (b) a normal PCG (step size for training image window = 100). From top to bottom: spectrogram, prediction from a AlexNet model, and prediction from a ResNet model.

illustrated in Fig. 7. In comparison with Fig. 6, VGGNet had a similar performance as AlexNet in that both made perfect classifications on the normal spectrogram image patches. Also, both models made mistakes in classification on two image patches which were located differently in the murmur spectrogram.

Likewise, GoogLeNet made perfect classifications on the murmur spectrogram as ResNet did as seen in Fig. 6. For the normal spectrogram in both figures, ResNet had more correct hits than GoogLeNet.

In summary, the comparison in Section 5.2 demonstrates that increasing the granularity during training, image extraction led to improved performance for ResNet. In both cases, AlexNet gave close to perfect classification results on the two test spectrograms. Maintaining the same granularity as in Fig. 6, we made a further comparison in Section 5.3 after running classifications with fine-tuned VGGNet and GoogLeNet models. Figure 7 indicates that VGGNet made good classifications on both spectrograms whereas GoogLeNet had misclassified most of the image patches extracted

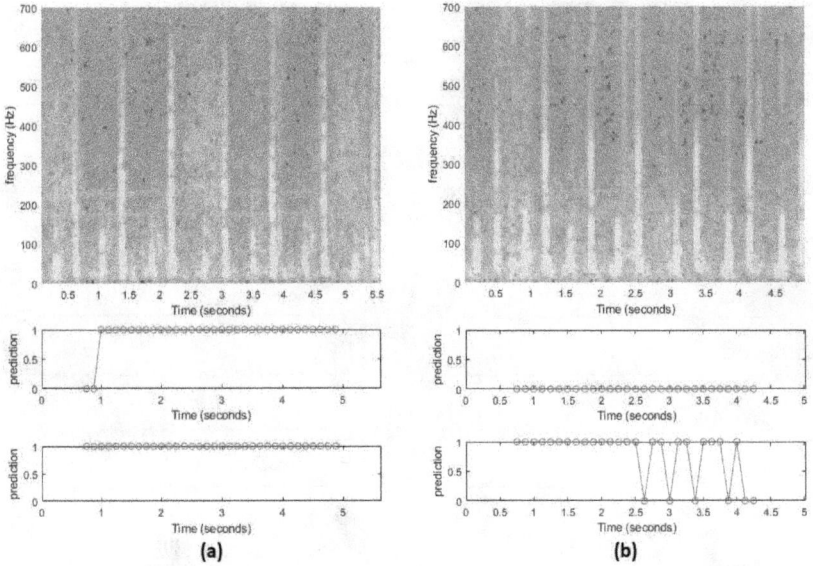

Fig. 7. Predictions on consecutive image patches extracted from spectrograms computed on (a) a murmur PCG and (b) a normal PCG (step size for training image window = 100). From top to bottom: spectrogram, prediction from a VGGNet model, and prediction from a GoogLeNet model.

along the normal spectrogram.

6. Experiments with Deep Recurrent Convolutional Neural Networks

We used the following parameter settings for training the bidirectional LSTM. Adaptive moment estimation (ADAM) solver was selected because it worked better with LSTMs than stochastic gradient descent with momentum (SGDM) solver. Learning rate was set at 0.01 with a minimum batch size of 50 and a maximum number of epochs of 200. A gradient threshold of 1.0 was also set to stabilize the training process to avoid large gradients.

We conducted a five-fold cross validation on the stability of the trained classifier. Data selection for training and testing was on a subject level. In each fold, we put data from twenty percent of the subjects into the testing set and the remaining into the training set. With the training image window step size set at 100, every ten consecutive spectrogram images were sampled and aggregated as one trial. Because PCG signals vary in length from subject to subject, the number of training and testing trials were different in various folds.

Experiments on deep CNNs indicate that AlexNet archived the best performance. Therefore within each trial, every image was fed into the fine-tuned AlexNet model for computing feature tensors (size of 6x6x256). They were computed as the outputs from the last maximum pooling layer, which was selected based on a previous study.[25] After reshaping the feature tensors into vectors, the bidirectional LSTM began training and took about one hour to complete.

Table 3 lists the classification results from cross-validations. Most folds demonstrated a performance boost over those gained in using deep CNNs only. The average of the overall accuracy reached 94.01%, which was a four-percent improvement over the best result achieved with deep CNNs.

Table 3. Classification Accuracies of Deep Recurrent CNNs.

Fold	Sensitivity	Specificity	Overall accuracy	F-score
1	74.69%	93.33%	85.10%	0.82
2	100.00%	91.12%	94.16%	0.92
3	96.82%	99.53%	98.38%	0.98
4	80.21%	100.00%	93.55%	0.89
5	98.85%	98.90%	98.87%	0.99
Average	90.11%	96.58%	**94.01%**	0.92

7. Discussions

The four deep CNN models, in comparison, demonstrated consistent improvement on the ILSVRC benchmark tasks. However, the same trend did not hold in the cardiac murmur classification task. Our explanation is that deeper models (ResNet being the deepest among the four) have more complexity and parameters. Therefore, they were more data thirsty in fine tuning. This had been verified through our experiments in which data augmentation with denser image patch extractions led to improved performance of the deep CNNs, most notably for ResNet.

We used a simple voting strategy during testing. In a different voting strategy, the probability of a PCG recording was classified as either murmur or normal and can be computed as the average probabilities assigned to its randomly selected window patches.

The comparisons were conducted on two randomly selected testing spectrograms with randomly selected fine-tuned deep CNN models. With a different selection on both testing data and models, the results could be slightly different but the observed difference should remain the same.

Besides the visual features extracted from deep CNNs, we also experimented with simpler features extracted from spectrograms. Among many, we computed two time-frequency (TF) moments, namely instantaneous frequency and spectral entropy, which are in itself one dimensional. We then fed them to the bidirectional LSTM for training. Experimental results show that these features led to an overall accuracy at around 75 percent, much lower than those achieved with deep CNNs. This is another proof of the power from visual feature extractions through deep CNN models.

Overall, our approach on using deep recurrent CNNs demonstrated a performance boost over using deep CNNs only. The majority of the cross validation folds demonstrated an absolute performance gain over the deep CNN approach. This indicates that temporal features captured with LSTMs is a great addition to the spatial and spectral features learned with deep CNNs.

8. Conclusions

The classification between cardiac murmur and normal PCGs is a challenging problem because of subtle differences. This work successfully employs deep CNNs with transfer learning and data augmentation to learn from a small dataset of PCG recordings. The power of deep CNNs on automatic feature extraction enables accurate classifications without the need of segmentation. Four state-of-the-art deep CNN architectures were compared on classification performance.

In the ILSVRC benchmark tasks, deeper models showed higher performance than their counterparts with less number of layers. Training with the limited PCG dataset, the deeper models do not share the same performance gains. In fact, the least deep model in selection demonstrated better performance in all comparisons. Fine tuning the deep CNN models is data thirsty and data augmentation improved performance for all the deep CNN models. The result can be used as a guidance for deep model selections in a similar problem given limited amount of training data.

Adding to the spatial and spectral features computed with deep CNNs, we improved our approach using LSTMs to extract temporal features. Experimental results indicate a performance boost after including the temporal features. A best performance on classifying PCGs was achieved at 94.01% using the fine-tuned AlexNet with the LSTM network.

In conclusion, we demonstrated an approach using deep recurrent convolutional neural networks to extract spatial, spectral, and temporal features from PCG signals. Experimental results indicated that the deep recurrent CNN based approach is a powerful and practical solution to the problem of automatic cardiac murmur classification.

References

1. World statistics on cardiovascular disease. `www.who.int/mediacentre/factsheets/fs317/en/` Accessed: 2017-11-14.
2. S. Sanei, M. Ghodsi, and H. Hassani, An adaptive singular spectrum analysis approach to murmur detection from heart sounds, *Medical Engineering & Physics*. **33**(3), 362 – 367 (2011). doi: https://doi.org/10.1016/j.medengphy. 2010.11.004. URL `http://www.sciencedirect.com/science/article/pii/S1350453310002729`.
3. F. Safara, S. Doraisamy, A. Azman, A. Jantan, and S. Ranga, Wavelet packet entropy for heart murmurs classification, *Advances in Bioinformatics*. **2012** (2012). doi: http://dx.doi.org/10.1155/2012/327269.
4. A. T. Balogh. *Analysis of the Heart Sounds and Murmurs of Fetuses and Preterm Infants*. PhD thesis, Pazmany Peter Catholic University (2012).
5. O. Russakovsky, J. Deng, H. Su, J. Krause, S. Satheesh, S. Ma, Z. Huang, A. Karpathy, A. Khosla, M. Bernstein, A. C. Berg, and L. Fei-Fei, ImageNet Large Scale Visual Recognition Challenge, *International Journal of Computer Vision*. **115**(3), 211–252 (2015). doi: 10.1007/s11263-015-0816-y.
6. C. Liu, D. Springer, Q. Li, B. Moody, R. A. Juan, F. J. Chorro, F. Castells, J. M. Roig, I. Silva, A. E. W. Johnson, Z. Syed, S. E. Schmidt, C. D. Papadaniil, L. Hadjileontiadis, H. Naseri, A. Moukadem, A. Dieterlen, C. Brandt, H. Tang, M. Samieinasab, M. R. Samieinasab, R. Sameni, R. G. Mark, and G. D. Clifford, An open access database for the evaluation of heart sound algorithms, *Physiological Measurement*. **37**(12), 2181 (2016). URL `http://stacks.iop.org/0967-3334/37/i=12/a=2181`.
7. C. Potes, S. Parvaneh, A. Rahman, and B. Conroy. Ensemble of feature-based and deep learning-based classifiers for detection of abnormal heart sounds. In *Computing in Cardiology Conference*, pp. 621–624 (2016). doi: 10.23919/CIC.2016.7868819.
8. M. Zabihi, A. B. Rad, S. Kiranyaz, M. Gabbouj, and A. K. Katsaggelos. Heart sound anomaly and quality detection using ensemble of neural networks without segmentation. In *Computing in Cardiology Conference,* pp. 613–616 (2016). doi: 10.23919/CIC.2016.7868817.
9. E. Kay and A. Agarwal. Dropconnected neural network trained with diverse features for classifying heart sounds. In *Computing in Cardiology Conference,* pp. 617–620 (2016). doi: 10.23919/CIC.2016.7868818.

10. The effectiveness of data augmentation in image classification using deep learning, cs231n.stanford.edu/reports/2017/pdfs/300.pdf Accessed: 2017-11-14.

11. N. Srivastava, G. Hinton, A. Krizhevsky, I. Sutskever, and R. Salakhutdinov, Dropout: A simple way to prevent neural networks from overfitting, *Journal of Machine Learning Research.* **15**, 1929–1958 (2014). URL http://jmlr.org/papers/v15/srivastava14a.html.

12. S. Ioffe and C. Szegedy, Batch normalization: Accelerating deep network training by reducing internal covariate shift, *CoRR.* **abs/1502.03167** (2015). URL http://arxiv.org/abs/1502.03167.

13. J. Yosinski, J. Clune, Y. Bengio, and H. Lipson, How transferable are features in deep neural networks?, *CoRR.* **abs/1411.1792** (2014). URL http://arxiv.org/abs/1411.1792.

14. Z. Huang, Z. Pan, and B. Lei, Transfer learning with deep convolutional neural network for sar target classification with limited labeled data, *Remote Sensing.* **9**(9) (2017). doi: 10.3390/rs9090907. URL http://www.mdpi.com/2072-4292/9/9/907.

15. P. Thodoroff, J. Pineau, and A. Lim, Learning robust features using deep learning for automatic seizure detection, *CoRR.* **abs/1608.00220** (2016). URL http://arxiv.org/abs/1608.00220.

16. P. Bashivan, I. Rish, M. Yeasin, and N. Codella, Learning representations from EEG with deep recurrent-convolutional neural networks, *CoRR.* **abs/1511.06448** (2015). URL http://arxiv.org/abs/1511.06448.

17. P. Xi, R. Goubran, and C. Shu. Cardiac murmur classification in phonocardiograms using deep convolutional neural networks. In *Proceedings of the International Conference on Pattern Recognition and Artificial Intelligence* (2018).

18. P. Bentley, G. Nordehn, M. Coimbra, and S. Mannor. The PASCAL Classifying Heart Sounds Challenge 2011 Results. http://www.peterjbentley.com/heartchallenge/index.html .

19. N. Ranganathan, V. Sivaciyan, and F. Saksena, *The Art and Science of Cardiac Physical Examination: With Heart Sounds and Pulse Wave Forms on CD.* Contemporary Cardiology, Humana Press (2007). URL https://books.google.ca/books?id=yeOBqe5u6V4C.

20. A. Krizhevsky, I. Sutskever, and G. E. Hinton. Imagenet classification with deep convolutional neural networks. In eds. F. Pereira, C. J. C. Burges, L. Bottou, and K. Q. Weinberger, *Advances in Neural Information Processing Systems 25*, pp. 1097–1105, Curran Associates (2012). URL http://papers.nips.cc/paper/4824-imagenet-classification-with-deep-convolutional-neural-networks.pdf.

21. K. Simonyan and A. Zisserman, Very deep convolutional networks for large-scale image recognition, *CoRR.* **abs/1409.1556** (2014). URL http://arxiv.org/abs/1409.1556.

22. C. Szegedy, W. Liu, Y. Jia, P. Sermanet, S. Reed, D. Anguelov, D. Erhan, V. Vanhoucke, and A. Rabinovich. Going deeper with convolutions. In *Computer Vision and Pattern Recognition (CVPR)* (2015). URL http:

//arxiv.org/abs/1409.4842.

23. K. He, X. Zhang, S. Ren, and J. Sun, Deep residual learning for image recognition, *CoRR*. **abs/1512.03385** (2015). URL http://arxiv.org/abs/1512.03385.

24. S. Hochreiter and J. Schmidhuber, Long short-term memory, *Neural Comput.* **9**(8), 1735–1780 (1997). doi: 10.1162/neco.1997.9.8.1735. URL http://dx.doi.org/10.1162/neco.1997.9.8.1735.

25. P. Xi, C. Shu, and R. Goubran, Comparing 2d image features on viewpoint independence using 3d anthropometric dataset, *International Journal of the Digital Human.* **1**, 412–425 (2016).

Chapter 12

Robust and Adaptive Vehicle Detection System Based on Energy Map Analysis by Using Surveillance Videos

Yan-Lin Chou and Daw-Tung Lin*

Department of Computer Science and Information Engineering
National Taipei University
151, University Road, New Taipei City, Taiwan
*dalton@mail.ntpu.edu.tw

Many automobile repair shops and parking lots are often equipped with a sensing coil to detect when a vehicle enters. However, the single sensing coil often produces false alarms (e.g., when motorcycles pass over the sensor or vehicles reverse from or stop at the gates). To overcome these problems, surveillance camera equipment is utilized and installed near the entrance gate to detect the incoming vehicles. Given that image-processing technology is now more developed, we propose using a camera to perform the task of a sensor and improve the accuracy of vehicle detection. This system is empowered such that it can adapt to the different factors of an outdoor environment. The background subtraction method is utilized to extract foreground information of a moving object from the field of view of the camera. Optical flow is also applied to determine the direction of the incoming vehicle. A foreground energy-map analysis is conducted to improve the reliability of vehicle detection. Finally, a 20-day test of the system was conducted at an automobile repair shop. The experimental results show a highly promising detection performance with a hit rate as high as 95.58%. The camera system is designed to replace the sensing coils to reduce the hardware costs and increase the detection efficiency.

1. Introduction

With advancement in technology, the traditional traffic management systems have evolved into intelligent automated traffic management systems,

---

*Corresponding author: Daw-Tung Lin.
The preliminary version of this article has been published in 2018 International Conference on Pattern Recognition and Artificial Intelligence.

which are capable of detecting vehicles with a high accuracy in all weather conditions.[1-3] Sina *et al.*[4] extracted raw traffic video from CCTV footage and used it to identify a specific vehicle and count the total number of vehicles per unit time. Pan *et al.* [5] combined background subtraction and edge detection algorithms to detect a vehicle. Moreover, they proposed a method that can automatically generate an adaptive region of interest (ROI) based on the height of a vehicle computed from the observed width of the road. Guo *et al.*[6] presented a vehicle detection method that is not sensitive to the time of day and can therefore be effective at night. Miller *et al.*[7] designed a vehicle detection method based on Hidden Markov Models (HMMs). They applied a modified Viterbi algorithm to the HMM sequential estimation framework to initialize and track vehicles. Moreover, they used the AdaBoost method to identify the vehicles. Seenouvong *et al.*[8] utilized the background subtraction method to extract information of a moving object within a ROI of the road to detect a vehicle. Meany *et al.*[9] employed background subtraction and machine learning algorithms to perform automatic vehicle counting by using remote video cameras. Choudhury *et al.*[10] applied Haar-like features for vehicle detection. Mehboob *et al.*[11] analyzed the vehicle trajectories in the video frame and tracked the trajectories over time. Vehicle counting was conducted by estimating the trajectories and comparing the trajectories with a Hungarian tracker. Ren *et al.*[12] combined feature point detection and foreground temporal-spatial image analysis to determine multiple parameters pertaining to traffic flow and to identify the types of vehicles from a video sequence. Chauhan *et al.*[13] used background subtraction and linear quadratic estimation methods to predict the path of a vehicle and to count all detected vehicles in urban traffic scenarios; their method attained an accuracy of 99%. Sahgal *et al.*[14] proposed a computer vision-based technique for vehicle queue detection at an urban traffic intersection.

Recently, many entrance gates have been equipped with sensing coils. Sensors are time-consuming to install and often trigger a false alarm when a non-vehicle object passes over them. Given that image-processing technology is more developed,[15] we propose using a camera to perform the task of a sensor. This would increase the value of the surveillance equipment, reduce equipment expenditure, and improve the accuracy of vehicle detection. This system is developed such that it can adapt to the different factors of an outdoor environment. The background subtraction method is utilized to extract foreground information of a moving object from the field of view (FOV) of a camera. Optical flow is also applied to determine the direction of the incoming vehicle. A foreground energy-map analysis is conducted to improve the reliability of vehicle detection. The concept of applying energy maps is very novel in the field of computer vision. Yi *et al.*[16] suggested that a crowd-movement path is similar to that of fluid movement and used this concept to establish a normal energy map. A higher energy represents the presence of more people in the region, while a lower energy represents the presence of fewer objects such as obstacles. Based on these factors, we can establish various customized energy maps. Thus, we suggest that the concept of an energy map can also be applied for the detection of traffic flow.

2. System Design and Considerations

2.1. *Vehicle detection system configuration*

Vehicle detection system reliability is affected by the position, angle, and FOV of a camera. Therefore, an algorithm is required to adjust these parameters to increase the reliability of the system. In this work, a general type camera is mounted at a high position to detect incoming vehicles, as shown in Fig. 2.

Fig. 1.   Actual automobile repair shop where the solution was tested in this study.

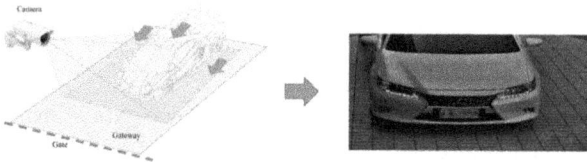

Fig. 2.   Video camera configuration for vehicles detection.

2.2. *Main issues and considerations*

Light   Pedestrians   Motorcycle   Backwards   Parking

Fig. 3.   Situations and events that are considered in this study.

When a sensor is deployed for automatic vehicle detection, false alarms are commonly triggered when a vehicle is either moving backward or parking temporarily. When an image-processing algorithm is incorporated into a camera, some of the problems encountered by the induction coil in the camera can be eliminated. However, the following issues persist: sensitivity to lighting change, non-target-vehicle object identification (pedestrian or motorcycle), false alarms for vehicles moving backward, and false alarms for vehicles parking temporarily. These situations are listed in Fig. 3 and are addressed as follows:

- Operation in all weather conditions: Because the vehicle detection system is installed in an outdoor environment, the outdoor lighting can affect the results of image-processing algorithms. Therefore, we utilized an adaptive background subtraction method (described in Section 3.1) to automatically adapt to the variable light conditions. Figure 4 shows the three main lighting conditions that affect detection when using the camera.

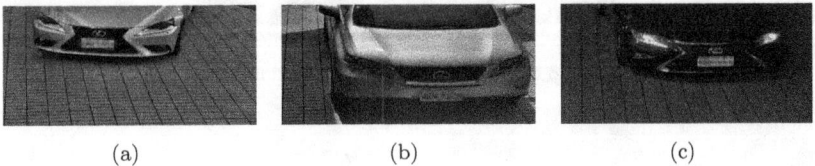

(a)   (b)   (c)

Fig. 4.   Different lighting conditions: (a) normal daylight; (b) strong daylight; (c) night.

- Pedestrians and motorcycles: An entrance-gate is usually an open space. Therefore, in addition to the target vehicles, other moving objects, such as pedestrians and motorcycles, appear in the FOV of the mounted camera. Examples are shown in Fig. 5. We constructed an algorithm that accurately identified and excluded these non-target objects.

(a)   (b)

Fig. 5. Examples of Pedestrians and motorcycles appearing in the FOV: (a) pedestrians and (b) motorcycles.

- Wrong way and backward movement: An automobile repair shop entrance gate is an open space; therefore, there is no specific path that a vehicle must follow to enter the shop. Due to these liberal constraints, there are two main vehicle movement patterns that must be accurately identified: (1) the vehicle leaving the entrance gate in a reverse direction (reverse event) and (2) the vehicle leaving the entrance gate in the wrong direction (wrong-way event) as illustrated in Fig. 6.

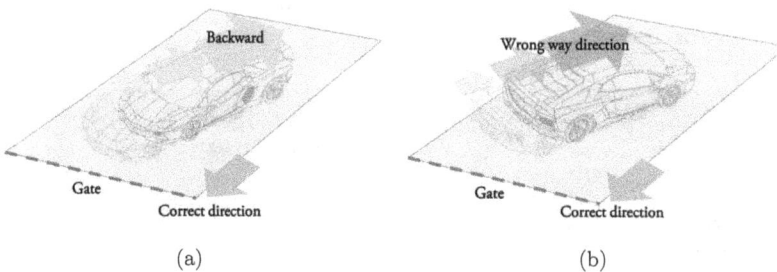

(a)   (b)

Fig. 6. Directions in which a vehicle enters the entrance gate of an automobile repair shop: (a) Reverse direction and (b) wrong direction.

- Temporary parking: Occasionally, an incoming vehicle must wait for guidance and instructions from the service personnel concerning how and when the vehicle should enter. Thus, an incoming vehicle might enter the FOV of the camera but not leave the FOV of the camera for a brief period of time because the vehicle might have temporarily parked, as depicted in Fig. 7. To resolve this problem, we compared the initial and final positions of the vehicle to identify a temporarily parked vehicle, as discussed in Section 3.3.

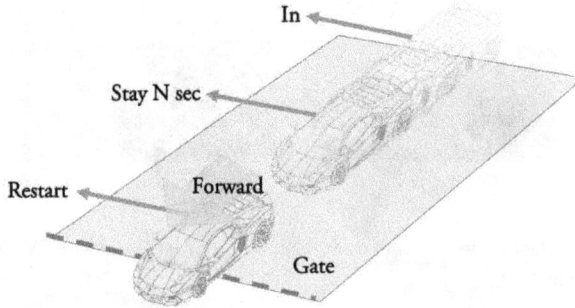

Fig. 7.   Temporary parking problem.

- License plate missing in the snapshot: To perform license plate recognition, the system must capture a snapshot of the vehicle. However, if the front of the vehicle has passed through the FOV of the camera after the vehicle detection algorithm was triggered, the license plate cannot be recognized as indicated in Fig. 8. In Section 3.4, we propose a foreground energy-map concept and an associated method to ensure that the license plate is visible in the captured snapshot.

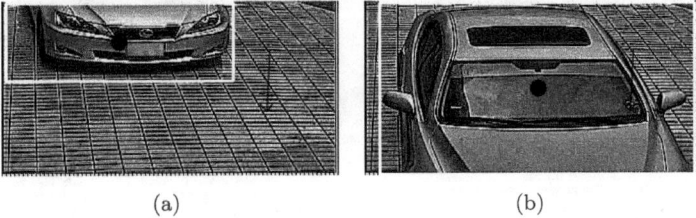

(a)   (b)

Fig. 8.   (a) Snapshot contains license plate; (b) license plate missing.

3. The Proposed Vehicle Detection System

We constructed and integrated a series of image-processing algorithms that are reliable and can detect vehicles in a complex environment under various weather conditions. Figure 9 shows a flow chart of the proposed vehicle detection system. First, an image was captured using the camera and then, it was pre-processed. The motion direction configuration was pre-defined to

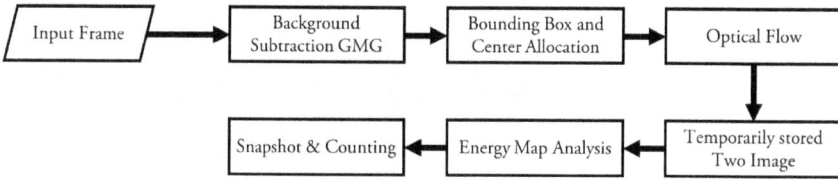

Fig. 9. System flow chart.

detect a specific direction of an incoming vehicle. Second, moving objects are extracted with the Gaussian Mixture and Gamma (GMG) background model segmentation method. Furthermore, pedestrians, motorcycles, and other non-target objects are filtered out by examining the object's width and area. The optical-flow method was then applied to determine the direction of the moving object in order to exclude reverse and wrong-way events. The center point of each moving object was recorded to exclude events in which a vehicle is temporarily parked. Then, to capture a snapshot of the license plate accurately, we utilized the energy-map method to determine the image that provided the clearest view of the license plate. Finally, the system counted the number of vehicles entering.

3.1. *Background subtraction by using the GMG model*

A fixed-background model is affected by changes in the lighting conditions and weather. Thus, we utilized the robust and adaptive GMG background subtraction algorithm.[17] The GMG model can adapt to changes in the lighting conditions and extract foreground information in all weather conditions. The GMG background model classifies the foreground and background of an image on the basis of Bayesian inference. As shown in Fig. 10(f), if the background, obtained from the GMG model, is stable, then no hole appears in the foreground. Then, a morphological filtering operation can be applied to remove noise and fill in small gaps to obtain a complete foreground object. In the GMG model, the foreground information is promptly discarded, thus allowing the model to adapt to environmental changes such as lighting conditions and object shadows. We also evaluated the Visual Background Extractor (VIBE), Mixture of Gaussian (MOG), and MOG2 methods and observed that the foreground integrity of the GMG method is higher than that of these algorithms, as illustrated in Fig. 10.

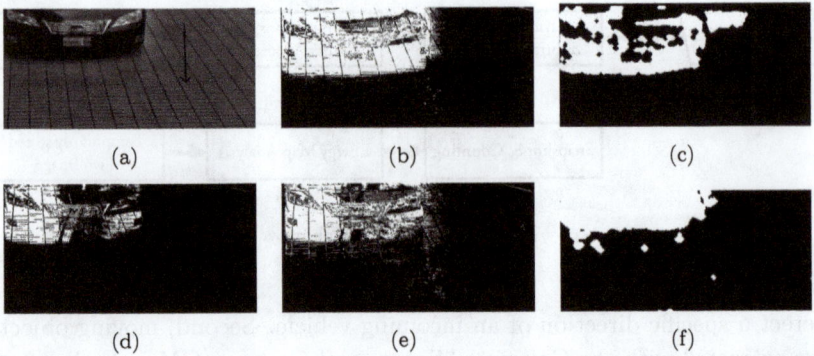

Fig. 10.   Different methods for obtaining the foreground: (a) original image; (b) frame difference; (c) VIBE; (d) MOG; (e) MOG2; (f) GMG model.

3.2. *Optical flow*

In Section 2.2, we mention that when reverse and wrong-way events occur, a false alarm is triggered by the vehicle detection system. Thus, we adopted an optical flow to detect the direction of the vehicle. After obtaining the direction, we excluded reverse and wrong-way events. The system then calculated a tolerance range of approximately 45° to determine if the direction of the vehicle was appropriate. Reverse and wrong-ways events are excluded if the angles exceeded the range. Figure 11 shows an example of our calculation results.

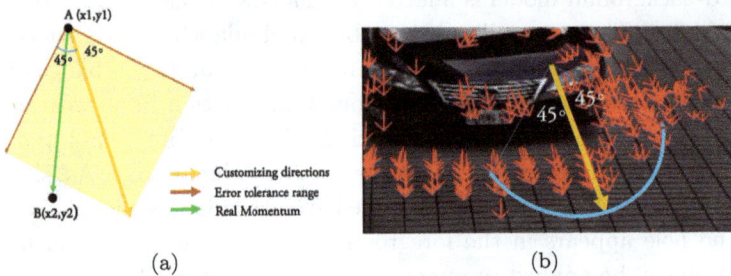

Fig. 11.   (a) Direction determination; (b) optical flow result.

3.3. *Bounding box and center allocation*

In Section 2.2, we introduce a situation of an automobile repair shop in which a vehicle often has to stop temporarily to await maintenance. To

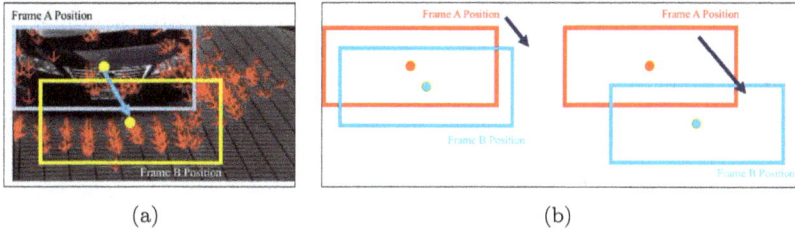

Fig. 12. (a) Measuring vehicle center-point changes; (b) smaller shift is identified as the same one (left), larger shift is identified as a new vehicle (right).

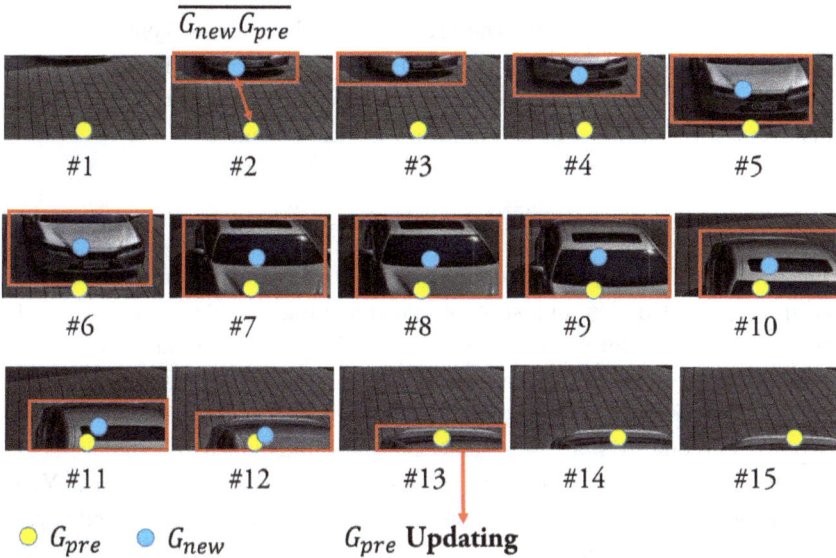

Fig. 13. The image sequence of incoming vehicle event and center allocation process.

avoid repeated counting and false alarms after the vehicle restarts, we compared the center point of the vehicle when it stops and when it is moving. If the difference is sufficiently small, the system determines the vehicle to be the same one. The center-point formula is expressed as $\overline{G_{new}G_{pre}} = \sqrt{(x_2 - x_1)^2 + (y_2 - y_1)^2}$, where $G_{new} = (x_1, y_1)$ is the current center-point location, and $G_{pre} = (x_2, y_2)$ is the previous center-point location. If $\overline{G_{new}G_{pre}}$ is greater than a certain threshold, then the vehicle is identified as a new vehicle; otherwise, the vehicle is identified as the same one, as shown in Fig. 12.

Figure 13 shows an image sequence of a vehicle entering. In frame #1, the vehicle detection system sets a default point G_{pre}, which was placed far away from the vehicle entry position. In frame #2, if the foreground area of the vehicle is larger than the threshold, the system initiates the calculation of the vehicles center position G_{new}. If $\overline{G_{new}G_{pre}}$ is greater than a certain threshold, then the vehicle is considered as a new vehicle. However, if the vehicle was moving forward, as appears in frame #10, and $\overline{G_{new}G_{pre}}$ is smaller than a certain threshold, then the vehicle is considered the same vehicle, temporarily parked in the FOV of the camera. In Image frame #13, if the foreground area of the vehicle is smaller than a certain threshold, then G_{new} is replaced by G_{pre}. For example, if a vehicle halts in the middle of the FOV of the camera and the vehicles center position G_{new} is replaced by G_{pre}, then G_{pre} is in the middle of the FOV of the camera. If the vehicle restarts and G_{pre} is smaller than the threshold, then this event is determined as a temporary parking event.

3.4. *Foreground energy-map analysis*

Once the vehicle image has been analyzed through the aforementioned procedure, we captured a snapshot of the incoming vehicle for license plate recognition. To ensure that an appropriate image is selected from a series of snapshots (e.g., Fig. 17(a) and (d)), we proposed the foreground energy-map analysis method and integrated the method into the vehicle detection system. The energy map represents the probability of a specific event occurring in a region and displays the energy levels in pseudo color. Yi *et al.*[16] applied this concept to demonstrate the probability that a pedestrian passes through a specific region in a station hall. Belardinelli *et al.*[18] utilized an energy map to illustrate the variation in momentum. In the figure, the red color represents a high-momentum region and the blue color represents a low-momentum region. Subsequently, a scoring factor is calculated on the basis of the vehicle foreground area on the energy map. Finally, the snapshot with the largest score is chosen. Algorithm 1 describes the proposed foreground energy-map analysis procedure.

First, we built an energy map based on the probability that vehicles appear in a region. The region is colored in red if the probability is high. Otherwise, the region is colored in colors such as yellow and blue. In the scenario considered here, the best timing to capture a snapshot is when the vehicle is entering the automobile repair shop (i.e., direction from top to bottom of the FOV of the camera). Thus, as shown in Fig. 17(c) and (f),

---

Algorithm 1 Foreground Energy Map Analysis

1: Build the energy map based on the probability of vehicles appear in the regions.
2: Divide the energy map into $n \times n = m$ blocks and set weighting coefficient $w(i), 1 \le i \le m$.
3: Compute Q_i (the sum of foreground pixels grey level in each block i) and set the block flag q_i.
4: Calculate $W = \sum_{i=1}^{m} q_i \times w_i$ for each block i.
5: **if** W is high **then**
6:    keep the snapshot image.
7: **end if**

---

the ROI is plotted in red at the top and in blue at the bottom of the energy map. The energy map is divided into $n \times n = m$ blocks as illustrated in Fig. 14.

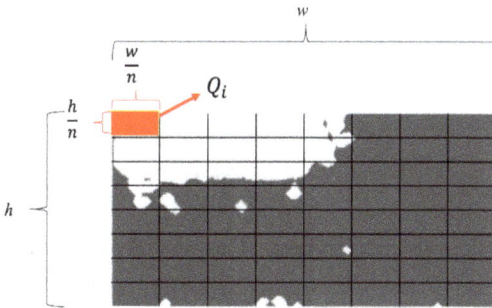

Fig. 14.   Energy map analysis conducted by dividing the image into $n \times n = m$ blocks.

Each block is assigned a weighting coefficient $w(i), 1 \le i \le m$. The red blocks in the figure indicate the possible vehicle entry region and thus have high weights. The yellow blocks represent the region that is near the edge of red blocks region and have lower weights. The blue blocks around the lower edge of the energy map are assigned the lowest weights because vehicles are not expected to enter from this location. The energy map is designed as presented in Fig. 15.

Once the energy map is completed, the foreground image can be used as an input for the energy-map analysis. For example, both foreground images in Fig. 17(b) and (e) were used to perform the energy-map analysis to determine the image that has the highest chance of containing the complete

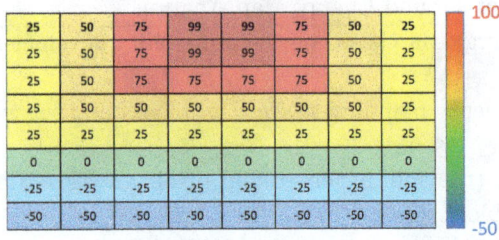

Fig. 15.   Example of an energy map.

license plate. Let Q_i be the sum of the foreground pixels gray level in each cell block i; then, the block flag q_i is set as follows.

$$q_i = \begin{cases} 1 \ if \ Q_i \geq E \\ 0 \ if \ Q_i < E \end{cases} \tag{1}$$

If Q_i is greater than the threshold E, then the block is flagged as $q_i = 1$ and regarded as the object foreground block; otherwise, the block is regarded as the background with $q_i = 0$. Let the total energy score be calculated as the follows.

$$W = \sum_{i=1}^{m} q_i \times w_i, \tag{2}$$

where w_i is the weighting coefficient for the block i. An energy map was developed according to the example presented in Fig. 15. Each block was assigned a score in the energy map. The red blocks in the figure represent the regions in which vehicles frequently appear and are assigned higher scores. The yellow blocks represent the region that is near the edge of an image and are assigned scores lower than those of the red blocks. The blue blocks are located at the lower edge of the energy map and are assigned the lowest scores because vehicles should not enter the automobile service shop by driving through this region. Once the energy map had been formed, the foreground image was used as an input for energy map analysis, and w_i was defined as the bonus score for each block i. Each w_i was multiplied with the flag of each block q_i; the sum of products was the calculated as the total score W of the image. Fig. 16(a) and (b) present the foreground image and the corresponding energy map, respectively. We observed that when a foreground object is located in the red color blocks, then a high value of W was attained, as presented in Fig. 16(b). Finally, the snapshot with the highest energy score W was selected. Then, W was utilized to compare the temporary images from a series of snapshots.

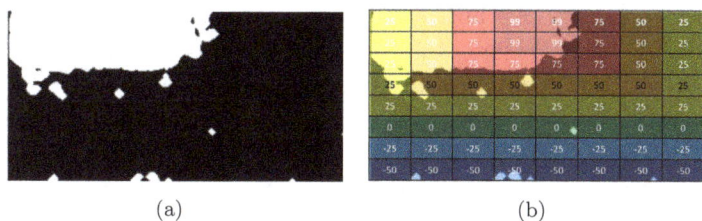

Fig. 16. An example of energy map analysis: (a) foreground image and (b) corresponding energy map.

We demonstrated several test results of the energy-map analysis method. If the vehicle moves away from the entrance gate, the total score is lower because the foreground pixels are closer to the edge of the image. If the vehicle is far from the entry position, the total score substantially decreases as well. Figure 17(c) shows a vehicle foreground image (Fig. 17(b)) of a vehicle that is completely located inside the entrance gate. Therefore, the image had a high energy score of W=2140. Figure 17(d) indicates a vehicle deviating from the FOV of the camera; therefore, the corresponding energy score W was as low as 290 (Fig. 17(f)). Thus, we adopted images with a high score as the candidates for further license plate recognition.

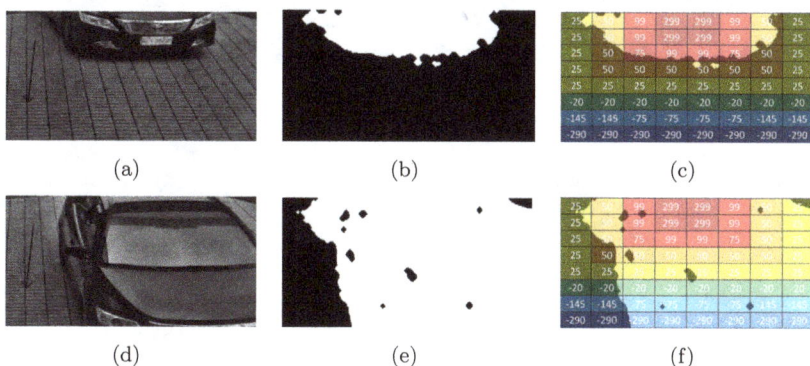

Fig. 17. (a) An image contains a license plate at time t; (b) foreground image; (c) the energy-map score W=2140; (d) when the detection proceeds at time $t + a$, the vehicle deviating from the FOV of the camera ; (e) foreground of (d); (f) the energy-map score W=290.

For a given image, the energy map was divided into small blocks. In general, the block size affects the reliability of the energy map for vehicle detection. On the basis of our empirical study, we observed that the accuracy of an energy map improves when it is divided into small blocks, as presented in Fig. 18. Figure 18(a) presents a 4×4 energy map that is divided into 16 blocks. An analysis of this energy map revealed that some energy map blocks cover many background pixels due to its rough resolution. Figure 18(b) presents an 8×8 energy map that is divided into 64 blocks. By comparing the energy scores of the 4×4 energy map of (Fig. 18(c)), and the 8×8 energy map of (Fig. 18(d)), we found that most of the foreground object pixels can be included appropriately in the 8×8 energy map blocks. This implies that a relatively precise energy score can be obtained when an energy map is divided into a relatively high number of energy blocks.

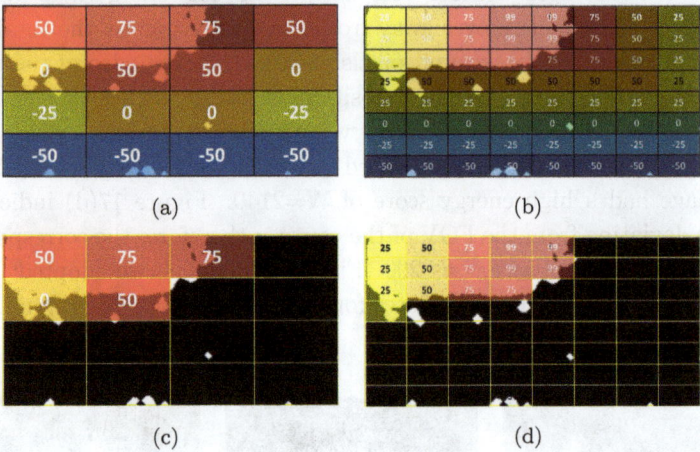

Fig. 18. Energy maps with (a) 4×4 blocks and (b) 8×8 blocks, Energy map scores obtained when an energy map is divided into (c) 4×4 blocks AND (d) 8×8 blocks.

4. Experimental Results

4.1. *Dataset*

To evaluate the deployed system, we collected a general type surveillance camera video from an automobile repair shop for a period of 20 days. Based on the timeline, we divided the test video into four time slots: (a) 7:00 a.m.~11:00 a.m., with soft daylight; (b) 11:00 a.m.~2:00 p.m., with stronger daylight; (c) 2:00 p.m.~7:00 p.m., with dim daylight; and (d) 7:00 p.m.~10:00 p.m., at night. Figure 19 presents the time schedule and environmental conditions of the recorded videos. We found that weather conditions varied in the 20-day video data, including sunny, cloudy, and rainy days. As shown in Fig. 19, two vertical black lines denote the business hours of the automobile repair shop — from 7:00 a.m. to 7:00 p.m. Finally, the ground truth was manually labelled and shown in Table 1. Therefore, we divided the data into two scenarios, one with and one without night records, and tested the reliability of the system. Scenario 1 was from 7:00 a.m. to 7:00 p.m. (business hours of the automobile repair shop), and scenario 2 was from 7:00 a.m. to 10:00 p.m. (before the system was shut down).

Fig. 19.   Time schedule and weather conditions of recorded video data.

4.2. *Experimental results and main issues analysis*

The proposed vehicle detection system was implemented on a personal computer with an Intel i5-760 quad-core CPU, 8 GB RAM, and 128 GB SSD. The performance was evaluated using the entire video dataset. Based on the two scenarios specified in Section 4.1, the test results are presented

Table 1. Experimental results.

	Scenario 1	Scenario 2
# of Ground Truth Vehicle	1360	1391
# of Detected Object	1360	1362
# of Detected Vehicle	1300	1302
Snapshot containing License Plate	1289	1291
# of Miss Vehicle	60	89
# of False Alarm	60	60
Correct Vehicle Detection Rate(%)	95.58%	93.60%
Snapshot Hit Rate(%)	99.16%	99.16%
Miss Rate(%)	4.41%	6.40%
False Alarm Rate(%)	4.41%	4.40%

in Table 1. For scenario 1, 1360 moving events were detected, with 1289 events being appropriate vehicle detections. The successful hit rate was approximately 95.58%. Sixty false alarm events occurred in total, representing a false alarm rate of approximately 4.41%. 60 vehicles were not detected in scenario 1; we classified them as missed detection events. The total missed detection rate was approximately 4.41%. We also noticed that the successful hit rate was lower in scenario 2 (93.60%). We observed a lower successful hit rate at night.

In addition, we reorganized the data for each time slot and present the detailed test results in Table 2. During the business hours, the system had a successful hit rate of over 95% for the time slot from 7:00 a.m. to 5:00 p.m. Due to the lack of a proper light source in the time slot of 7:0022:00 p.m., the hit rate decreased to 74.45%. The results demonstrate that the performance of the detection system is highly affected by light. Pedestrians generated a total of 39 false alarms, with a false alarm rate of 2.86%. Motorcycles generated a single false alarm, with a rate of 0.07%. Temporarily parked vehicles generated a total of 20 false alarms, with a rate of 1.46%. We conclude that pedestrians cause the highest number of false alarms.

4.2.1. *Details of false analyses in different weather conditions*

In Section 2.2, we discussed the challenges of image recognition in different weather conditions. We found that the proposed detection system has an optimal performance and provides an average successful detection rate of up to 96% during the daytime. We presented the experimental results obtained by using the system for vehicle detection during rainy weather

Table 2. Detail experimental results of 20-day data from 7:00AM to 10:00PM. *GT*: ground truth, *VC*: vehicle counting, *HR*: correct detection hit rate.

	07:00~11:00			11:00~14:00			14:00~17:00			17:00~:19:00			19:00~22:00			Overall Day and Night		
	GT	VC	HR	GT	VC	HR	GT	VC	HR	GT	VC	HR	GT	VC	HR	GT	VC	HR
Day1	-	-	-	-	-	-	20	19	95.00%	6	6	100%	3	0	0.00%	28	25	89.29%
Day2	25	25	100%	23	23	100%	23	23	100%	9	9	100%	0	0	-	80	80	100%
Day3	20	20	100%	15	14	93.33%	-	-	-	-	-	-	-	-	-	35	34	97.14%
Day4	26	26	100%	19	19	100%	20	20	100%	12	9	75.00%	4	1	25.00%	81	75	92.59%
Day5	25	24	96.00%	22	22	100%	25	25	100%	1	0	0.00%	0	0	-	73	71	97.26%
Day6	28	28	100%	24	24	100%	34	30	88.24%	12	7	58.33%	0	0	-	98	89	90.82%
Day7	20	18	90.00%	24	22	91.67%	16	16	100%	3	3	100%	0	0	-	63	59	93.65%
Day8	5	4	80.00%	8	8	100%	6	6	100%	2	2	100%	0	0	-	21	20	95.23%
Day9	32	30	93.75%	26	24	92.31%	24	22	91.67%	10	9	90.00%	5	0	0.00%	97	85	87.63%
Day10	17	17	100%	31	30	96.77%	18	18	100%	11	11	100%	5	0	0.00%	82	76	92.68%
Day11	18	18	100%	19	19	100%	21	20	95.23%	10	8	80.00%	0	0	-	68	65	95.58%
Day12	27	25	92.59%	16	14	87.50%	31	30	96.77%	9	9	100%	3	0	0.00%	86	78	90.70%
Day13	19	16	84.21%	19	19	100%	27	27	100%	11	9	81.82%	0	0	-	76	71	93.41%
Day14	8	8	100%	7	7	100%	7	6	85.71%	8	6	75.00%	0	0	-	30	27	90.00%
Day15	29	27	93.10%	24	23	95.83%	27	27	100%	6	6	100%	4	0	0.00%	90	83	92.22%
Day16	21	21	100%	29	29	100%	17	17	100%	15	13	86.67%	0	0	-	82	80	97.56%
Day17	25	25	100%	19	19	100%	36	35	97.22%	13	12	92.30%	1	0	0.00%	94	91	96.81%
Day18	8	8	100%	8	7	87.50%	13	11	84.62%	3	3	100%	1	0	0.00%	33	29	87.88%
Day19	26	24	92.30%	27	26	96.30%	31	31	100%	14	14	100%	4	1	25.00%	102	96	92.00%
Day20	20	16	80.00%	24	24	100%	28	28	100%	-	-	-	-	-	-	72	68	94.44%
Overall	399	381	95.49%	384	373	97.14%	424	411	96.93%	153	135	88.24%	31	2	6.45%	1391	1302	93.60%

in Table 2 in blue. On the basis of the results presented in Table 2, we observed that even in a rainy weather, the successful detection rate was high. We observed from the completeness of vehicle foreground detection results that despite the phenomenon of reflection from water, rainy days do not have much influence. The proposed detection system had an average successful detection rate of up to 92% in rainy weather.

However, the successful detection rate declined to 6.45% during the nighttime. By comparing scenario 1 and scenario 2, we found that the detection hit rate was very low at night. The foreground image of a vehicle is considerably small, and thus, the proposed system failed to function appropriately at night. We observed that foreground images contained residual data pertaining to the body of a vehicle; this data were highly volatile. In some cases, the system could not differentiate between the body of a vehicle and the dark background, as presented in Fig. 20.

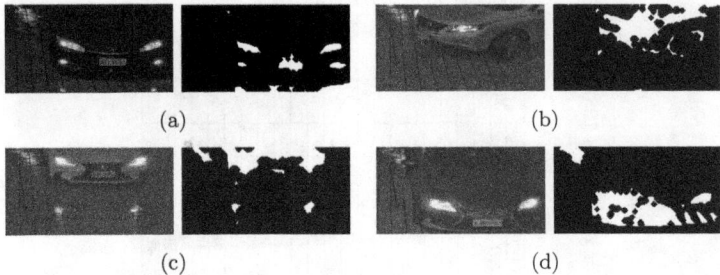

(a)   (b)

(c)   (d)

Fig. 20.   Failed detections during nighttime. In each case, the image on the left is the input image, and the one on the right is the object detection result.

4.2.2. *Pedestrian analysis*

The entrance of an automobile service shop is an open area and many pedestrians may pass through this area. These pedestrians may cause false alarms when a vehicle detection system is used. Therefore, in this section, we discuss the false alarm problem caused by pedestrians. Among the 3554 events that included pedestrians in scenario 1, only 39 events caused false alarms. The false alarm ratio was only 1.09%. Moreover, in scenario 2, the false alarm ratio was only 1.07% (number of false alarms / total number of events that included pedestrians = 39/3621). This result suggests that the proposed system can avoid most false alarms even during the nighttime. The test results are listed in the Table 4. The results revealed that most

Table 3. Results of counting vehicles in a rainy weather (Scenario 2: 7:00 AM ~ 10:00 PM). *GT*: ground truth, *VC*: vehicle counting, and *HR*: correct detection hit rate.

| | Scenario 2 | | | | | | | | | | | | | | | | | |
| | 07:00~11:00 | | | 11:00~14:00 | | | 14:00~17:00 | | | 17:00~19:00 | | | 19:00~22:00 | | | Full Day | | |
	GT	VC	HR	GT	VC	HR	GT	VC	HR	GT	VC	HR	GT	VC	HR	GT	VC	HR
Day1	25	25	100.00%	23	23	100.00%	20	19	95.00%	6	6	100.00%	3	0	0.00%	28	25	89.29%
Day2	20	20	100.00%	15	14	93.33%	23	23	100.00%	9	9	100.00%	0	0	0.00%	80	80	100.00%
Day3	25	24	96.00%	19	19	100.00%	20	20	100.00%				0	0		35	34	97.14%
Day4	28	28	100.00%	22	22	100.00%	25	25	100.00%	12	9	75.00%	4	1	25.00%	81	75	92.59%
Day5	20	18	90.00%	24	24	100.00%	34	30	88.24%	1	0	0.00%	0	0		73	71	97.26%
Day6	5	4	80.00%	24	22	91.67%	6	6	100.00%	12	7	58.33%	0	0		98	89	90.82%
Day7	32	30	93.75%	8	8	100.00%	24	22	91.67%	3	3	100.00%	0	0		63	59	93.65%
Day8	17	17	100.00%	26	24	92.31%	18	18	100.00%	2	2	100.00%	0	0		21	20	95.23%
Day9	18	18	100.00%	31	30	96.77%	21	20	95.23%	10	9	90.00%	5	0	0.00%	97	85	87.63%
Day10	27	25	92.59%	19	19	100.00%	31	30	96.77%	11	11	100.00%	5	0	0.00%	82	76	92.68%
Day11	19	16	84.21%	16	14	87.50%	27	27	100.00%	10	8	80.00%	0	0		68	65	95.58%
Day12	8	8	100.00%	19	19	100.00%	7	6	85.71%	9	9	100.00%	3	0	0.00%	86	78	90.70%
Day13	29	27	93.10%	24	23	95.83%	24	23	95.83%	11	9	81.82%	0	0		76	71	93.41%
Day14	21	21	100.00%	29	29	100.00%	29	29	100.00%	8	6	75.00%	0	0		30	27	90.00%
Day15	25	25	100.00%	19	19	100.00%	17	17	100.00%	6	6	100.00%	4	0	0.00%	90	83	92.22%
Day16	8	8	100.00%	8	7	87.50%	36	35	97.22%	15	13	86.67%	0	0		82	80	97.56%
Day17	26	24	92.30%	27	26	96.30%	13	11	84.62%	13	12	92.30%	1	0	0.00%	94	91	96.81%
Day18	8	8	100.00%	24	24	100.00%	31	31	100.00%	3	3	100.00%	1	0	0.00%	33	29	87.88%
Day19	26	24	92.30%	27	26	96.30%	28	28	100.00%	14	14	100.00%	4	1	25.00%	102	96	92.00%
Day20	20	16	80.00%	24	24	100.00%	28	28	100.00%				1	0		72	68	94.44%
Total	399	381	95.49%	384	373	97.14%	424	411	96.93%	153	135	88.24%	31	2	6.45%	1391	1302	93.60%

Table 4.   Detection results of pedestrians events.

	Scenario 1	Scenario 2
Video Length (day)	20	20
Time Period	07:00∼19:00	07:00∼22:00
# of Pedestrians	3554	3621
Fail Exclusion	39	39
Correct Exclusion	3515	3582
Miss Rate (%)	1.09%	1.07%
Correct Detection Rate (%)	98.91%	98.93%

pedestrian events could be avoided by using the proposed system, and only a small subset of pedestrian events would cause a false alarm. The false alarm examples are presented in Fig. 21. The false alarm example presented in Fig. 21(a) is based on the condition that a group of pedestrians entered the automobile service shop in a very short period of time. When a small group of people entered through the entrance, the crowd appeared very large and the area was close to the entrance, thus resulting in a false alarm. Fig. 21(b) presents another case in which a pedestrian held an umbrella, and thus, a false alarm was triggered.

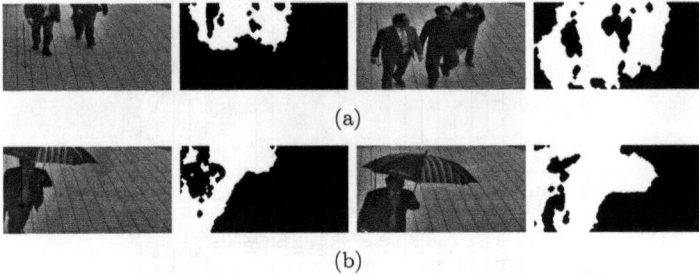

(a)

(b)

Fig. 21.   Cases in which false alarms were triggered due to pedestrians.

4.2.3. *Motorcycles analysis*

There are many employees who may enter the automobile service shop by riding a motorcycle. During the 20-day test, 55 motorcycles entered the automobile service shop. One of the motorcycles had goods hanging on both sides of the vehicle; thus, a false alarm was triggered. In summary, only one false alarm was triggered for motorcycles. The failure rate of detection was 1.82%, and the overall detection success rate by excluding the false alarm

Table 5. Detection results of motorcycles events.

	Scenario 1	Scenario 2
Video Length (day)	20	20
Time Period	07:00~19:00	07:00~22:00
# of Motorcycles	55	55
Fail Exclusion	1	1
Correct Exclusion	54	54
Miss Rate (%)	1.82%	1.82%
Correct Detection (%)	98.18%	98.18%

caused due to motorcycles was 98.18%, as presented in Table 5. The system performed very well when the false alarm due to motorcycles was excluded. Only one false alarm occurred due to motorcycles, as presented in Fig. 22. Because the motorcycle was carrying a large item, the foreground width of the vehicle increased, thus causing the false alarm.

(a)

Fig. 22. False alarm caused by a motorcycle that carried a large item.

4.2.4. *Wrong direction and backward movement analysis*

The problem pertaining to the reverse movement of a vehicle is discussed in Section 2.2. Many vehicles may not follow the correct direction when entering the automobile service shop. This behavior may cause the vehicle detection system to generate false alarms. During the 20-day test, a total of 182 wrong direction and backward movement events occurred. We used the optical flow method to successfully exclude all the wrong direction and backward movement events, thus achieving a 100% accurate detection rate. Table 6 presents the detection results. The proposed optical flow verification method can effectively determine the vehicle momentum.

Section 2.2 described the problem of reverse movement of the vehicle. Many vehicles may not follow the correct direction to enter the automobile service shop. This behavior may cause the vehicle detection system to generate false alarms. Within the span of the 20-day experiments, there were a total of 182 wrong way and backward movement events that occurred.

Table 6. Detection results of wrong direction and backward movement events.

	Scenario 1	Scenario 2
Video Length (day)	20	20
Time Period	07:00~19:00	07:00~22:00
# of Wrong way and backward events	182	182
Fail Exclusion	0	0
Correct Exclusion	182	182
Miss Rate (%)	0.00%	0.00%
Correct Detection Rate (%)	100.00%	100.00%

Table 7. Detection results of temporary parking events.

	Scenario 1	Scenario 2
Video Length (day)	20	20
Time Period	07:00~19:00	07:00~22:00
# of Temporary Parking Events	275	275
Fail Exclusion	20	20
Correct Exclusion	255	255
Miss Rate (%)	7.27%	7.27%
Correct Detection Rate (%)	92.73%	92.73%

We used the optical flow method to successfully exclude all the wrong way and backwards movement events, achieving 100% correct detection rate. Table 6 presents the detection results. We conclude that the proposed optical flow verification method can effectively determine the momentum of a vehicle.

4.2.5. *Temporary parking event analysis*

As described in Section 2.2, often, several vehicles enter the automobile service shop simultaneously. When this situation occurs, an incoming vehicle can be temporarily blocked within the FOV of the mounted camera. During the 20-day test, a total of 275 temporary parking events occurred. The vehicle detection system generated 20 false alarms and was able to successfully identify 255 temporary parking events. Thus, the false alarm rate for the temporary parking event was 7.27%, as presented in Table 7. A few false alarms were caused by a broken foreground image. The other false alarms were due to a mismatch of the center-of-gravity point of the vehicle, as presented in Fig. 23.

(a)

(b)

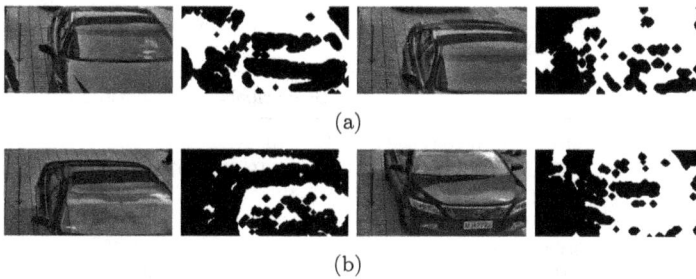

Fig. 23.   False alarms due to temporary parking events.

Table 8.   Experimental results of missing detection of vehicles.

	Scenario 1	Scenario 2
Vehicle Ground Truth	1360	1391
# of Detected Vehicles	1360	1362
Hit	1300	1302
Miss	60	89
False Alarm	60	60
Hit Rate (%)	95.58%	93.60%
Miss Rate (%)	4.41%	6.40%
False Alarm Rate(%)	4.41%	4.40%

4.2.6. *Missing detection of vehicles*

Table 8 reveals that some vehicles were not detected during the test. In scenario 1, a total of 1360 objects were detected, of which 60 were false alarms, and 60 vehicles were entirely missed. Thus, a missed detection rate of 4.41% was observed. In scenario 2, the number of missed detections was 89, and the missed detection rate was 6.40%. These results demonstrate that the vehicle detection system frequently fails to detect vehicles at night. By comparing scenario 1 and scenario 2, we found that the detection success rate is very low at night due to dark images.

4.2.7. *Snapshot without including the license plate*

In Section 2.2, we specified a problem pertaining to a missing license plate. We obtained the snapshots taken while conducting the experiments and developed energy maps to analyze the 1302 vehicle images. Among these images, 1291 images of vehicles contained license plates. Thus, the rate

Table 9.   Experimental results of snapshots without including the license plate.

	Scenario 1	Scenario 2
Video Length (day)	20	20
Time Period	07:00~19:00	07:00~22:00
Snapshot of vehicle counting	1300	1302
Snapshot with license plate	1289	1291
Missing license plate	11	11
Hit Rate (%)	99.16%	99.16%
Miss Rate(%)	0.84%	0.84%

of taking a snapshot without including a license plate was only 0.84%, as
presented in Table 9. These results highly support the assertion that the use
of energy maps can effectively solve the problem of identifying the vehicle
images that do not contain license plates.

By using the energy map analysis algorithm specified in Section 3.4,
appropriate vehicle images could be selected. However, in some cases, the
license plate may not be present in the selected snapshot for a vehicle.
Figure 24 presents such a failure case. In Fig. 24, (a) and (d) present
two video frames of an incoming vehicle. Fig. 24 (b) and (e) denote the
foreground object images of Fig. 24 (a) and (d), respectively. Fig. 24 (a) was
captured because the light of the vehicles headlight was observed. However,
the vehicle did not enter the camera FOV when the snapshot was taken.
Fig. 24 (d) displays a vehicle entering the FOV of the camera. For this
case, we used the energy map method to analyze Fig. 24 (b) and (e), and
determined which foreground image had a higher probability of containing
the license plate. Fig. 24 (c) and (f) present the results obtained after
conducting an energy map analysis on Fig. 24 (b) and (e), respectively.
The energy map analysis result shows that Fig. 24 (c) had a higher energy
score than Fig. 24 (f). Thus, we selected Fig. 24 (b) as the most suitable
snapshot for the vehicle. However, Fig. 24 (b) does not contain a license
plate.

Figure 25 presents another failure case that does not contain a license
plate. In this case, Fig. 25 (a) displays a vehicle that is turning and entering
into the FOV of the camera, but we cannot see the license plate. Fig. 25
(c) displays an image in which the front of the vehicle had gradually turned
to the correct direction. Therefore, we used energy map analysis. Fig. 25
(c) and (f) present the energy map analysis results of Fig. 25 (b) and (e),
respectively. The result displays that Fig. 25 (c) had a higher energy score

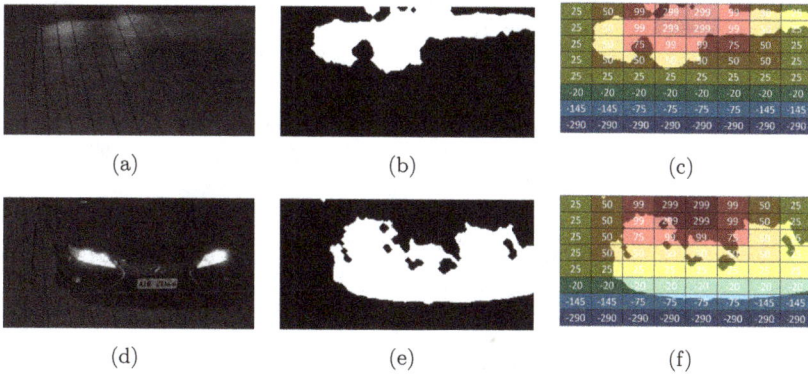

Fig. 24.   Failed case in which the snapshot does not contain a license plate. The energy score for (c) is 2066 and that for (f) is 728.

than Fig. 25 (f). Thus, we selected Image Fig. 25 (a) as the final snapshot. However, Fig. 25 (a) does not contain a license plate.

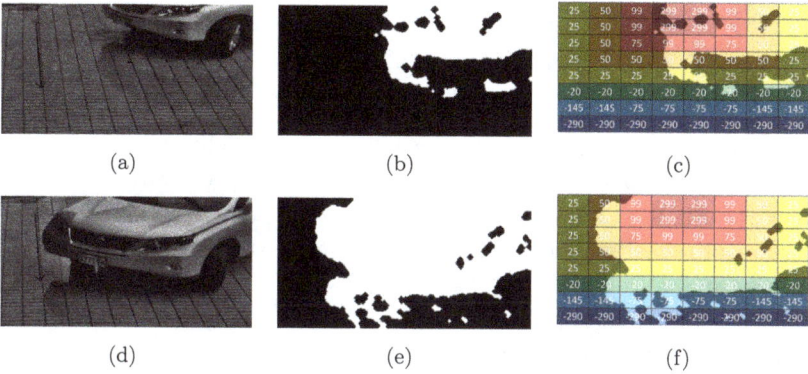

Fig. 25.   Failed case in which the snapshot does not contain a license plate. The energy score for (c) 1967 and that for (f) is 1641.

4.2.8. *Overall false alarms analysis*

All the false alarm cases are listed in Table 10 on the basis of the results of the experiments. The data recorded by a surveillance camera mounted in an automobile service shop during a 20-day test were analyzed. A total of 60 false alarms occurred; thus, the overall false alarm rate was 4.40%. Note that 39 false alarms were due to pedestrians; thus, the corresponding false

Table 10. Overall false alarms analysis.

	Scenario 1	Scenario 2
Video Length (day)	20	20
Time Period	07:00∼19:00	07:00∼22:00
# of Detected Objects	1360	1362
Total False alarms	60	60
# of Pedestrians	39	39
# of Motorcycles	1	1
# of Wrong way and backward movements	0	0
# of Temporary parking events	20	20
Overall False alarm rate (%)	4.40%	4.40%
False alarm rate of Pedestrian (%)	2.86%	2.86%
False alarm rate of Motorcycles (%)	0.07%	0.07%
False alarm rate of Wrong way (%)	0.00%	0.00%
False alarm Rate of Temporary parking (%)	1.46%	1.46%

alarm rate was 2.86%. Moreover, one false alarm was due to a motorcycle, and the corresponding false alarm rate was 0.07%. Temporary parking events caused 20 false alarms, and the corresponding false alarm rate was 1.46%. Pedestrians caused the highest number of false alarms.

4.3. *Performance comparison*

Our algorithm was implemented in all weather conditions and complex environments. However, most other algorithms are specifically designed for highway and normal road environment, where false alarms do not occur. Five vehicle detection methods were compared in this study. Zheng *et al.*[19] used a Convolutional Neural Network (CNN) to construct a virtual coil and make the counting decisions. Yuan *et al.*[20] proposed neighborhood gradient prediction for extracting a feature and applying this feature to detect a vehicle. Tourani *et al.*[21] utilized edge detection, motion detection, and a Kalman filter to detect a vehicle. Song *et al.*[22] proposed a vehicle counting method that applied background subtraction and considers the ROI. As shown in Table 11, our algorithm exhibits promising performance in a complex environment and various lighting conditions.

5. Conclusion

This paper presented a complete solution for outdoor vehicle detection in the open area of an automobile repair shop entrance gate. The background subtraction method was utilized to extract foreground information of a

Table 11. Performance comparison.

			Method		
	Zheng et al.[19]	Yuan et al.[20]	Tourani et al.[21]	Song et al.[22]	Our method
Test Site	Highway (one-way)	Road (one-way)	Road (one-way)	Highway (one-way)	Automobile Service Shop (open space area)
Dataset Length	20 min	48 hours	3 mins	52 hours	280 hours, 20 days
All-weather	√	√	√	√	√
Pedestrain					√
Motorcycle			√		√
Reversing					√
Temporary stop					
Correct Detection Rate	92.3%	97.5%	95.9%	97.46%	Day-time 95.58% Day/Night 93.60%

moving object. Optical flow was then applied to determine the direction of an incoming vehicle. A foreground energy-map analysis was proposed to improve the reliability of the snapshot captured during vehicle detection. The proposed system was implemented and tested for 20 days at an automobile repair shop in all weather conditions and complex environments. The experimental results showed a highly promising detection performance with a hit rate as high as 95.58%. We conclude that the proposed computer vision system successfully excludes many specific unwanted events and has reliable vehicle detection performance. It can replace sensors, thus improving its acceptance by industry. In our energy-map analysis, the energy map was generated manually. Recently, machine learning or deep learning techniques have improved and presented promising results for vehicle counting and intelligent transportation system applications.[23-25] In the future, the energy map could be automatically generated using deep learning algorithms, increasing the adaptability of the system.

Acknowledgments

This work was supported in part by the Ministry of Science and Technology, Taiwan, Grant 105-2622-E-305-00-CC3 and by the Orbit Technology Incorporation.

References

1. B. Coifman, D. Beymer, P. McLauchlan, and J. Malik, A real-time computer vision system for vehicle tracking and traffic surveillance, *Transportation Research Part C: Emerging Technologies*, **6**(4), 271–288 (1998).
2. N. Buch, S. A. Velastin, and J. Orwell, A review of computer vision techniques for the analysis of urban traffic, *IEEE Transactions on Intelligent Transportation Systems*, **12**(3), 920–939 (2011).
3. A. Hanif, A. B. Mansoor, and A. S. Imran, Performance analysis of vehicle detection techniques: A concise survey. In *World Conference on Information Systems and Technologies*, pp. 491–500 (2018).
4. I. Sina, A. Wibisono, A. Nurhadiyatna, and B. Hardjono, Vehicle counting and speed measurement using headlight detection. In *Proc. Conf. Advanced Computer Science and Information Systems*, pp. 149–154 (2013).
5. X. Pan, Y. Guo, and A. Men, Traffic surveillance system for vehicle flow detection. In *Proc. Int. Conf. Computer Modeling and Simulation*, pp. 314–318 (2010).
6. J.-M. Guo, C.-H. Hsia, K.-S. Wong, and J.-Y. Wu, Night-time vehicle lamp detection and tracking with adaptive mask training. In *IEEE Trans. Vehicular Technology*, pp. 4023–4032 (2015).

7. N. Miller, M. A. Thomas, J. A. Eichel, and A. Mishra, A Hidden Markov Model for vehicle detection and counting. In *Proc. Conf. Computer and Robot Vision*, pp. 269–276 (2015).

8. N. Seenouvong, U. Watchareeruetai, C. Nuthong, and K. Khongsomboon, A computer vision based vehicle detection and counting system. In *Proc. Int. Conf. Knowledge and Smart Technology*, pp. 224–227 (2016).

9. S. Meany, E. Eskew, R. Martinez-Castro, and S. Jang, Automated vehicle counting using image processing and machine learning. In *Proc. SPIE*, vol. 10170 (2017).

10. S. Choudhury, S. P. Chattopadhyay, and T. K. Hazra, Vehicle detection and counting using haar feature-based classifier. In *2017 8th Annual Industrial Automation and Electromechanical Engineering Conference*, pp. 106–109 (2017).

11. F. Mehboob, M. Abbas, R. Jiang, A. Rauf, S. A. Khan, and S. Rehman, Trajectory based vehicle counting and anomalous event visualization in smart cities, *Cluster Computing*, pp. 1–10 (2017).

12. J. Ren, C. Zhang, L. Zhang, N. Wang, and Y. Feng, Automatic measurement of traffic state parameters based on computer vision for intelligent transportation surveillance, *International Journal of Pattern Recognition and Artificial Intelligence.* **32**(04), 1855003 (2018).

13. N. S. Chauhan, F. Rahman, R. Sarker, and M. M. H. Pious, Vehicle detection, tracking and counting using linear quadratic estimation technique. In *2018 2nd International Conference on Inventive Systems and Control* (2018).

14. D. Sahgal, A. Ramesh, and M. Parida, Real-time vehicle queue detection at urban traffic intersection using image processing, *International Journal of Engineering Science and Generic Research.* **4**(2) (2018).

15. K. B. Saran and G. Sreelekha, Traffic video surveillance: Vehicle detection and classification. In *Proc. Int. Conf. Control Communication and Computing India*, pp. 516–521 (2015).

16. S. Yi, H. Li, and X. Wang, Understanding pedestrian behaviors from stationary crowd groups. In *Proc. Computer Vision and Pattern Recognition*, pp. 3488–3496 (2015).

17. A. B. Godbehere, A. Matsukawa, and K. Goldberg, Visual tracking of human visitors under variable-lighting conditions for a responsive audio art installation. In *Proc. American Control Conference*, pp. 4305–4312 (2012).

18. A. Belardinelli, F. Pirri, and A. Carbone, Motion saliency maps from spatiotemporal filtering. In *Proc. Int. Workshop on Attention in Cognitive Systems*, pp. 112–123 (2009).

19. J. Zheng, Y. Wang, and W. Zeng, CNN based vehicle counting with virtual coil in traffic surveillance video. In *Proc. Int. Conf. Multimedia Big Data*, pp. 280–281 (2015).

20. Y. Yuan, Y. Zhao, and X. Wang, Day and night vehicle detection and counting in complex environment. In *Proc. Int. Conf. Image and Vision Computing New Zealand*, pp. 453–458 (2013).

21. A. Tourani and A. Shahbahrami, Vehicle counting method based on digital image processing algorithms. In *Proc. Int. Conf. Pattern Recognition and*

Image Analysis, pp. 1–6 (2015).

22. J. Song, H. Song, and W. Wang, An accurate vehicle counting approach based on block background modeling and updating. In *Proc. Int. Conf. Image and Signal Processing,* pp. 16–21 (2014).

23. J. Chung and K. Sohn, Image-based learning to measure traffic density using a deep convolutional neural network, *IEEE Transactions on Intelligent Transportation Systems.* **19**(5), 1670–1675 (2018).

24. H. Wang, M. Mazari, M. Pourhomayoun, J. Smith, H. Owens, and W. Chernicoff, An end-to-end traffic vision and counting system using computer vision and machine learning: The challenges in real-time processing, *SIGNAL 2018 Editors.* p. 13 (2018).

25. S. Awang and N. M. A. N. Azmi, Vehicle counting system based on vehicle type classification using deep learning method. In *IT Convergence and Security 2017,* pp. 52–59 (2018).

Chapter 13

Automatic High-Speed Compressive Tracking with Motion Prediction

Hongjun Li[*] and Wei Hu

School of Electronic and Information, Nantong University,
Nantong, 226019, China
*lihongjun@ntu.edu.cn

Compressive tracking algorithm is a simple and efficient tracking algorithm, which has good accuracy and a robust performance. Despite much success that has been demonstrated, numerous issues remain to be addressed. First, the samples selected by the algorithm do not have discriminative representation and the number of samples is relatively huge affecting the computational complexity. Furthermore, the search window of the algorithm is fixed, so when the target scale changes, noise is introduced into the Bayes classification model easily and leads to the loss of tracking. In this chapter an automatic compressive tracking based on motion prediction is proposed. The number of samples is reduced and the tracking speed is improved by using motion prediction, the tracking accuracy is also improved by adjusting the tracking window size adaptively. Extensive experiments in subjective and objective comparison are performed on the OTB datasets and the VOT challenge 2014 datasets. Experimental results show that the accuracy, robustness and computational complexity of our tracker have been improved. The proposed algorithm is significantly better than several state-of-art algorithms on the OTB datasets and the VOT challenge 2014 datasets. The computational efficiency of the proposed algorithm is reduced by 75% compared to compressive tracking and nearly 10% of the DSST tracker which is the winner of VOT 2014.

1. Introduction

With the rapid development of electronic technology, computer vision has become a hot research topic. Video object tracking is an issue which contains image processing[1], pattern recognition[2], signal processing and so on. Object tracking remains a challenging problem due to the change in appearance caused by pose, illumination, occlusion, motion and so on. An effective appearance model is of prime importance for the success of a tracking algorithm and has attracted much attention in recent years.

Numerous effective representation schemes have been proposed for robust object tracking in recent years. Isard and Blake[3] introduced the particle filter theory into the field of machine vision last century. Collins et al.[4] considered the object tracking as a binary classification problem and used the forward learning binary classifier to classify the target and the background. Parag et al.[5] proposed an adaptive boosting linear weak classifier. Hidayatullah et al.[6] used camshift to improve multi-hue and multi-object tracking performance. Candès et al.[7] proposed the theory of compressive sensing, and Zhang et al.[8] introduced it into the field of object tracking. However, the explosive growth of video information aggravates the burden on computers[9]. If the target tracking process time can be reduced, it will help us a lot. So, reducing the complexity of the algorithm to improve the efficiency needs further study.

Recently, Yang et al.[10] proposed a compressive tracking method based on SIFT[11], to solve the problem of non-adaptive scale. Zhang et al.[12] proposed an adaptive method for learning the parameters of compressive tracking. Fiza et al.[13] predicted the position of the image by the motion history. The compressive sensing theory[14] shows that if the dimension of the feature space is sufficiently high, these features can be projected to a randomly chosen low-dimensional space which contains enough information to reconstruct the original high-dimensional features. The dimensionality reduction method via random projection[15] is data-independent, non-adaptive and information-preserving. Although these algorithms improve the robustness of compressive tracking, there still exists several problems. First, the calculation of the tracking process is huge, second, the size of the search window cannot change adaptively, and it introduces the noise into the classifier easily. Furthermore, when the objects scale changes, it is difficult to detect the targets.

To solve these problems, this chapter analyzed the compressive tracking algorithms in detail and designed a novel tracking algorithm based on motion prediction. The algorithm reduces the number of the candidate samples collected and improves the operating speed of the algorithm by utilizing motion prediction. By using the adaptive size of the search window algorithm, it adapts the scales of the target and avoids the noise into the module of the classifier. The proposed compressive tracking algorithm runs in real-time and performs favorably against state-of-the-art trackers on challenging sequences in terms of efficiency, accuracy and robustness.

We proposed a high speed compressive tracking based on motion prediction with an adaptive size of search window (ASSWCT), which learns motion direction for search and scale estimation. Several advantages of ASSWCT is summarized as follows: (1) predict motion direction to reduce the candidate region; (2) change the size of search range adaptively by the motion vector; (3) collect the positive and negative samples according to the success rate; (4) change the size of the tracking window adaptively according to the size of the target; (5) run in real-time and perform favorably against state-of-the-art trackers on challenging sequences in terms of efficiency, accuracy and robustness.

The remainder of the chapter is organized as follows. In section 2, we introduce compressive tracking. Section 3 presents a high speed compressive tracking algorithm based on motion prediction and the details are shown in Section 4. Section 5 is devoted to experimental results and analysis, and Section 6 concludes the chapter.

2. Compressive Tracking

The compressive tracking algorithm proposed by Zhang et al.[12] is divided into three parts, namely, feature extraction, feature compression, classifier construction and update.

2.1. *Compressed Sensing*

A random matrix $R \in \mathbb{R}^{n \times m}$ whose rows have unit length projects data from the high-dimensional feature space $x \in \mathbb{R}^m$ to a lower-dimensional space $v \in \mathbb{R}^n$

$$v = Rx \tag{1}$$

where $n \ll m$. Each projection v is essentially equivalent to a compressive measurement in the compressive sensing encoding stage. If the random matrix R in (1) satisfies the Johnson-Lindenstrauss lemma, x can be reconstructed with minimum error from v with high probability if x is K-sparse. This strong theoretical support motivates us to analyze the high-dimensional signals via their low-dimensional random projections.

2.2. *Feature Extraction*

As the coefficients in the measurement matrix can be positive or negative, the compressive features compute the relative intensity difference in a way like the generalized Haar-like features. Haar-like features are similar to Haar wavelet, whose characteristic value is the difference between two matrix pixels. Usually, Haar-like feature can be calculated by the integral image method. The large set of Haar-like features are compressively sensed with a very sparse measurement matrix. The compressive sensing theories ensure that the extracted features of our algorithm preserve almost all the information of the original image. Therefore, we can classify the projected features in the compressed domain efficiently without the curse of dimensionality.

2.3. *Feature Compression*

A very sparse random measurement matrix which can compress features, is defined as:

$$R_{ij} = \sqrt{s} \times \begin{cases} 1, & p=\dfrac{1}{2s} \\ 0, & p = 1-\dfrac{1}{s} \\ -1, & p=\dfrac{1}{2s} \end{cases} \qquad (2)$$

Acholioptas proved that this type of matric with $s=1$ or $s=3$ satisfies the Johnson-Lindenstrauss lemma. This matrix is easy to compute which requires only a uniform random generator. More importantly, when $s=3$, it is sparse where two thirds of the computation can be avoided. Furthermore, only the nonzero entries of R need to be stored which makes the memory requirement also very light. The features can then be compressed by function (1), where $x \in R^m$ is the original feature and $R \in R^{n \times m}$ is the measurement matrix. Therefore, the projected features can be classified in the compressed domain efficiently without the curse of dimensionality.

2.4. *Classifier Construction and Update*

We assume all elements in v are independently distributed and modeled with a naive Bayes classifier,

$$H(v) = \log\left(\frac{\prod_{i=1}^{n} p(v_i \mid y =1)p(y=1)}{\prod_{i=1}^{n} p(v_i \mid y = 0)p(y=0)} \right) = \sum_{i=1}^{n} \log\left(\frac{p(v_i \mid y =1)}{p(v_i \mid y = 0)} \right) \qquad (3)$$

where we assume uniform prior, $p(y=1) = p(y=0)$, and $y \in \{0,1\}$ is a binary variable which represents the sample label.

Diaconis and Freedman[17] show that random projections of high dimensional random vectors are almost Gaussian. Thus, the conditional distributions $p(v_i \mid y=1)$ and $p(v_i \mid y=0)$ in the classifier $H(v)$ are assumed to be Gaussian distributed with four parameters $(\mu_i^1, \sigma_i^1, \mu_i^0, \sigma_i^0)$ where,

$$p(v_i \mid y=1) \sim N(\mu_i^1, \sigma_i^1), p(v_i \mid y=0) \sim N(\mu_i^0, \sigma_i^0) \qquad (4)$$

where $\mu_i^1(\mu_i^0)$ and $\sigma_i^1(\sigma_i^0)$ are the mean and standard deviation of the positive(negative) class. The scale parameters in (4) are incremental updated by

$$\mu_i^1 \leftarrow \lambda\mu_i^1 + (1-\lambda)\mu_i^1$$

$$\sigma_i^1 \leftarrow \sqrt{\lambda(\sigma_i^1)^2 + (1-\lambda)(\sigma^1)^2 + \lambda(1-\lambda)(\mu_i^1 - \mu^1)^2} \qquad (5)$$

where $\lambda > 0$ is a learning parameter, $\sigma^1 = \sqrt{\dfrac{1}{n}\sum_{k=0|y=0}^{n-1}(v_i(k) - \mu^1)^2}$,

$\mu^1 = \dfrac{1}{n}\sum_{k=0|y=0}^{n-1}v_i(k)$. Parameters μ_i^0 and σ_i^0 are updated with similar rules. The above equations can be easily derived by the maximum likelihood estimation.

3. Automatic High-speed Compressive Tracking Based on Motion Prediction

3.1. *Motion Prediction*

In Ref. 8, the search strategy considers the area as the candidate region which is around the upper left corner of the previous target of the 20 Euclidean distances. The center is the position of the left vertex of the target in the previous image, and the other white pixels are the left vertexes of the candidate region. Then, features of every candidate region which provides 50 compressive Haar-like features are extracted. Last, these features of different candidate regions are calculated by a naive Bayes classifier, and the optimal region is selected as the target region in the current frame.

In the process of determining the target region, using such a broad search strategy is not a good idea and wastes computing time. So, the motion prediction is introduced into the search strategy to predict the motion direction of the target. Then, search the target meticulously in the predicted direction and roughly in other directions. There are many algorithms to predict motion trends, such as motion prediction combined with Mean Shift, and Motion History Image. When the tracking algorithm combines with the motion prediction, the robustness will be improved. However, the complexity of calculation is reduced by little, therefore, we will take an effective strategy to predict the motion, and try to reduce the computing complexity.

Assuming that the algorithm can track the target stably and the tracking result of the previous frames is correct, we can get the motion trend from the two previous frames. The positions of the previous frames are (x_1, y_1) and (x_2, y_2) respectively, the motion vector β is defined as:

$$\beta = (x_2, y_2) - (x_1, y_1) \tag{6}$$

The motion vector β represents the motion direction in the previous frames. If the direction of the motion doesn't change suddenly, the direction of motion in the current frame is the same as the vector β. We take the search strategy that will search candidate regions meticulously in the predicted direction and roughly in other directions. In the meticulous strategy, a matrix A which is the same dimension as the compressive tracking and is divided into four quadrants is the same as the Cartesian Coordinate System, which is shown in function (7).

$$
A_1 = \begin{bmatrix} 1 & \cdots & 1 & 0 & \cdots & 0 \\ \vdots & \ddots & \vdots & \vdots & \ddots & \vdots \\ 1 & \cdots & 1 & 0 & \cdots & 0 \\ 0 & \cdots & 0 & 0 & \cdots & 0 \\ \vdots & \ddots & \vdots & \vdots & \ddots & \vdots \\ 0 & \cdots & 0 & 0 & \cdots & 0 \end{bmatrix}
A_2 = \begin{bmatrix} 0 & \cdots & 0 & 1 & \cdots & 1 \\ \vdots & \ddots & \vdots & \vdots & \ddots & \vdots \\ 0 & \cdots & 0 & 1 & \cdots & 1 \\ 0 & \cdots & 0 & 0 & \cdots & 0 \\ \vdots & \ddots & \vdots & \vdots & \ddots & \vdots \\ 0 & \cdots & 0 & 0 & \cdots & 0 \end{bmatrix}
A_3 = \begin{bmatrix} 0 & \cdots & 0 & 0 & \cdots & 0 \\ \vdots & \ddots & \vdots & \vdots & \ddots & \vdots \\ 0 & \cdots & 0 & 0 & \cdots & 0 \\ 1 & \cdots & 1 & 0 & \cdots & 0 \\ \vdots & \ddots & \vdots & \vdots & \ddots & \vdots \\ 1 & \cdots & 1 & 0 & \cdots & 0 \end{bmatrix}
A_4 = \begin{bmatrix} 0 & \cdots & 0 & 0 & \cdots & 0 \\ \vdots & \ddots & \vdots & \vdots & \ddots & \vdots \\ 0 & \cdots & 0 & 0 & \cdots & 0 \\ 0 & \cdots & 0 & 1 & \cdots & 1 \\ \vdots & \ddots & \vdots & \vdots & \ddots & \vdots \\ 0 & \cdots & 0 & 1 & \cdots & 1 \end{bmatrix} \tag{7}
$$

The quadrant which is in the same direction as vector β will be searched meticulously, and it makes sure that the candidate region is concentrated in the motion direction. If the target turns around suddenly, the region will not be in the predicted quadrant and the target will be lost. So, another matrix B is defined as:

$$
B = \begin{pmatrix} 1 & 0 & \cdots & 0 & 1 \\ 0 & & & & 0 \\ \vdots & & \ddots & & \vdots \\ 0 & & & & 0 \\ 1 & 0 & \cdots & 0 & 1 \end{pmatrix} \tag{8}
$$

In function (8), B is a matrix which diagonal value is 1. Take OR operation between matrix A and B. The new candidate region can conclude almost all the probable regions.

The operating time of the compressive tracking is represented as O:

$$O = N_1 N_2 N_3 \tag{9}$$

where the number of the samples and the features are N_1 and N_2 respectively, N_3 is the operating time of each feature.

The operating time of the compressive tracking with motion prediction is represented as O_1:

$$O_1 = K N_1 N_2 N_3 \tag{10}$$

as demonstrated in equation (9) and (10), the operating time O_1 drops by nearly three-quarters, so the speed of tracking will be improved.

3.2. *Search Window Optimization*

The search size of candidate regions is uniform for different videos in compressive tracking. If the size of the search window can change adaptively according to the intensity of motion, the efficiency will be improved. Therefore, we calculate the motion distance between the adjacent two frames, and change the size of the search range in line with the distance. If the target is stationary, the strategy will use the uniform window size to search. Otherwise, the size of the window will be adjusted according to the motion distance.

3.3. *Samples Selecting Optimization*

The methods of the positive and negative sample collection are uniform in CT. The positive samples are the points offset four pixels and the negative samples are the points offset between 4 and 30 pixels, In David's video[18], the target is 75 pixels wide and 95 pixels high. The successful rate of the region offset 4 pixels is 0.9. In the Biker video, the target is 16 pixels wide and 26 pixels high. When the region offsets 4 pixels, the successful rate is only 0.78. If the target gets smaller, the successful rate will be lower and these positive samples will not suitable. Therefore, our strategy is to try to change the offsets adaptively according to the size of target.

As shown in Figure 1, the target size is $w \times h$. The largest offset value is l and the points of the farthest positive samples are on the circle whose radius is l. We can calculate the offset value l of positive samples with the function:

$$\begin{cases} \dfrac{wh - wn - hm + mn}{wh + wm + hn - mn} > 0.9 \\ m^2 + n^2 = l^2 \end{cases} \qquad (11)$$

In function (11), we can obtain $\tilde{l} < \dfrac{1}{19}\min(w, h)$. This means the offset value is approximate $\dfrac{1}{19}$ wide or high of the target. If the successful rate is lower than 0.5, we will get negative samples. This strategy, gets the positive and negative samples more representative, because these samples are collected according to the success rate.

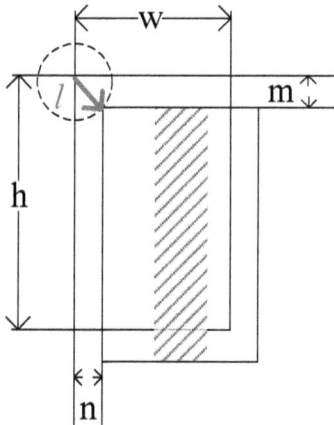

Fig. 1. Sample selecting strategy.

3.4. *Tracking Window Optimization*

In the CT algorithm, the size of the tracking window is fixed in the entire process. When the size of the target becomes smaller, the tracking window will contain a lot of background noise and the noise will influence the Bayes classifier causing the loss of target. If the size of the target gets larger, it will influence the collection of negative samples and will also influence the Bayes classifier. These can lead to the loss or offset of the target. To solve this problem, we proposed the algorithm which can set the size of the search window adaptively.

In the tracking process, it collects the candidate regions around the position of the previous frames and finds the tracking location with the maximal classifier response. Then, samples the image around the location to get the positive and negative samples, and uses samples to update the Bayes classifier. In this chapter, when we get the optimal location, the strategy will sample around the location with pixel ranges, and change the size of each candidate region and find the maximal classifier response.

The center of the tracking window doesn't change. Extract features in each region and classify by the Bayes classifier. The maximal classifier response is the final tracking result. Then, extract the feature of the result and use those to update the classifier. Although the collected number of of the candidate regions increases, the number is still much lower than the CT algorithm and this strategy can improve the robustness.

4. The Proposed Algorithm: Compressive Tracking with Adaptive Size of Search Window (ASSWCT)

In this chapter, we named the Compressive Tracking with Improved Speed ISCT and Compressive Tracking with Adaptive Size of Search Window ASSWCT. In ISCT, we added three modules, such as motion prediction module, motion distance module and sample modules. These modules can decrease the number of the samples and improve the speed of the operation. In ASSWCT, we add re-sample module and window changing module to improve the robustness based on the ISCT.

4.1. *Alogrithm1: ISCT*

Initialization:
Select the tracking target area in first frame manually, construct and update the Bayes classifier.
Input:
Second video frame
1. Sample a set of image patches, then extract and compress these patches to get the feature vector v.
2. Use the classifier $H(v)$ in function (3) to classify each vector v and find the maximal classifier response as the tracking result.
3. Use four strategies: motion prediction, search window optimization, sample selecting optimization and tracking window optimization to sample a set of image patches to get the positive and negative samples, and then update the Bayes classifier.
4. Record the position of tracking.

Tracking:
Input:
The t-th video frame
1. Calculate the motion vector by the previous frames. Use motion prediction and search window optimization to sample a set of image patches, and then extract and compress these patches to get the feature vector v.
2. Use the classifier $H(v)$ in function (3) to classify each vector v and find the maximal classifier response as the tracking result.
3. Use a sample selecting optimization strategy to sample a set of image patches to get the positive and negative samples and update the Bayes classifier.
4. Record the position of tracking.
Output:
Tracking position and classifier parameters.

4.2. *Algorithm2: ASSWCT*

The initialization in the ASSWCT is like ISCT.

Tracking:
Input:
The t-th video frame
1. Calculate the motion vector by the previous frames. Use motion prediction and search window optimization to sample a set of image patches, and then extract and compress these patches to get the feature vector v.
2. Use the classifier $H(v)$ in function (3) to classify each vector v and find the maximal classifier response as the temporary tracking result.
3. Sample a set of image patches. Change the size of the search window, extract and compress these patches to get the feature vector v_1 by function (1). Use the classifier $H(v)$ to classify each vector v_1 and find the maximal classifier response as the final tracking result.
4. Use the final size of the window and sample a set of image patches to get positive and negative samples by sample selecting optimization.
5. Update the Bayes classifier and record the tracking position.
Output:
Tracking position and classifier parameters.

5. Experiments

5.1. *Performance Evaluation*

We use three metrics to evaluate the efficiency of the trackers. The first metric is the Successful Rate (SR). To measure the performance on a sequence of frames, we count the number of successful frames whose SR is larger than the given threshold. If the SR is larger than 0.5 in one frame, the tracking result is considered a success. The second metric is the Center Location Error (CLE) which measures the Euclidean distance between the center of the tracking box and the center of ground truth box. It is a widely used evaluation metric of precision tracking. The third is computational complexity. We use Frames Per Second (FPS) to analyze the algorithm complexity. Higher FPS is a benefit to the real application.

5.2. Experiment Setup

We evaluate tracking algorithms with challenging sequences on an Online Tracking Benchmark (OTB)[18] dataset. OTB datasets contain 100 challenging sequences. It is worth noting that the most challenging sequences are used for evaluation. The two trackers we proposed were compared with several state of the art methods such as the CT, Fast Compressive Tracking (FCT)[19], and Convolutional Networks without Training (CNT)[20], Discriminative Scale Space Tracking (DSST)[21]. For a fair comparison, all the evaluated trackers are initialized with the same parameters. The algorithms are implemented in MATLAB, which runs on a Core i5 Quad-Core 2.5Ghz CPU with 4GB RAM. In Compressive Tracking algorithm, given a target location at the current frame, the positive samples search range is set as 4 pixels and gets 45 positive samples. Set the search range between 8 and 30 pixels as the negative sample candidate regions and get 50 negative samples randomly. The search radius for the object location detection is set as 20 pixels. The dimensionality of projected space is set as $n = 50$ and the learning parameter λ is set as 0.85. In ISCT and ASSWCT algorithm, the size of search windows for positive and negative samples changes adaptively. The initialize search radius is set as 10 pixels. The other parameters are set the same as the Compressive Tracking. In the CNT algorithm, we will take the parameters configured in the literature. For a fair comparison, all parameters are fixed for all the experiments to demonstrate the robustness and stability. The parameters have a relation with the accuracy and speed, however, we don't consider the parameters optimization.

5.3. Experiment on OTB Dataset

5.3.1. Experiment on the sequence attributes

The videos in the benchmark dataset are annotated with attributes, which describe the challenges that a tracker facing in each sequence-e.g., Illumination Variation, Scale Variation, Occlusion, Deformation, Motion Blur, Fast Motion, In-Plane Rotation, Out-of-Plane Rotation, Out-of-View, Background Clutters, Low Resolution. These attributes are useful for diagnosing and characterizing the behavior of trackers in such a large dataset, without analyzing each individual video. As space is limited, we report results for some attributes mentioned in OTB dataset in the following section. Figure 2 and Figure 3 are the results of the tracking, where the results of CT are marked in red and a solid line, the results of ISCT are marked in yellow and a dotted line, the result of DSST is marked in purple and a dotted line, the results of ASSWCT are marked in black and a dotted line and the CNT is marked in green and a solid line.

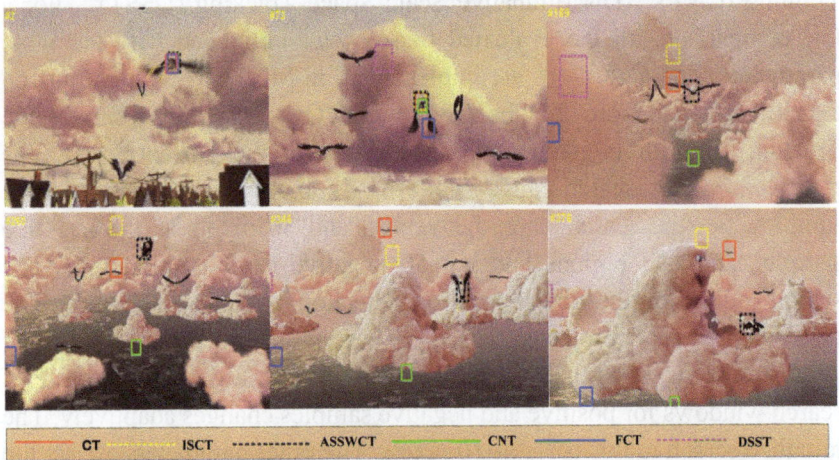

Fig. 2. Tracking results.

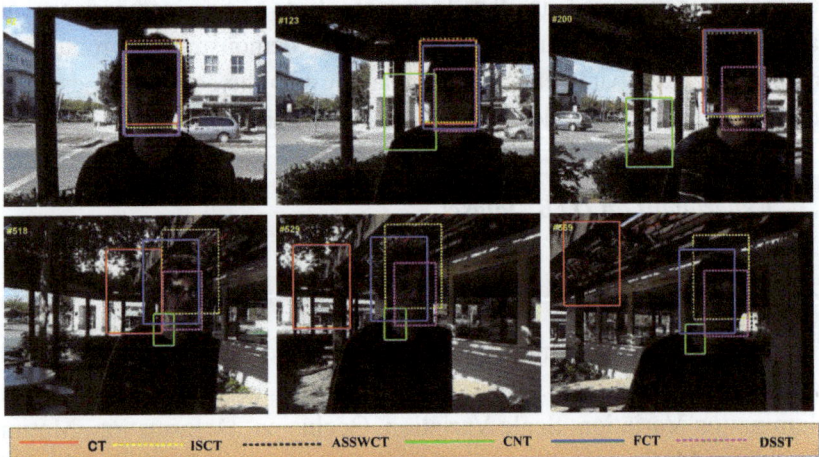

Fig. 3. Tracking results.

5.3.2. Qualitative evaluation

We selected 15 challenge sequences in OTB dataset, and use three standard evaluation metrics, namely Successful Rate (SR), Center Location Error (CLE) and Tracking Speed (TS). Table 1 and Table 2 show the quantitative results averaged over 10 times. Bold fonts indicate the best performance while the italic fonts indicate the second one. The total number of evaluated frames is 7531.

Table 1. Success rate and tracking speed.

Sequence	Tracking Speed/Successful Rate				
	FCT	ISCT	ASSWCT	CNT	DSST
Basketball	*24.11*/0.78	**18.77**/*0.91*	32.31/**0.98**	4644/0.07	43/0.05
Bird1	11.57/0.21	**8.80**/0.20	*9.47*/**0.39**	2593/*0.31*	16.5/0.02
Bird2	3.60/0.46	**2.20**/0.57	*2.39*/**0.59**	648/0.56	12.9/0.56
Board	25.98/0.10	**16.52**/0.13	*20.70*/*0.45*	4510/0.21	41.9/**0.70**
ClifBar	2.48/0.69	**1.44**/0.69	*1.64*/0.70	767/*0.85*	5.2/**0.90**
Crossing	3.0/0.95	**1.56**/0.97	*1.59*/0.83	795/**1.0**	3.8/*0.98*
Fish	9.76/*0.97*	**4.76**/0.84	*5.54*/**0.98**	3130/0.28	40.4/0.94
RedTeam	18.49/0.21	*10.78*/0.52	**10.55**/*0.59*	531/**1.00**	18.2/0.56
Subway	5.0/0.92	*2.68*/0.94	**2.62**/**0.95**	1137/0.22	6/0.90
Suv	17.94/0.14	**10.11**/0.63	*10.36*/0.59	6067/**0.99**	56.2/*0.96*
Trellis	12.18/0.37	**7.02**/0.30	*7.19*/0.57	3650/0.29	89.4/**0.99**
Walking	20.27/0.54	*14.85*/0.46	**13.84**/0.54	2679/**0.99**	18.6/*0.98*
Walking2	12.21/0.39	**7.53**/0.39	*7.63*/0.38	3224/**1.0**	39.4/*0.9*
Dudek	40.13/0.78	**27.19**/*0.92*	*33.67*/**0.93**	7550/0.67	348.3/0.9
Coupon	8.30/0.51	**4.70**/0.74	*5.21*/0.75	2209/0.34	368.9/**0.98**
Total/ Average	214.5/0.54	**138.9**/0.60	*164.6*/*0.69*	48918/0.59	1152.9/**0.73**
FPS	36	**53**	*47*	0.15	6.5

In Table 1, ISCT processes all images using 138.9 seconds, ASSWCT in 164.6 seconds, CT in 216.5 seconds and FCT in 214.5 seconds. ASSWCT reduces 51.9 seconds, almost one third of the whole tracking time. Furthermore, compared with CT, the successful rate of ASSWCT improves almost 31 percent. ASSWCT has great advantages in terms of real-time, although some sequences are lower than CNT and DSST. The value of FPS in ISCT and ASSWCT is nearly 50. In the terms of success rate, CNT, DSST and ASSWCT all have good performance.

In Table 2, We compared Center Location Error in 15 challenge sequences in OTB dataset. ASSWCT performs better than other trackers in an average result. Considering three standard evaluation metrics, ASSWCT algorithm achieves the best or second-best result in most sequences in terms of success rate, center location error, and FPS.

Table 2. Center location error.

Sequence	Center Location Error(CLE)					
	CT	FCT	ISCT	ASSWCT	CNT	DSST
Bird1	117.85	25.87	126.59	**25.65**	74.50	323.8
Bird2	43.25	53.02	17.92	**17.75**	44.66	18.3
Board	67.98	107.96	138.65	116.33	93.60	**43.1**
ClifBar	3.64	4.28	**2.95**	3.98	9.22	4.8
Crossing	8.29	3.03	5.57	6.39	**1.48**	1.65
Fish	21.21	9.55	11.54	10.82	30.02	**5.96**
RedTeam	7.02	7.78	7.42	5.11	**2.68**	3.25
Subway	12.80	5.38	8.54	7.64	140.56	**2.35**
Suv	73.12	86.00	56.12	57.59	**3.42**	5.92
Trellis	56.86	55.59	49.72	48.80	39.61	**4.45**
Walking	5.5	5.51	7.41	6.01	1.81	1.67
Walking2	55.7	61.26	62.35	63.97	**2.47**	3.55
Dudek	27.54	30.32	23.99	23.06	43.70	**14.6**
Coupon	18.75	21.18	21.09	18.68	24.40	**3.7**
Average	42.42	46.54	35.61	**28.08**	39.98	46.05

5.4. *Experiment on VOT 2014 Dataset*

5.4.1. *Experiment on the sequence attributes*

Figure 4 and Figure 5 are the results of the tracking, where the results of CT are marked in red and a solid line, the results of FCT are marked in blue and a solid line, the results of ISCT are marked in yellow and a dotted line, the results of DSST are marked in purple and a dotted line, the results of ASSWCT are marked in black and a dotted line and those of CNT are marked in green and a solid line. The ASSWCT tracker performs better than some state-of the art trackers.

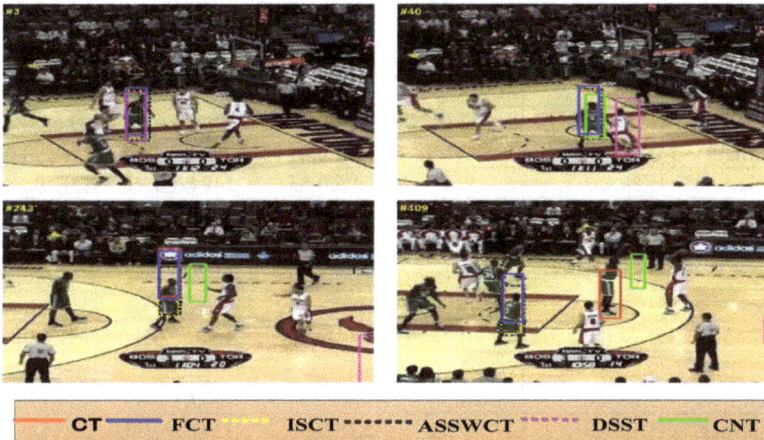

Fig. 4. Basketball.

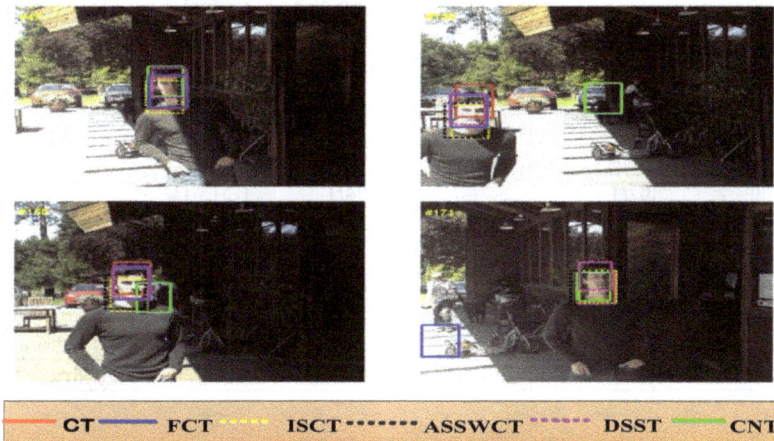

Fig. 5. Sunshade.

5.4.2. *Qualitative evaluation*

We compared the performance of ASSWCT with other competing trackers in the VOT2014 challenge. As we can see in Table 3, ASSWCT tracker performs well in terms of accuracy, the accuracy is like the state of the art tracker CNT and a little lower than the DSST tracker. However, the CNT costs a lot of time in tracking and DSST is nearly 10 times slower than the ASSWCT tracker.

Table 3. Results of CT, FCT, CNT, DSST and ASSWCT on the VOT2014 benchmark.

Sequences	Tracking Speed/Successful Rate				
	CT	FCT	ASSWCT	CNT	DSST
ball	11.85/*0.58*	*9.75*/0.15	**6.24/0.73**	3466.6/0.1	29.08/0.14
basketball	20.41/0.03	*20/0.13*	**15.6/0.61**	4220.7/0.01	87.42/0.01
bicycle	5.37/0.3	*4.74/0.3*	2.96/0.55	1494.8/**0.71**	8.02/0.54
car	6.12/0.46	*5.63/0.46*	**4.14**/0.52	1401.8/*0.7*	11.58/**0.84**
david	12.56/0.27	*11.93/0.28*	**8.04**/0.40	4237.1/*0.9*	146.8/**0.99**
diving	3.51/*0.18*	3.26/0.15	2.4/0.2	1197.1/0.12	34.99/0.16
drunk	25.90/0.4	*24.37/0.33*	19/0.32	6729.8/*0.44*	250.41/**0.96**
fernando	9.94/0.22	*9.23/0.24*	**8.12**/0.31	1646/0.07	151.84/*0.27*
fish1	9.26/0	*7.14/0*	5.7/0	2382.5/0	10.69/0
fish2	9.22/0.01	*7.66/0.01*	5.8/0.01	1702.1/0.01	43.31/0.01
gymnastics	3.76/0.33	*2.85/0.33*	2.15/0.35	1141.2/0.33	33.15/0.33
hand1	4.76/0.1	*3.81/0.1*	2.57/0.1	1340/0.1	13.03/0.1
hand2	5.49/0.06	*4.48/0.09*	3.0/0.1	1435.4/0.07	21.81/0.06
jogging	5.46/0.22	4.99/0.22	3.4/0.25	1656.3/0.22	21.56/0.21
motocross	*3.61/0.03*	3.83/0.01	3.0/0.05	901.73/0.01	86.85/0.01
polarbear	9.58/0.45	*9.04/0.76*	6.64/0.80	2069.4/0.47	36.43/*0.79*
skating	*10.55*/0.1	10.73/0.13	7.8/0.05	2194.1/*0.14*	29.05/**0.23**
sphere	5.34/0.1	*4.25/**0.81***	3.19/0.17	1088.5/0.06	36.38/0.33
sunshade	3.86/0.45	*2.96/**0.62***	2.04/*0.50*	923.92/0.47	10.76/0.48
surfing	5.67/1	*4.58/1*	2.94/1	1513.1/1	9.79/0.94
torus	5.99/0.35	*4.49/0.11*	3.15/*0.64*	1414.5/0.09	15.41/**0.84**
trellis	11.30/0	*8.81/0.09*	5.66/0.01	3075/*0.37*	94.69/**0.91**
tunnel	17.99/0.05	*16.2/0.07*	**11.76**/0.04	3970/**0.97**	89.93/*0.93*
woman	9.99/0.17	*9.15/0.16*	6.24/0.17	3220.1/*0.9*	59.63/*0.87*
Total/Average	217.49/0.25	*193.88/0.27*	**141.54**/*0.35*	54421.75/0.34	1332.6/**0.45**
FPS	46	*52*	**71**	0.2	7.5

In Table 3, the tracked object in the Surfing sequence is a person, all the trackers performed well, since the person does not move his limbs such that the body articulation creates a problem. However, it does not attain the highest score on every sequence. As the experiments show, there are several failed cases. These limitations stem from the data not following the assumptions of the method. The sequences (Fish, Skating, Motocross, Jogging, and Hand), which contain strong out-of-pane rotation, fast changes and similar background. ASSWCT can cover these only partially, using an adaptive window size. Also, we didn't consider any re-initialization, so we can found out that some of our tracking accuracy is not better than the VOT2014 Challenge results mentioned. Our future work will focus on re-initialization for object tracking under heavy occlusion and revising the motion prediction accuracy and robustness. ASSWCT takes less than 2 minutes to process all 25 videos (~10000 frames), it is computationally efficient. The complexity is reduced about 75% compared to compressive tracking and nearly 90% compared to DSST tracker which is the winner in VOT 2014. The mean FPS of ASSWCT is 10 times as that of DSST, and fast than FCT, CT and CNT.

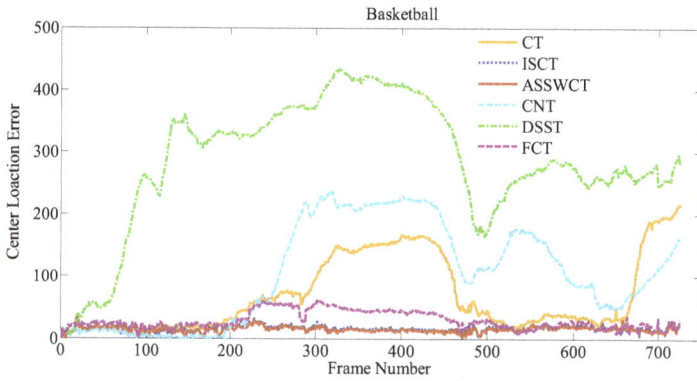

Fig. 6. A frame-by-frame comparison of the center location error (in pixels) on the challenging sequences Basketball.

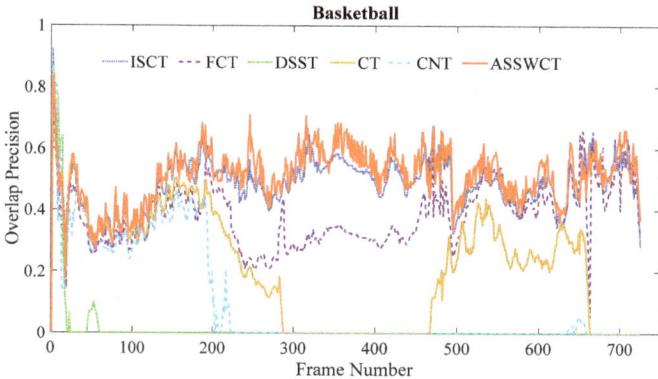

Fig. 7. A frame-by-frame comparison of the overlap precision (in pixels) on the challenging sequences Basketball.

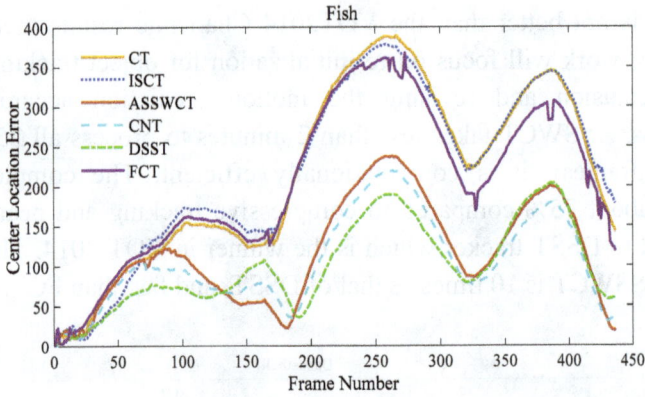

Fig. 8. A frame-by-frame comparison of the center location error (in pixels) on the challenging sequences Fish.

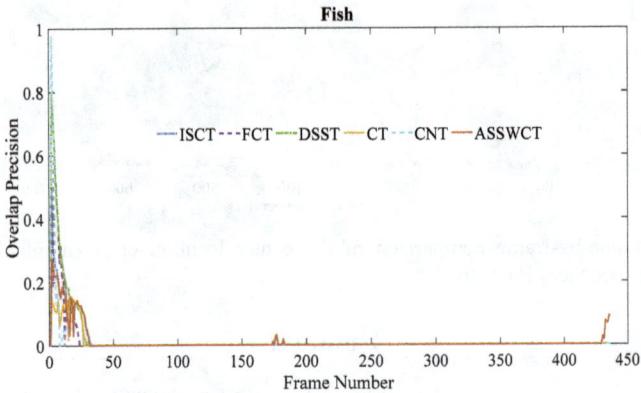

Fig. 9. A frame-by-frame comparison of the overlap precision (in pixels) on the challenging sequences Fish.

Figure 6 and Figure 9 illustrate the results on two sequences in the VOT2014 challenge dataset. The figures show the Successful Rate and Center Location Error value of different trackers in the Basketball video and Fish video in full frames. ASSWCT provides promising results compared to competing trackers on these sequences. In the Basketball video, ASSWCT performs much better than other trackers. In the Fish video, all the trackers performed poorly. From Figure 8 we can find that DSST, ASSWCT and CNT are better than other trackers. From Figure 9, all the trackers performed badly, but ASSWCT is still a little better than other trackers.

6. Conclusions

We proposed an automatic compressive tracking method based on a motion prediction algorithm named ASSWCT. The algorithm predicts the motion direction by previous frames and reduces the number of the candidate regions to improve the speed of the tracking process. It can also change the search range adaptively according to the motion distance calculated from the motion vector. The algorithm reduces a lot of time in the tracking procedure. Furthermore, the algorithm combines meticulous search with rough search to improve the robustness of tracking. According to the tracking result in the first step which has located the tracking position roughly, ASSWCT re-samples images and adjusts the size of the search window to improve the robustness of tracking. The simulation results show that ASSWCT is significantly better than the similar tracking performance.

Acknowledgments

This work was supported by the University Science Research Project of Jiangsu Province (16KJB510036); the Science and Technology Program of Nantong (MS12016025); Nantong University-Nantong Joint Research Center for Intelligent Information Technology (KFKT2017B04).

References

1. Li H, Suen C Y., A novel Non-local means image denoising method based on grey theory, *Pattern Recognition*, 49(1), 217–248 (2016).
2. Li H, Suen C Y., Robust face recognition based on dynamic rank representation, *Pattern Recognition*, 60(12), 13–24 (2016).
3. M. Isard and A. Blake, A mixed-state CONDENSATION tracker with automatic model-switching, In *Proc. IEEE Int. Conference on Computer Vision*, pp.107–112, Bombay, India (1998).

4. R. Collins, Y. Liu, M. Leordeanu. Online selection of discriminative tracking features, *IEEE Trans. Pattern Anal.*, 27(10), 1631–1643 (2005).
5. T. Parag, F. Porikli, A. Elgammal, Boosting adaptive linear weak classifiers for online learning and tracking, In *Proc. IEEE Int. Conference on Computer Vision and Pattern Recognition*, pp.1–8 (2008).
6. P. Hidayatullah and H. Konik, CAMSHIFT improvement on multi-hue and multi-object tracking, In *Proc. IEEE Int. Conference on Electrical Engineering and Informatics*, pp. 1–8, September 2011.
7. J. Candès, T. Tao, Decoding by linear programming, *IEEE Trans. Inform Theory*, 51(12), 4203–4215 (2005).
8. K. H. Zhang, L. Zhang, M. H. Yang, Real-time compressive tracking, *European Conference on Computer Vision*, pp. 864–877 (2012).
9. J. F. Henriques, C. Rui, P. Martins, J. Batista, High-Speed Tracking with Kernelized Correlation Filters. *IEEE Trans. Pattern Anal.*, 37(3), 583–596 (2015).
10. H. Yang, X. Jiang, S. Gao, Adaptive Compressive Tracking Algorithm Based on SIFT Features, in *Third International Conference on Robot, Vision and Signal Processing*, pp. 78–81 (2015).
11. D. G. Lowe, Distinctive image features from scale-invariant key points, *International Journal of Computer Vision*, 60(2), 91–110 (2004).
12. W. Z. Zhang, J. G. Ji, Z. Z. Jing, W. F. Jing, Y. Zhang. Adaptive real-time compressive tracking, *International Conference on Network and Information Systems for Computers*, pp. 236–240 (2015).
13. Fiza Murtaza, H. Y. Muhammad, A. Sergio, Multi-view human action recognition using histograms of oriented gradients description of motion history images, *International Conference on Frontiers of Information Technology*, pp. 297–302 (2015).
14. E. J. Candes, T. Tao, Near-optimal signal recovery from random projections. Universal Encoding Strategies? *IEEE Trans. Inform Theory*, 52(12), pp. 5406–5425 (2006).
15. Ella, Bingham and Heikki, Mannila, Random projection in dimensionality reduction: Applications to image and text data, in Proceedings of the Seventh ACM SIGKDD *International Conference on Knowledge Discovery and Data Mining*, pp. 245–250 (2001).
16. M. Danelljan., G. Hager, F.S. Khan, M. Flesberg, Accurate scale estimation for robust visual tracking, in *Proceedings of the British Machine Vision Conference*, pp. 1 (2014).
17. P. Diaconis and D. Freedman, Asymptotics of graphical projection pursuit, *The Annals of Statistics,* 12(3), 793–815 (1984).
18. http://cvlab.hanyang.ac.kr/tracker_benchmark/
19. K. H. Zhang, L. Zhang, M. H. Yang, Fast compressive tracking, *IEEE Trans. Pattern Anal.*, 36(10), 2002–2015 (2014).

20. K. H. Zhang, Q. S. Liu, Y. Wu, M. H. Yang, Robust visual tracking via convolutional networks without training, *IEEE Trans. Image Process.*, 25(4), pp. 1779–1792 (2016).
21. M. Danelljan., G. Hager, F. S. Khan, M. Flesberg, Discriminative scale space tracking, *IEEE Trans. Pattern Anal.*, 39(8), 1561–1575 (2016).

Chapter 14

"How to Rate a Video Game?" — A Prediction System for Video Games Based on Multimodal Information

Vishal Batchu and Varshit Battu*

*International Institute of Information Technology Hyderabad,
Gachibowli, Hyderabad 500032,
vishal.batchu@students.iiit.ac.in[†]*

Video games have become an integral part of most people's lives in recent times. This led to an abundance of data related to video games being shared online. However, this comes with issues such as incorrect ratings, reviews or anything that is being shared. Recommendation systems are powerful tools that help users by providing them with meaningful recommendations. A straightforward approach would be to predict the scores of video games based on other information related to the game. It could be used as a means to validate user-submitted ratings as well as provide recommendations. This work provides a method to predict the G-Score, that defines how good a video game is, from its trailer (video) and summary (text). We first propose models to predict the G-Score based on the trailer alone (unimodal). Later on, we show that considering information from multiple modalities helps the models perform better compared to using information from videos alone. We created our own dataset named VGD (Video Game Dataset) and provide it along with this work. The approach mentioned here can be generalized to other multimodal datasets such as movie trailers and summaries etc. Towards the end, we talk about the shortcomings of the work and some methods to overcome them.

1. Introduction

Video games are almost everywhere these days, from individual consumers who play video games for fun to serious E-Sports professionals. The video game industry is a billion dollar industry, it was valued at $44.9 billion back in 2007 which rose to $91.5 billion in 2015. The increase in the rate

---

*battu.varshit@research.iiit.ac.in
[†]https://iiit.ac.in

of development of games and the number of people who play these games spiked up hand in hand throughout the world over the recent years. This increase in the sheer number of games marketed required people to rely on a trusted resource that would give them information about these games since it is infeasible for a human to keep the details of every single game ever released in memory. Another trend observed in recent times is that there is an exponential increase in the amount of data shared online. This, however, comes with certain unforeseen consequences such as a reduction in the quality of data present online and the spread of bogus information i.e false information being shared online. Considering the video game industry, people often rely on various sites to provide them with ratings, reviews etc of games before purchase. Since most ratings and reviews are submitted by a wide array of users, maintaining them is hard and hence, we end up having a lot of incorrect/unwanted entries. Another issue we often face with simple methods of input is that users might unknowingly select the wrong option such as an incorrect rating or a genre for a video game. Reviews and descriptions don't face this issue since textual inputs have lesser tendency to be incorrectly entered, however not many people would be willing to spend their time adding textual information and hence we see a wide use of simple input methods. Recommendation systems are quite popular since they allow us to provide meaningful options to users for various purposes. Deep learning has shown a lot of promise at this task. We define the G-Score of a game as a value that determines how good a game is based on critic and user game ratings. In order to mitigate the issues mentioned earlier and to offer useful recommendations to users, we propose several deep neural network architectures that would predict the G-Score from the trailer and the summary of a video game. We believe that the use of summaries along with the trailers would aid the model to predict the G-Score better than the use of trailers alone. This would also aid game developers while creating trailers to see how well they score before a public release since the predicted G-Scores could be used to refine and improve the trailers. In order to train our models, we created the VGD dataset and provide it with this work.

2. Related Work

There have been multiple works in areas related to video and text classification, however, they often deal with domain specific information. Nominal work has been done on video game trailers in the past. We use video game trailers along with reviews to perform a cross-domain analysis in order to predict ratings.

Video Analysis and Classification - Zhang et al.[1] proposed a supervised learning technique for summarizing videos by automatically selecting key-frames. They use Long-Short-Term Memory to model the variable-range temporal dependency among frames so that both representative and compact video summaries can be generated. Venugopalan et al.[2] looked into how linguistic knowledge, taken from large text corpus, can aid the generation of natural language descriptions of videos. Haninger et al.[3] quantified and characterized the content in video games rated T (for "Teen") and measured how accurate the ESRB-assigned content descriptors displayed on the game box are to the real game. Simonyan et al.[4] investigated architectures of discriminatively trained deep Convolutional Networks for action recognition in videos. Capturing the complementary information from still frames and motion between frames was a challenge they addressed. Kahou et al.[5] presented an approach to learn several specialist models using deep learning techniques. Among these were a convolutional neural network focusing on capturing visual information in detected faces, a deep belief net which focused on the representation of the audio stream, a K-Means based "bag-of-mouths" model, which extracts visual features around the mouth region and a relational auto-encoder, which addressed spatiotemporal aspects of videos. Le et al.[6] presented unsupervised feature learning as a way to learn features directly from video data. They presented an extension to the Independent Subspace Analysis algorithm to learn invariant spatiotemporal features from unlabeled video data. Zhou et al.[7] formalize multi-instance multi-label learning in which each training example was associated with not only multiple instances, but also multiple class labels. They proposed algorithms for scene classification based on the relationship between multi-instance and multi-label learning.

Text Analysis and Classification - Glorot et al.[8] proposed a deep learning approach that learns to extract a meaningful representation for each review in an unsupervised manner. Sentiment classifiers trained with this high-level feature representation clearly outperform state-of-the-art methods. Zhang et al.[9] showed empirical exploration on the use of character-level convolutional networks (ConvNets) for text classification. They built large-scale datasets to show that character-level convolutional networks can achieve state-of-the-art results. Iyyer et al.[10] presented a simple deep neural network that competes with and sometimes outperforms models on sentiment analysis and factoid question answering tasks by taking only a fraction of the training time. Baker et al.[11] describe the application of Distributional Clustering to document classification. Their approach clustered words into groups based on the distribution of class labels of each word. Unlike techniques such as Latent Semantic Indexing, they were able to compress the feature space, while maintaining the classification accuracy. Poria et al.[12] used the extracted features in multimodal sentiment analysis of short video clips representing one sentence each. They use the combined feature vectors of textual, visual, and audio modalities to train a classifier which was based on multiple kernel learning, and which is known to be good at heterogeneous data. Zhang et al.[13] mentioned that this learning problem was addressed by using a method called M_{LNB} which adapts the traditional naive Bayes classifiers to deal with multi-label instances. Feature selection mechanisms were incorporated into M_{LNB} to improve its performance.

3. Dataset

We created a dataset named VGD that consists of the trailer, summary, developer, age rating, user-score, critic-score and genre of 1,950 video games. The data was collected from metacritic.com[a]. The dataset along with the code used can be found at https://goo.gl/Z8bNN3 for replicability and future use. This is the first dataset of its kind and we believe it would be quite helpful to the research community.

3.1. *Preprocessing*

The first step in preprocessing involved the removal of certain games that had missing details (a lot of games did not have trailers).

Trailers - The trailers extracted from the website had a resolution of 720p (with a few exceptions). We reduced the resolution to 360p since 720p required more space and mostly consisted of redundant information from the view of a neural network. We put an upper limit of 3 minutes for each trailer, trimming trailers that were larger to the 3-minute mark.

Summaries - We removed non-ASCII characters from the summaries since some of the summaries had terms from other languages like Japanese, Korean, French etc. However, since they are quite small in number, including them would not provide much value in terms of generalizability of the approach.

The final dataset consists of 1,950 video game trailers and summaries.

---

[a]http://www.metacritic.com/game

Table 1. Distribution of VGD according to Genre classes, G-Score classes and Age Ratings.

Genre	Entries
Role-Playing	522
Strategy	329
Action	734
Sports	200
Miscellaneous	165

Age Rating	Entries
Mature	449
Adults Only	2
Everyone 10+	365
Teen	704
Everyone	409
Other	522

G-Score (S)	Entries
0-10	0
11-20	3
21-30	7
31-40	19
41-50	89
51-60	263
61-70	433
71-80	693
81-90	416
91-100	27

3.2. *Statistics*

Various statistics related to the dataset are provided, that show the diversity of the dataset. Video games were collected from a wide range of over 730 developers. Games span across various age ratings from E (Everyone) to M (Mature) which provided us with a wide collection of games.

Genres - We clustered the genres into 5 groups based on similarity as specified in Table 2 and present the number of games belonging to each group in the sub-tables of Table 1.

Game scores - We define the G-Score of a game as an average of critic and user ratings, details are specified in Section 4. We observed that most games have G-Scores above 40 and only a small fraction of games have a G-Score below 40 as shown in Table 1. This results in some inter-class bias.

Table 2.   Our proposed grouping of genres into 5 classes based on similarity.

Genre-Class	Genres
Role-Playing	Adventure, First-Person, Third-Person, Role-Playing
Strategy	Turn-Based, Strategy, War-Game, Puzzle, Platformer
Action	Action
Sports	Fighting, Sports, Racing, Wrestling
Miscellaneous	Simulation, Flight, Party, Real-Time

The main reason for this is that most video games that would potentially have a bad G-Score would either not have trailers or not have any associated critic/user ratings since most people would not play the game in the first place and hence would not be present in the dataset.

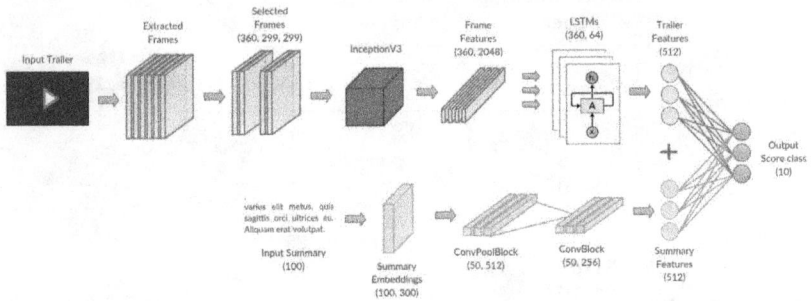

Fig. 1.   An overview of our pipeline corresponding to Model-1. We start with the trailers and summaries as inputs and predict the G-Score classes as outputs. The Inception-V3 pre-trained model is used to extract features of video frames. ConvPoolBlocks and ConvBlocks are described in Figure 4. The output sizes at each of the layers are mentioned in the figure.

4. Score Prediction

Each video game has a user rating R_u and critic rating R_c associated with it. We define the G-Score of a game (S) as follows,

$$S = \frac{R_u + R_c}{2} \tag{1}$$

and aim to predict this G-Score. The G-Score essentially represents how good a game is.

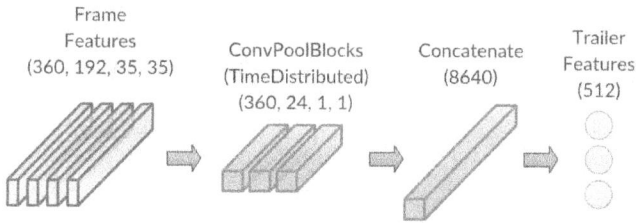

Fig. 2. The section of Model-2 that differs from Figure 1. The frame features we consider for input here are different from earlier since we use features from an intermediate layer of Inception-V3 and not the final outputs of Inception-V3.

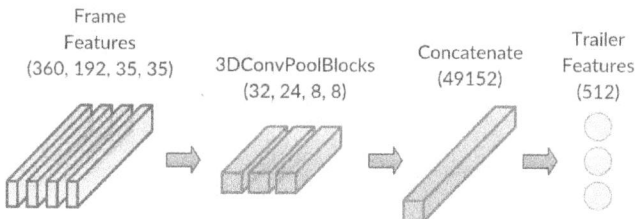

Fig. 3. The section of Model-3 that differs from Figure 1. The frame features are the same as Figure 2 that we use in Model-2.

Critic ratings were collected from a large number of critics and a weighted average was computed to form the final critic rating R_c. The weights of individual critics depend on the overall stature of the critic. Formally, if R_c^i corresponds to the rating of critic i and α^i is the weight associated with critic i and there are M critics then,

$$R_c = \sum_{i=1}^{M} \alpha^i * R_c^i$$

The number of critics that review games vary from game to game since popular games often get a larger number of ratings as compared to others that are not so popular. Critic weights α^i are based on how well the critics performed in the past (well written, insightful reviews etc). This is determined by Metacritic staff who handle the website from where we collected our data.

The user rating R_u was computed as an average of all user ratings submitted for the game. Formally, if R_u^i corresponds to the rating of user i and there are N users then,

$$R_u = \sum_{i=1}^{N} R_u^i$$

Regardless of the number of users and critics that rate a game, we computed the final score using Equation 1. We considered both trailers and summaries as inputs in order to predict this G-Score using our proposed model. We quantized the G-Scores to 10 classes since predicting the G-Score directly is a regression problem which is harder to tackle compared to classification problems.

4.1. *Trailers*

Each video game has an associated trailer that we used in order to predict the G-Score.

Trailer frame selection - Since videos are captured with a frame-rate of 24 fps, it was infeasible to use because of the sheer number of frames. Hence, we propose a method to pick frames in a certain manner that would allow us to maximize the information we obtain from game trailers. Firstly, we reduced the frame-rate to 4 fps while extracting the frames from the video. We then followed the frame selection algorithm, mentioned in Algorithm 1, in order to select frames. This allowed us to capture important information at various parts of trailers. The reason we skip frames is that most trailers have a sequence of events that go on for a while before transitioning to the next sequence of events. Upon observation, we used a skip of 150 frames as a good approximation. We skipped the first 50 frames since most trailers have textual information during the start of the video such as the developer titles, age ratings etc.

Trailer features - We used the pre-trained Inception-V3[14] model to extract features from each of the frames selected in the previous step. The model was pre-trained on ImageNet,[15] and hence, generalized well to a

---

Algorithm 1 Frame selection for trailers:

1: Consider we have a set of N frames $F_1, F_2, ..., F_N$
2: $f_{start} = 50$
3: **while** $f_{start} < N$ **do**
4:     **for** $j = 0$, j++, while $j < 10$ **do**
5:         **if** $f_{start} + j <= N$ **then**
6:             Select frame $F_{f_{start}+j}$
7:         **else**
8:             Break
9:     f_{start}+ = 150

---

wide range of images. We extracted the features of the *Avg_Pool* layer (the penultimate layer in the network) which gave us a feature representation of 2048 elements per frame. Considering all the frames, we got a vector having dimensions $(M, 2048)$ where M is the number of frames we selected by the frame selection algorithm 1 as our final trailer features.

4.2. *Summaries*

Considering all the summaries we had, we created a dictionary where each word was given an index. We then went through each of the summaries replacing words with their corresponding indexes. Finally, we resized the summaries to a size of 100 by trimming them if they were larger and padding them with zeros if they were smaller.

4.3. *Method*

Model-1 - We proposed a deep learning based architecture, as outlined in Figure 1, that used a combination of recurrent and convolution based networks which allowed us to process both trailer features and summaries in order to predict the G-Score of a video game. The frame features were fed to multiple levels of LSTMs[16] that finally output a vector of size 512. The summaries were fed to an embedding layer that dynamically generated embeddings having a size of 300. These embeddings were then fed to a convolution-based network, as depicted in Figures 1 and 4, that output a vector of size 512. Finally, these vectors were concatenated and passed along to a linear layer that output the G-Score class. We also performed experiments on multiple other model architectures, which gave us the best results.

ConvPoolBlock   ConvBlock

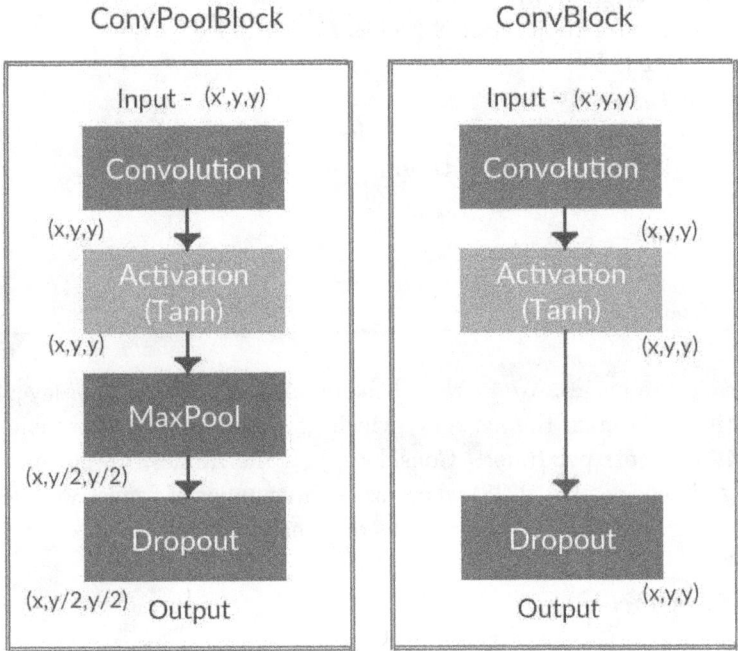

Fig. 4.   ConvPoolBlocks and ConvBlocks are used in order to process the summaries in our proposed models. A ConvPoolBlock consist of Convolution, Tanh, MaxPool and Dropout layers. A ConvBlock consists of Convolution, Tanh and Dropout layers.

Model-2 - We used a time distributed CNN over extracted frame features (these frame features however, were taken from an intermediate layer of the Inception-V3 network) to generate a small embedding for each frame which were then concatenated and fed to a fully connected layer in order to produce the final output vector as illustrated in Figure 2. Summaries were passed through a CNN, similar to what was done earlier. The outputs from both the LSTM and CNN were concatenated and a linear layer was applied to predict the final output. One significant advantage of this approach was that the model had a very small number of parameters since the time distributed CNN shares weights across time. This would be an ideal model to use in memory constrained scenarios such as mobile computing.

Model-3 - We used a 3D CNN[17] over the frames to generate an output embedding for the trailer as outlined in Figure 3. Summaries were passed

Gran Turismo 6

Sample Game Trailer Frames

+

Game Summary

"Gran Turismo 6 is a comprehensive racing simulator that allows fans to drive a prolific collection of cars on the world's most legendary racetracks."

⇩

Predicted Score Class

40-50

Fig. 5.   Qualitative example where the model predicts incorrect G-Score class for Gran Turismo 6. The true G-Score for Super Mario Odyssey is 93 and the true G-Score for Gran Turismo 6 is 81.

through a CNN, similar to what was done earlier. The outputs were then concatenated and passed to a linear layer to predict the final G-Score class.

We also tried generating sentence embeddings using Doc2Vec[18] for each of the summaries, but they didn't give us the best results, and hence we

Super Mario Odyssey

Sample Game Trailer Frames

+

Game Summary

"Mario embarks on a new journey through unknown worlds, running
and jumping through huge 3D worlds in the first sandbox-style Mario
game since Super Mario 64 and Super Mario Sunshine."

⇩

Predicted Score Class

90-100

Fig. 6. Qualitative example where the model predicts the correct G-Score class for Super Mario Odyssey.

stuck to dynamic embeddings as mentioned earlier. The three models mentioned here consider both the trailer and summary as inputs. In order to validate our claim that the use of summaries gives us accuracy improvements, we also performed the same experiments without considering summaries on each of the proposed models and report accuracies in Table 3.

This shows that using summaries along with trailers gives us significant improvements of over 5%.

4.4. *Implementation Details*

We implemented the proposed models in the Keras[19] framework over the Tensorflow[20] backend. The reason we chose this was because of the ease of implementation in Keras and the efficiency and optimization of models in Tensorflow. We used the Cross-entropy loss at the output since we were essentially dealing with a multi-class classification problem, and used the Adam optimizer with a learning rate of 1e-4 and a decay of 1e-6 in order to train the model. We also tried using the SGD optimizer but Adam gave us faster convergence and hence we used that to train our final models. We used *tanh* activations instead of ReLU throughout the model as it helped us achieve better accuracies. We also included multiple Dropout[21] layers throughout the network since that allowed the model to generalize well.

To evaluate our model, we performed a 10-fold cross-validation and provide results. Further details on Model-1 (our best model) can be found in the code submitted along with this work at https://goo.gl/fYiEfq.

5. Results

On each of our proposed models, we performed a 10-fold cross-validation and considered the mean as our final accuracy. We observed a significant increase in accuracy with the inclusion of summaries as inputs along with the trailers. Model-1 gave us the best results in terms of accuracy. We believe the main reason for this was that Inception-V3 was trained on ImageNet, which is a huge dataset of more than 1M images. Hence, it provided us with feature representations that were rich and meaningful.

Model-2 had a very small number of parameters which is why it is well suited for use in portable devices and memory constrained situations such as mobile processing. This, however, comes at a cost of lower accuracy than Model-1.

5.1. *Qualitative Analysis*

A few qualitative results have been provided where the network performed well in one case but failed in another. Gran Turismo 6, shown in Figure 5, had a true G-Score of 81 but we predicted a G-Score class of 40-50. The main reason this failed was that the trailer had multiple overlay texts and

Table 3. Results on predicting G-Scores using 10-fold cross-validation. We present mean accuracies on all three of our models considering trailers only as inputs as well as both trailers and summaries as inputs. Improvements obtained with each of the models are also mentioned.

Model	Input	Accuracy
Model-1	Trailer Only	65.2
	Trailer and Summary	**70.5**
	Improvement	+5.3%
Model-2	Trailer Only	63.3
	Trailer and Summary	66.6
	Improvement	+3.3%
Model-3	Trailer Only	64.5
	Trailer and Summary	68.8
	Improvement	+4.3%

game-play irrelevant clips. A simple solution to frames containing overlay text is to ignore them before feeding them to model. We could also process these frames separately, extracting the text from them and using them as inputs along with the summaries of games. Since non game-play scenes do not contribute any significant information when scoring a game, the model would misinterpret this information, hence resulting in incorrect G-Scores. In the example provided, refer to Figure 5, the frame containing the person would get a feature representation from Inception-V3 that has no relevance to the game and would ultimately contribute to noise. Handling non game-play scenes in trailers is an issue that is hard to tackle and is one of the shortcomings of this work. An approach towards this would be to train a model that takes a frame as an input and predicts if the frame is a game-play scene or not given the video as a reference.

5.2. *Empirical Validation*

We validate our claim that summaries provide information that is quite useful while predicting the G-Score of a video game. Hence, using both the trailers and summaries allowed us to predict with a higher accuracy. We conducted a significance test, where we performed experiments on predicting the G-Score of a video game based on the trailer alone, and showed that we gained significant accuracy improvements of over 5% when we used both the summaries and trailers in order to predict the G-Score as mentioned in Table 3. Most of the time, we had the summary at our disposal along with the trailers of games and hence, using information from multiple modalitiesd helped us develop models that performed better.

6. Conclusion and Future Work

In this work, we showed how valuable multimodal knowledge is at performing a task at hand. In most real-life scenarios we would have multimodal information available which could be utilized to train better models. We also provided a new VGD dataset that is a dataset on video games, a first of its kind. We proposed multiple models that work under different scenarios such as memory constrained settings etc. We plan to apply our approach to movie trailers and summaries in order to show the generalizability of our approach. We plan to take care of overlay texts that occur in trailers by processing them separately in order to produce better results. Finally, we also plan to include audio in order to improve our prediction accuracies.

References

1. K. Zhang, W.-L. Chao, F. Sha, and K. Grauman, Video summarization with long short-term memory. In *European Conference on Computer Vision*, pp. 766–782 (2016).
2. S. Venugopalan, L. A. Hendricks, R. Mooney, and K. Saenko, Improving lstm-based video description with linguistic knowledge mined from text, *arXiv preprint arXiv:1604.01729* (2016).
3. K. Haninger and K. M. Thompson, Content and ratings of teen-rated video games, *JAMA.* **291**(7), 856–865 (2004).
4. K. Simonyan and A. Zisserman, Two-stream convolutional networks for action recognition in videos, 2014.
5. S. E. Kahou, X. Bouthillier, P. Lamblin, C. Gulcehre, V. Michalski, K. Konda, S. Jean, P. Froumenty, Y. Dauphin, N. Boulanger-Lewandowski, et al., Emonets: Multimodal deep learning approaches for emotion recognition in video, *Journal on Multimodal User Interfaces,* 2016.
6. Q. V. Le, W. Y. Zou, S. Y. Yeung, and A. Y. Ng, Learning hierarchical invariant spatio-temporal features for action recognition with independent subspace analysis. In *CVPR 2011*, 2011.
7. Z.-H. Zhou and M.-L. Zhang, Multi-instance multi-label learning with application to scene classification. In *Advances in Neural Information Processing Systems*, 2007.
8. X. Glorot, A. Bordes, and Y. Bengio, Domain adaptation for large-scale sentiment classification: A deep learning approach, 2011.
9. X. Zhang, J. Zhao, and Y. LeCun, Character-level convolutional networks for text classification, 2015.

10. M. Iyyer, V. Manjunatha, J. Boyd-Graber, and H. Daumé III, Deep un-ordered composition rivals syntactic methods for text classification, 2015.
11. L. D. Baker and A. K. McCallum, Distributional clustering of words for text classification, 1998.
12. S. Poria, E. Cambria, and A. Gelbukh, Deep convolutional neural network textual features and multiple kernel learning for utterance-level multimodal sentiment analysis, 2015.
13. M.-L. Zhang, J. M. Peña, and V. Robles, Feature selection for multi-label naive bayes classification, 2009.
14. C. Szegedy, V. Vanhoucke, S. Ioffe, J. Shlens, and Z. Wojna, Rethinking the inception architecture for computer vision, *CoRR*, 2015.
15. J. Deng, W. Dong, R. Socher, L.-J. Li, K. Li, and L. Fei-Fei, ImageNet: A Large-Scale Hierarchical Image Database. In *CVPR09*, 2009.
16. S. Hochreiter and J. Schmidhuber, Long short-term memory, *Neural Comput.*, 1997.
17. S. Ji, W. Xu, M. Yang, and K. Yu, 3d convolutional neural networks for human action recognition, *IEEE Trans. Pattern Anal. Mach. Intell.*, 2013.
18. J. H. Lau and T. Baldwin, An empirical evaluation of doc2vec with practical insights into document embedding generation, 2016.
19. F. Chollet et al., Keras. `https://github.com/fchollet/keras` (2015).
20. M. Abadi, A. Agarwal, P. Barham, E. Brevdo, Z. Chen, C. Citro, G. S. Cor-rado, A. Davis, J. Dean, M. Devin, S. Ghemawat, I. Goodfellow, A. Harp, G. Irving, M. Isard, Y. Jia, R. Jozefowicz, L. Kaiser, M. Kudlur, J. Levenberg, D. Mané, R. Monga, S. Moore, D. Murray, C. Olah, M. Schuster, J. Shlens, B. Steiner, I. Sutskever, K. Talwar, P. Tucker, V. Vanhoucke, V. Vasude-van, F. Viégas, O. Vinyals, P. Warden, M. Wattenberg, M. Wicke, Y. Yu, and X. Zheng. TensorFlow: Large-scale machine learning on heterogeneous systems. URL `https://www.tensorflow.org/` 2015.
21. N. Srivastava, G. E. Hinton, A. Krizhevsky, I. Sutskever, and R. Salakhut-dinov, Dropout: A simple way to prevent neural networks from overfitting., *Journal of Machine Learning Research*, 2014.

Index

www.ingramcontent.com/pod-product-compliance
Lightning Source LLC
Chambersburg PA
CBHW050544190326
41458CB00007B/1909